Raising Mentally Strong Kids is a comprehensive guide to raising resilient children in our complex world. Each chapter is packed with immediately usable parenting strategies, and a deep philosophy that children and families of our era need pervades this book.

MICHAEL GURIAN, founder of the Gurian Institute and bestselling author of *The Wonder of Boys* and *The Wonder of Girls*

When two dads who also happen to be pioneers in brain science and parenting psychology tackle the biggest challenges facing kids today, the product is a dynamic, science-based response to that often-heard plea from parents: "I wish these kids came with a manual!" Well, now you have a great one—a clear road map to helping your children create a better life for themselves and a better relationship for you both!

PHILLIP C. "DR. PHIL" MCGRAW, PH.D.

Parents are to nurture children so they have the resources to surmount life's challenges. Key to resilience is developing mental and emotional strength. In this easy-to-read manual, Drs. Amen and Fay unlock the essentials of effective parenting and offer vital lessons for any stage of child-rearing.

JEFFREY K. ZEIG, PH.D., The Milton Erickson Foundation

Each of our kids needs all the love, encouragement, and strength we—individually and collectively—can help them generate. Drs. Fay and Amen are masters at sharing all the best practices to raise *strong kids* who become all they can be and develop into great, inspiring leaders in their respective occupations and life.

MARK VICTOR HANSEN, co-creator of the Chicken Soup for the Soul, ASK!, and One Minute Millionaire series of books that have sold over 500 million copies

Raising Mentally Strong Kids is a valuable resource for anyone looking to raise mentally strong kids in today's complex world. By applying the principles outlined in this book, you can create lasting changes that will impact generations to come. As a testament to its effectiveness, four generations of my family have undergone SPECT brain scans, and integrating that information into family relationships has resulted in significant positive changes across generations!

DR. EARL R. HENSLIN, PSY.D., B.C.E.T.S., diplomate in the American Academy of Traumatic Stress and author of *This Is Your Brain on Joy*

Raising Mentally Strong Kids will give any parent who wants to have kids who are confident, competent, and cooperative the step-by-step solutions.

LEWIS HOWES, *New York Times* bestselling author of *The School of Greatness* and *The Greatness Mindset*

What if we could empower our children to be more resilient, have a strong sense of self-worth, and *healthfully* overcome the challenges they face in life? This book is the road map to equipping our kids with the tools they'll need to thrive in a rapidly changing world.

SHAWN STEVENSON, bestselling author of *Eat Smarter* and *Sleep Smarter*

Dr. Fay and Dr. Amen's book reveals not just the *what* to do about child and brain development and function but *why* things impact, improve, and change our behaviors, which makes these concepts deeply motivating and actionable. You may find yourself asking, "Where was this book when I was a kid?" until you happily realize that not only can you apply these ideas to help your children thrive, but yourself as well.

DR. DARRIA LONG, national bestselling author of *Mom Hacks*, national TV health contributor, emergency physician, and mom

Raising Mentally Strong Kids is an essential and urgently needed book for anyone interacting with children. Dr. Daniel Amen and Dr. Charles Fay share their amazing expertise to give parents and grandparents a guide to raise kids to be resilient, strong, and confident in a shifting world. Highly recommended!

STEVEN MASLEY, MD, FAHA, FACN, CNS, bestselling author of *The 30-Day Heart Tune-Up*

Dr. Fay and Dr. Amen understand the current climate and struggles that parents and teachers face while raising emotionally resilient and mentally strong kids. The authors present timeless and empowering principles within each chapter, making them easily comprehensible and applicable to readers' unique situations. To enhance its practicality, they include a concise set of action steps at the end of each chapter. This powerful book spoke to my heart and soul, causing me to recommit to being a more intentional and effective father. It has become required reading for my coaching clients and the educational institutions I work with.

LARRY KERBY, MBA, speaker, parenting enthusiast and life coach

This is a refreshing and innovative parenting book, and a must-read for parents interested in raising kids with their brain health and character in mind. This book provides the science, insight, and practical steps on how to raise mentally and emotionally healthy, capable, kind, and responsible children. This book has the potential to raise up healthier families, which have the opportunity to foster healthier communities!

SHARON MAY, PH.D., founder of Safe Haven Marriage Intensives

In an age when children are struggling more than ever, Drs. Amen and Fay have written a masterful book to help us raise mentally strong kids—backed by neuroscience and in support of parents who are also trying to find their way forward. This should be a guide for all parents today.

DR. UMA NAIDOO, the Mood Food MD, nutritional psychiatrist and biologist, professional chef, and author of the bestselling *This Is Your Brain on Food*

A SAMPLE OF OTHER BOOKS BY DANIEL G. AMEN

Change Your Brain Every Day: Simple Daily Practices to Strengthen Your Mind, Memory, Moods, Focus, Energy, Habits, and Relationships, Tyndale, 2023

You, Happier: The 7 Neuroscience Secrets of Feeling Good Based on Your Brain Type, Tyndale, 2022

Your Brain Is Always Listening: Tame the Hidden Dragons That Control Your Happiness, Habits, and Hang-Ups, Tyndale, 2021

The End of Mental Illness: How Neuroscience Is Transforming Psychiatry and Helping Prevent or Reverse Mood and Anxiety Disorders, ADHD, Addictions, PTSD, Psychosis, Personality Disorders, and More, Tyndale, 2020

Change Your Brain, Change Your Grades, BenBella, 2019

Feel Better Fast and Make It Last: Unlock Your Brain's Healing Potential to Overcome Negativity, Anxiety, Anger, Stress, and Trauma, Tyndale, 2018

Memory Rescue: Supercharge Your Brain, Reverse Memory Loss, and Remember What Matters Most, Tyndale, 2017

Stones of Remembrance: Healing Scriptures for Your Mind, Body, and Soul, Tyndale, 2017

Captain Snout and the Superpower Questions: How to Calm Anxiety and Conquer Automatic Negative Thoughts (ANTs), Zonderkidz, 2017

The Brain Warrior's Way: Ignite Your Energy and Focus, Attack Illness and Aging, Transform Pain into Purpose, with Tana Amen, New American Library, 2016

The Brain Warrior's Way Cookbook: Over 100 Recipes to Ignite Your Energy and Focus, Attack Illness and Aging, Transform Pain into Purpose, with Tana Amen, New American Library, 2016

Time for Bed, Sleepyhead: The Falling Asleep Book, Zonderkidz, 2016

Change Your Brain, Change Your Life: The Breakthrough Program of Conquering Anxiety, Depression, Obsessiveness, Lack of Focus, Anger, and Memory Problems (revised), Harmony Books, 2015, 42-week *New York Times* bestseller

Healing ADD: The Breakthrough Program That Allows You to See and Heal the 7 Types of ADD (revised), Berkley, 2013

The Daniel Plan: 40 Days to a Healthier Life, with Rick Warren and Mark Hyman, Zondervan, 2013, debuted as a #1 *New York Times* bestseller

Unleash the Power of the Female Brain: Supercharging Yours for Better Health, Energy, Mood, Focus, and Sex, Harmony Books, 2013

Use Your Brain to Change Your Age: Secrets to Look, Feel, and Think Younger Every Day, Crown Archetype, 2012, *New York Times* bestseller

Change Your Brain, Change Your Body: Use Your Brain to Get and Keep the Body You Have Always Wanted, Harmony Books, 2010, *New York Times* bestseller

The Brain in Love: 12 Lessons to Enhance Your Love Life (formerly titled *Sex on the Brain*), Three Rivers Press, 2007

A SAMPLE OF OTHER BOOKS BY CHARLES FAY

Bullying: When Your Child Is the Target, Love and Logic Institute, 2016

Love and Logic Magic for Early Childhood: Practical Parenting from Birth to Six Years, with Jim Fay, Love and Logic Institute, 2015

Stepparenting: Keeping It Sane, Love and Logic Institute, 2015

From Bad Grades to a Great Life!: Unlocking the Mystery of Achievement for Your Child, Love and Logic Institute, 2011

Parenting for Success: Happy, High Achieving Kids, Love and Logic Institute, 2008

RAISING
MENTALLY
STRONG KIDS

How to Combine the Power of Neuroscience with
Love and Logic® to Grow Confident, Kind, Responsible,
and Resilient Children and Young Adults

DANIEL G. AMEN, MD
& CHARLES FAY, PHD

Foreword by **JIM FAY,** Cofounder of the Love and Logic Institute

TYNDALE
REFRESH®

Think Well. Live Well. Be Well.

MEDICAL DISCLAIMER

The information presented in this book is the result of years of practice experience and clinical research by the authors. The information in this book, by necessity, is of a general nature and not a substitute for an evaluation or treatment by a competent medical or psychological specialist. If you believe you are in need of medical or psychological intervention, please see a health care professional as soon as possible. The case studies in this book are true. The names and circumstances of many of those profiled have been changed to protect the anonymity of patients.

Visit Tyndale online at tyndale.com.

Visit Daniel G. Amen, MD, at danielamenmd.com.

Tyndale, Tyndale's quill logo, *Tyndale Refresh*, and the Tyndale Refresh logo are registered trademarks of Tyndale House Ministries. Tyndale Refresh is a nonfiction imprint of Tyndale House Ministries, Carol Stream, Illinois.

Raising Mentally Strong Kids: How to Combine the Power of Neuroscience with Love and Logic to Grow Confident, Kind, Responsible, and Resilient Children and Young Adults

Cover designed by Eva M. Winters

Interior designed by Laura Cruise

Published in association with the literary agency of WordServe Literary Group, www.wordserveliterary.com.

Scripture quotations are taken from The Holy Bible, English Standard Version® (ESV®), copyright © 2001 by Crossway, a publishing ministry of Good News Publishers. Used by permission. All rights reserved.

For information about special discounts for bulk purchases, please contact Tyndale House Publishers at csresponse@tyndale.com, or call 1-855-277-9400.

Library of Congress Cataloging-in-Publication Data

A catalog record for this book is available from the Library of Congress.

ISBN 978-1-4964-8479-6

Printed in the United States of America

30	29	28	27	26	25	24
7	6	5	4	3	2	1

Contents

Foreword

By Jim Fay, Cofounder of the Love and Logic Institute

By the time you open this book, I will have worked with kids, parents, and educators for 70 years. I'd like to tell you that it was always a great success, but unfortunately the first segment of that time was spent using some of the old traditional methods of rant, rave, and rescue. These worked with sweet, compliant kids but often backfired with strong-willed and stubborn kids. I coined the terms *Helicopter* parent and *Drill Sergeant* parent because I realized that I was a bit of both.

I'd also like to brag that I raised my first two kids, but they were really raised by my father inside my head. Every time I opened my mouth his words and voice came out. I tried to be more patient, but I always defaulted to discipline with decibels and a Helicopter rescue every time something went wrong. My dad was still running my life. I didn't like it, even though I had grown to love him.

In 1968, as a teacher, I was stumbling all over myself because of my lack of classroom management skills. The sweet kids were afraid of me, and the defiant, uncooperative ones viewed me as weak. As a result, I barely made it through the year and was about to give up. But having been raised by a stubborn Irishman who harped on the notion that nothing is worth doing unless it's unpleasant, I couldn't see myself walking away from this misery. I couldn't give up on teaching. I had to master it, so I desperately clawed my way through a master's degree at the University of Denver. That helped a bit. What really made the difference was the gift of being able to work with some tremendous experts in the field, attend a dizzying number of their trainings, and share all of this with my son, Charles. Though he was in early elementary school at the time, he listened with great interest, and he didn't complain much when I used him as a test subject. Our relationship blossomed over our discussions of human nature, psychological theories, and muscle cars. Before long, I discovered that I had a knack for turning theories into practical skills.

I also had the benefit of being able to experiment with many students, watch many highly effective and not-so-effective teachers and parents, and see very clearly what worked and what didn't. As the years went by and I had massive amounts of clinical practice, I discovered truths about parenting through organic, practical ways. This was extremely useful, but my methods of study and experimentation were quite primitive compared to those of neuroscientists conducting formal university research.

My dream was to get parents and teachers thinking and talking differently about adult-child relationships. About that time, I met Dr. Foster Cline, an innovative psychiatrist. Together we created the beginnings of the Love and Logic philosophy, and we established the Love and Logic Institute. As we started teaching these practical applications of psychological principles, I was amazed at how excited people were about their simplicity and effectiveness. We were constantly hearing, "Wow! This stuff really works!"

As the years went by, my dream became that of refining the techniques and simplifying them, making them easier to learn and apply. At that time, my little Charles had become a well-respected researcher, author, and public speaker called Dr. Charles Fay. As he formally joined our team, we continued the innovative discussions we'd started when he was a small boy. Through his insights, experience, and tireless work, Love and Logic became respected throughout the world.

Work and parenting were going well, but a cloud was still hanging over me. In my insecurity, I continued to wonder, *What if my discoveries fall flat in the face of the modern research being done on the brain? What if someday I'll face the fact that none of them is relevant? What if someday I have to stand before the world and apologize for steering people in the wrong direction?*

Fortunately, I got sick . . . very sick. Diagnosed with a serious autoimmune disorder called myasthenia gravis, I sought help from a famous neuroscientist and psychiatrist named Dr. Daniel Amen. He helped me with my condition, practically curing me of this uncurable disease. I quickly discovered that he was already quite familiar with Love and Logic and was enthusiastic about the match between what he was seeing in brain scans and what our approach could do to help parents and children develop stronger, healthier brains and behavior. This brilliant scientist and psychiatrist erased years of worry.

What a relief, I thought. *What a comfort to know that Love and Logic and the science of the brain fit together like a well-oiled machine. With both, children and families have more power to choose healthy brains and healthy futures.* That's why I am so excited about this book that I can hardly contain myself. I'm excited for you, the reader, because never before has there been a more powerful combination of approaches pulled together into one practical book. It's tremendously exciting and rewarding to know that family after family will enjoy more harmony and joy because of what Daniel and Charles have put together here.

Jim Fay

Introduction

Are you ready for some practical, scientifically sound strategies for raising kids who respect and love you so much that they adopt your deepest-held values? What if these techniques helped you avoid unwinnable arguments and power struggles? How would it be if these strategies also helped your kids develop the strong brains and behavioral habits required for confidence and resilience in this challenging world?

For over 80 combined years, we've been helping parents raise respectful, responsible, and mentally strong kids and young adults. As such, the pages of this book have not been penned by rookies, but by two men who have devoted their careers and their lives to the science and the practice of parenting. Just as important, both of us have raised families of our own and experienced the highs, the lows, and the humbling nature of family life and shaping little bundles of joy into grown adults.

We know what parenting used to be like and what it's like now. Yes, we're old enough to recall the days when the biggest technological challenges parents faced were the television and the telephone with a 15-foot cord. Some children, believe it or not, were defying their parents by sneaking more TV time and by running the phone cord under their bedroom doors. Those cords often blended with the shag carpet, making them difficult for a harried parent to detect.

While simpler, those times came with serious challenges that impacted practically every family. Alcohol has always been a problem. Marijuana and other drugs were becoming more popular and accessible. More kids were feeling free to show blatant disrespect, and many were tuning out from school. Teen pregnancy was another big concern. Over the past four decades these and many other challenges have reached epic proportions for many families.

With the growth of the internet and the advent of wireless technology, a universe of information is now available through a device small enough to fit in the pocket of even the snuggest-fitting jeans. Now we parent in an age where the devices available to our children contain more temptations than we faced during our entire childhood. Sure, some of the information out there is healthy and beneficial. Unfortunately, a large amount is deceptive, dark, and dangerous. The companies designing these devices and the software they rely on have mastered the science of addiction: Provide exciting content in random, unpredictable ways so that users always have a sense of missing out if they aren't constantly online. Provide content that targets their deepest needs to be noticed, adored, and valued as part of a social network. Get kids' brains addicted to dopamine, the reward chemical, by making the use of these devices more exciting than just about anything else (except, of course, risky sex, drugs, and other dangerous behaviors).

As we all know at heart, real joy comes from authentic relationships, a sense of purpose, helping others, and pursuing healthy challenges that lead to feelings of competence. We also know that a life filled with unhealthy distractions always leads to disappointment, anxiety, and deep depression. While most of us understand that, many of us feel overwhelmed by the thought of being in charge of providing a safe, happy home and raising our kids so they make good decisions, have healthy relationships, act kindly to others, become productive members of society, don't crumble in the face of challenges, and take responsibility for their goals and actions.

Here's the good news: You are smarter than your kids' smartphones. You've got more wisdom than their wireless devices. You've got way more hope and heartfelt motivation than the largest hard drive on earth. To make matters even better, you're reading a book like no other, one that marries 40 years of research on how to build healthy brains with 40 years of psychological strategies for taking good care of yourself while raising kids who understand an unequivocal truth: The quality of their lives—and the lives of others—will depend on the quality of their choices. And it doesn't have to be hard.

I'M DANIEL AMEN, MD

I was raised in a Lebanese family of seven children, where I found myself in the middle in terms of age. Why is that important? In our culture, the oldest boy was regarded as very special and so was the oldest girl. Of course, the baby was spoiled. Even though my mother was involved and loving, you can probably imagine how busy she must have been. So was my father. They worked extremely hard to take care of us, but the mix of cultural preferences and the juggling of so many children and other responsibilities left me feeling irrelevant.

When I turned 18, the Vietnam War was still raging, and I became an infantry medic where my love of medicine was born. But a year into it, I realized I didn't really like being shot at and got myself retrained as an X-ray technician and fell in love with medical imaging. When I was a second-year medical student, I married my childhood sweetheart, but two months later she became suicidal. I took her to see a wonderful psychiatrist, Stanley Wallace, MD, and came to realize that if he helped her, which he did, it wouldn't just help her, but it would also help me and our subsequent children and grandchildren. I fell in love with psychiatry because I realized it could help generations of people. I have loved it every day for the past 45 years.

There was one problem: I fell in love with the only medical specialty that virtually never looks at the organ it treats. As such, my love of psychiatry and my love of medical imaging were at odds. As my med school professors used to say, "How do you know unless you look?" In other words, how can we understand what's really going on inside the body . . . inside the brain . . . unless we scan the organs we're interested in? It didn't make sense that psychiatrists were not looking at the brain, and I knew this needed to change. I had no idea I would be part of the change.

In 1991, I went to a lecture on brain SPECT (single photon emission computed tomography) imaging. SPECT looks at blood flow and activity in the brain and basically tells physicians three things: is the brain healthy, underactive, or overactive? Over the next few years, my psychiatric practice radically changed. And in the last 33 years Amen Clinics has performed over 250,000 brain SPECT scans on patients from 155 countries. We have learned countless lessons from our brain-imaging work. The most important one is that, rather than seeing psychiatric problems as "mental illnesses," we see them as brain health issues. This one idea changes everything. Get your brain right and your mind will follow. It led me to repeatedly emphasize the following:

When their brains are troubled, children, teens, and young adults are sadder, sicker, and less successful in all they do, including schoolwork, sports, and relationships. A troubled brain means a troubled life, whereas a stronger and healthier brain means a stronger and healthier life.

In this book, I will provide you with a wealth of information to help you and your children develop strong brains. As you can see, it's been my life's passion, and it is an honor to share it with you. Looking at the big picture, you will learn how to:

1. **Develop a love affair with your brain.** You need to love the three-pound mass between your ears—because your brain controls how you think, act, feel, and manage those difficult situations that leave you wanting to lecture, threaten, scream, or use some other ineffective parenting strategy. Obviously, the brain helps you remain thoughtful rather than reactive, one of the hallmarks of great parenting. When you fall in love with your brain, you start taking better care of it. You feed it, exercise it, and rest it. Your brain also helps you consistently demonstrate *firmness* and *kindness*. Decades of research shows this combination of *firmness* and *kindness* to be one of the primary factors differentiating successful from unsuccessful parents.[1]

2. **Teach your child to love and protect their brain.** As you may already know, modeling is one of the most powerful ways of teaching your kids. As they see you falling head over heels in love with your brain, this will help them want a similar love affair. They will be responsive to learning that the brain is soft; the skull is hard and has multiple sharp ridges. When the head experiences any form of impact, the brain ricochets inside this hard and sharp casing. In brain scans, I have seen children as young as 8 suffering from serious head injuries from playing football for only one season. You read that right: brain damage at 8 years old! In fact, I recently worked with a patient who had been an all-American soccer player in high school and college. Even though she never had a concussion, her brain was not healthy—and hadn't been for years. The brain trauma she endured *and never knew about* made every aspect of her life as a parent, a wife, an employee, and a friend harder.

3. **Educate your child about *how* to care for their brain.** It's not hard. I started teaching my daughter Chloe when she was 2 years old how to make choices to care for her brain (you'll learn more about it in chapter 1). Show by example how to avoid anything that hurts the brain (e.g., trauma, drugs, alcohol, the standard American diet) and how to do things that help it (such as eating right, exercising, getting great sleep, learning new things, resisting inaccurate and negative thinking, avoiding overexposure to screens, and taking high-quality supplements).

I'M CHARLES FAY, PHD

Two extremely good-hearted parents, who openly admitted they had no idea what they were doing when it came to parenting, raised my two older sisters and me. As I often say, my mom, Shirley, had the toughest job of the two, staying home with the three of us kids. My father, Jim, a circus and nightclub musician, soon grew tired of the travel and begged for a job teaching music and art at an inner-city school. He got the job.

It wasn't long before a severely troubled student was placed in my dad's classroom. Scott displayed all the hallmarks of a cold sociopath: lack of empathy, extreme cruelty, obsession with starting fires, and absolutely no respect for authority. This was the late 1960s, and most teachers received little or no training in how to manage a student like Scott. Demands, lectures, and threats of punishment were not working. In fact, all they did was enrage Scott such that he'd take his extreme anger out on his classmates and the classroom pet. By early spring of that school year, my dad's nerves were shot and he found himself in a life-altering situation with Scott:

"You need to sit down and stop bothering your classmates!" my father growled.

Smirking, Scott replied with a quick burst of extreme profanity. Desperate and enraged, my father slapped him just hard enough to cause a small cut on his lip. Years later, my father admitted that his first thought was, *I'm a worthless, horrible person. I love my students, and look what I've just done.*

His second thought was, *I love teaching, but this is the end of my career.*

Up to this point, corporal punishment was still commonplace, and Scott's single mother was also at her wits' end with Scott. They couldn't find a replacement who wanted to work in that tough school, so my father managed to keep his job. It felt like a miracle to him except one unavoidable fact poked at his conscience: "I have no skills for working with challenging kids. I'm even having problems with the easy ones I have at home! I need to learn some positive ways of getting children to behave without yelling or threatening."

Intensely motivated by his guilt and desire to discover positive techniques, my dad spent practically all of his spare time reading books on human behavior, studying educational and psychological research, and attending trainings with some of the most renowned experts of the day. Fascinated by his passion, I began studying the same materials, starting around the age of 8. He even managed to get me into many of the seminars he was attending. I was struggling greatly with my math and English classes at school, but I was devouring the content that my dad and I were learning together. Some of my fondest childhood memories involved my father and I discussing the subject of human nature.

When he started using the skills on me and my sisters, I was caught by surprise. At 15, I became obsessed with having a dirt bike. The old dad would have said, "For crying out loud! Do you think money grows on trees?"

My new dad softly replied, "I can understand a young person wanting one. What's your plan for paying for it?"

I hatched a plan to finance my new passion with some odd jobs around town. After months of hard work, I purchased a heavily used Yamaha from a friend. My father responded with just two things: "I'm happy for you, son" and "Feel free to keep that as long as all of the safety rules we've discussed are followed and you're keeping up with your chores."

I didn't follow the safety rules, and I didn't stay up on my chores.

"This is so sad," he expressed with heartfelt empathy a month later. "I love you too much to nag, remind, or see you get hurt. That's why I paid to have someone to do those chores you've been neglecting. Glenn the handyman was willing to take your dirt bike for trade."

My dad never raised his voice, and he didn't back down. As the weeks passed, my anger morphed into respect. My dad cared enough about me to set limits and hold me accountable. He cared enough about me to do so with love and firmness, rather than anger and frustration.

As my father, Jim Fay, and his good friend, Foster Cline, MD, expanded their learning, they studied thousands of children, families, and schools around the globe and produced a variety of much-loved Love and Logic materials. Studying by their side and earning my doctorate in school and clinical psychology, I furthered the approach, ensuring that it remained consistent with recent research and the demands today's parents and educators face. I've also traveled the globe, sharing these powerful skills with a variety of parents and educators facing a dizzying array of real-world challenges.

As you read this book, the comprehensive medical and neuropsychiatric practices pioneered by my friend Dr. Amen will change your parenting. You'll also benefit from the marriage of his work with the deep, yet simple-to-implement psychological ideas embedded in the Love and Logic approach. The basic principles include:

1. **Mutual dignity:** Children largely learn how to treat others and themselves by how we treat them and how we allow them to treat us. Both require that we set limits that allow us to take good care of ourselves and the people around us.

2. **Shared control:** When we try to hoard control, we lose it, but when we share some, we gain it. Children become happier and more respectful when we allow them to learn responsibility, give them plenty of small choices, and let them live with the consequences of their choices. Kids also become stronger when they learn they can handle these consequences.

3. **Shared thinking:** The brain becomes strong only when we encourage children to own and solve the problems they encounter or create. When we bark orders at them and describe exactly what they should think and do, we stunt their development. The results are similar when we operate in a permissive manner and rescue them from the limits and consequences they face. In contrast, when we remain firm and loving, guiding them toward developing solutions to the dilemmas they encounter, their brains become strong and capable of facing bigger, real-world problems—and parenting becomes easier.

4. **Sincere empathy:** When we respond to children's mistakes or misbehavior with anger and frustration, we take ownership of their problem, making ourselves an easy target for their blame. When we respond with empathy, we make it harder for them to see us as the source of the problem. As you read this book, you will begin to see very clearly how empathy opens the brain to learning. You'll also discover how it lowers your stress and anxiety about being a parent.

5. **Loving relationships:** Nothing works without healthy, loving relationships. When we parent according to the first four principles of Love and Logic, this fifth becomes more or less automatic. When it does, life is far more gratifying, and our children begin to adopt our values on a subconscious basis. When they bond with us, they bond with our deepest-held beliefs.

There is great hope!

A few years back, I received a surprise call from Sam, one of my childhood buddies. We'd known each other from kindergarten through high school, and we'd had great fun goofing around. "Hey, Charles, I ran into your dad the other day, and he gave me your number," Sam said. "I'd like to introduce you to my wife, Phoebe. Let's get dinner some time."

The following Friday, I was sitting across the table from someone I hadn't seen for almost 40 years. It wasn't long before Sam asked, "So when did you end up becoming a psychologist? When we were kids, you weren't too excited about school. That's kind of a big switch. What happened?"

"Well I'd always been interested in it, but I didn't think I was smart enough to go to college. When we were kids, I was bitten by a tick and became sick with Rocky Mountain spotted fever. I also had chronic strep infections. This made it tough to learn. As I've gotten healthier, I've seen that my learning problems were related to those illnesses," I told him.

"That's such a coincidence!" Sam replied. "Dr. Daniel Amen had discovered some similar problems with our daughter, Jana. They have caused some serious learning and behavior problems, but things are getting better. And, by the way, Dr. Amen raves about Love and Logic. He's made it part of our treatment plan."

I had heard of Dr. Amen and was amazed that a preeminent, world-famous psychiatrist and author would include the Love and Logic approach as part of the treatment he provided his patients.

As the conversation flowed with Sam and Phoebe, I learned that they had adopted Jana and that she'd come with a long list of labels, including attention deficit hyperactivity disorder (ADHD), oppositional defiant disorder, sensory integration disorder, behavior disorder, and learning disability.

"Two things really made a world of difference," Phoebe chimed in. "The first has been the brain scan. It helped us see that her brain was not physically healthy. This was actually good news, because it motivated us to learn about how we could improve things by changing her diet, incorporating exercise, helping her get on a better sleep schedule, and addressing her biochemical issues with some very simple supplements."

Sam continued, "Your Love and Logic approach was so helpful too. It encouraged us to let go and allow her to make plenty of small mistakes. Because we were new parents and super worried about her because of her problems, we were micromanaging everything. We were terrified of her making any sort of mistake."

Phoebe interrupted, "And we were major Helicopter parents. We rescued her from everything."

"Yes. It was bad," Sam agreed. "We were working way harder on her life than she was, constantly trying to make everything perfect. It was backfiring big-time. Then we decided to let go and give her a chance to blow it. It was perfect. She was arguing with us about her homework, so Phoebe just empathized, 'Oh, we love you, Jana. In fact, we love you too much to argue about your homework. We will love you regardless of whether you get it done and earn a good grade or don't get it done and do poorly. Your dad and I decided that we help only when it's fun for us.'"

"She was so mad . . . mad because I wasn't," Phoebe continued. "She stormed off, shouting, 'Fine! I guess I will just fail because of you.' She blew the assignment and had to live with the consequences at school. They were small. It was no big deal, but this started our habit of allowing her to learn like you guys always teach: 'Hope and pray that your kids will make plenty of affordable mistakes when they are young so that they are mentally strong and have a good sense of cause and effect when the price tags become life and death.'"

"Things have dramatically improved because Dr. Amen is helping us make great progress with her brain health issues, while Love and Logic is helping us remain more empathetic, set better limits, and stay out of arguments with her and each other," Sam said. "It's a great combo of approaches."

After dinner that evening, I sat at my kitchen table, wondering how such a wonderful union had been created: A powerful brain-health approach married to the psychological skills my father and I had been teaching and refining for years. It wasn't long before I developed a friendship with Dr. Amen and focused on refining this partnership.

In 2021, we made this powerful pairing official as Love and Logic joined the Amen Clinics family. As you read the concepts and skills included in this book, we're confident that you'll be inspired and hope-filled, ready to tackle the great challenges of raising children from the womb to the workplace. It doesn't have to be hard.

Enjoy the journey!

Dr. Amen and Dr. Fay

PART 1

PRACTICAL NEUROPSYCHOLOGY FOR PARENTING SUCCESS

You will learn that the secret to successful parenting lies in the marriage of neuroscience and practical psychology, or practical neuropsychology as we call it. It is only when you address both the brain and the mind of your child (and yourself) that you can effectively raise mentally strong kids and young adults. This powerful combination arms you with solutions that work, even in difficult times and with challenging kids. By the end of Part 1, you will have the tools and strategies to help you:

- Develop a brain-centric attitude toward yourself and your children
- Have realistic expectations based on your child's stage of development
- Set clear goals for yourself as a parent and for your child
- Adopt a parenting style that fosters better decision-making in kids
- Promote bonding and relationship with your child
- Establish clear, enforceable family rules and limits
- Learn how to allow kids to make mistakes and deal with affordable consequences
- Stop being a doormat and set healthy boundaries for yourself and your children
- Think clearly and logically, and help your child do so from a young age
- Reinforce your child's positive behavior
- Raise kids with grit who don't crumble in the face of obstacles
- Stop beating yourself up for not being a perfect parent
- Give clear, unemotional consequences when your child's behavior is out of line
- Get your child to mind the first time you say something (yes, we said the first time!)
- Choose the best foods and supplements to support your child's brain (and your own), mind, and body
- Help your child learn to cultivate their own happiness
- Flip the switch on underachievement so your child can reach their potential
- Prevent your child from getting into trouble with technology
- Know what to do when brain/mental health issues arise

HEALTHY BRAINS: THE FOUNDATION OF MENTAL STRENGTH, RESPONSIBILITY, EMOTIONAL CONTROL, AND SUCCESS

You have to be your child's frontal lobes until theirs develop, but you also have to give them the tools to know how to take the driver's seat once their brain does mature.

Have you ever known someone who just doesn't get it? The kind of person who continually makes the same mistakes over and over, leading you to wonder, *What were they thinking?* Maybe you have a friend or relative, or even a spouse, who has the best intentions but keeps tripping up and creating unnecessary drama in the family.

Imagine that this friend is driving on the highway in stop-and-go traffic and sees someone in their rearview mirror tailgating them. This infuriates them and sends their thoughts spinning to how they're going to get back at the tailgater by slamming on the brakes. But while your friend is fixated on the rearview mirror, envisioning their revenge—BOOM!—they rear-end the car in front of them. They were so caught up in the moment, they neglected to consider the consequences of their actions.

Now think of someone else you know, someone who's got it together. You know, the kind of person who's rational and makes such good decisions that they could never be cast in a reality TV show because they would be too boring. Let's say this person finds themselves in the same traffic scenario. They might glance in the rearview mirror and, feel fleetingly irritated, but then they let it go and get back to focusing on the road in front of them. No fender bender for this friend.

What's the fundamental difference between these two types of people? Brain health.

At Amen Clinics, we've been looking at the brain for over 30 years. We have over 250,000 brain scans from people in more than 150 countries—the world's largest database of brain scans related to behavior. After looking at all these scans over the last few decades, one thing is very clear: When your brain works right, you work right. When your brain is troubled—for whatever reason—you're more likely to have trouble in your life.[1] Everything you (and your kids) do either helps or hurts your brain function and brain development—and every aspect of your present-day and future lives. And your brain health has a major impact on your child's brain health and mental strength.

We'll give you the brain basics you need to know to help yourself and your child fall in love with the gray matter between your ears. We'll show you how to love and care for the brain, so you can have a drama-free relationship and experience more success at home, in school, and in life. When your brain is healthy, parenting is easier. We promise. We'll also outline how combining better brain function with Love and Logic's psychology-based child-rearing strategies is the ultimate secret to parenting success. It's the marriage of these two pieces of the parenting puzzle that puts you on the path to raising mentally strong kids and having more fun while doing it.

BRAIN BASICS

Brains run schools, families, friendships, businesses, churches—and you. Yet most people rarely think about their brains, least of all their children's brains. Yet mental strength starts with a healthy brain. It's so important to know about the brain, love it, and maybe even become a bit obsessed with it—especially for your kids' sake. And it's equally critical to teach your children at an early age to love and care for their own brains. It will make parenting so much easier while setting them up for the mental fortitude that will help them succeed in every area of life! And remember, although it's better to start early, it's never too late to teach your child, adolescent, or young adult about brain health.

Let's take a deeper look at the supercomputer inside your head. The human brain typically weighs about three pounds and is the consistency of soft butter, tofu, or custard, and it is housed in a hard skull that has sharp bony ridges.[2] It's no surprise that the brain can be damaged from repeatedly heading soccer balls or from being pounded by helmet-to-helmet tackles in football!

The brain is a symphony of parts that work together to create and sustain a life. It is the organ responsible for learning, loving, creating, and behaving. And it is the most complex and amazing organ in the universe.

Fun Facts about the Brain

- It is 2 percent of the body's weight.
- It uses 20 to 30 percent of your calorie intake and 20 percent of the body's oxygen and blood flow.
- Information travels up to 268 mph in the brain.
- Its storage capacity equals six million years of the *Wall Street Journal*.
- Males have 10 percent more neurons.
- Females have more connections.

BRAIN DEVELOPMENT: FROM BIRTH TO ADULTHOOD

The age of 18 might be when your kid legally becomes an adult. Their brain, though, hasn't completely matured yet. The truth is, the brain doesn't fully develop until about age 25 (up to age 28 in males). Until this time, kids need your help. And during the development period, you need to provide children with the tools and techniques they need to encourage healthy brain habits.

An easy way to grasp brain development is to think about where your mind was at different ages. When you were 5, what was interesting to you? Trucks, dolls, playing in the sandbox, snacks? The decisions you made were simple: whatever choices your mom or dad gave you. When you were 12, your interests changed, maybe toward making friends at school, building crafts, or reading books on your own. You certainly thought about decisions differently: *What will I wear today? If I ignore Mom long enough, will she give up on trying to get me to do my chores? Ugh, I hate chores.* Once 18 rolled around, toys and playing took on a completely different meaning. Perhaps you had your first car, a job, and possibly even a boyfriend or girlfriend. Every year of your own development brought change in your focus and ability to make decisions.

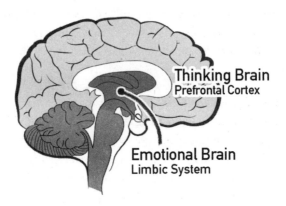

Here is a timeline of how the brain develops from birth to adulthood.

Prenatal and newborns: By the time a baby is born, its brain already boasts 100 billion neurons. However, only a relatively small number of neurons are myelinated, and they have fewer connections. Over time, myelin, a white fatty substance that works like insulation, surrounds the cells and keeps the energy focused and moving in one direction. A child's brain forms trillions of connections in the first 10 years, so you don't want anything to interrupt myelination.

About three-quarters of the brain develops outside the womb, in response to environment and experience, as well as genetics. Early childhood experiences create a background for development and learning, as well as influence the way the brain is wired. In turn, the wiring affects feelings, language, and thought. Experiences mold and sculpt the brain. Nature and nurture always work together.

Brain development is fast during the first year. By 12 months old, a baby's brain on the outside resembles that of a normal young adult. In terms of outward and psychological development, here's what's happening for babies and toddlers. From birth to 18 months, babies are completely dependent, unable to delay wants or needs, think that they and their mother are much the same person, and learn mostly through their senses.

Parenting tips: Research shows that even prior to conception, parents' lifestyle habits lay the foundation for their baby's overall physical and mental health and well-being.[3] In the womb, a baby's brain begins to develop. If a mom-to-be smokes (or is exposed to secondhand smoke), eats junk food, drinks too much alcohol, is chronically stressed, or has infections during the pregnancy, it can have a negative influence on the baby's developing brain. On the other hand, if a mom avoids smoking, eats nutritious meals, takes prenatal vitamins, manages her stress, and is healthy throughout the pregnancy, it boosts a baby's brain health. Take care of your own brain health to improve your newborn's brain health.

Early childhood: Toddlers begin to realize that they are separate, independent people and begin to exert independence by saying "No!" and "I want to do it myself." This new independence often frightens them, so they often have fears and tend to be more clingy. They develop a sense of confidence if they are allowed to exert independent behavior (under adequate supervision) versus a sense of self-consciousness if they are overcontrolled.

By age 3, a baby's brain has formed about 1,000 trillion connections—about twice as many as adults have. Starting at about age 3, rapid social, intellectual, emotional, and physical development occurs. Brain activity in this age group is more than twice that of adults. New synapses form throughout life, but never again will the brain be so able to easily master new skills or adapt to setbacks.

The preschool years lead to continued independence and discovery. Kids at this age show initiative and curiosity—you know, those questions that never seem to stop. They are also highly imaginative, may have imaginary friends, and have some trouble separating reality from fantasy. So it's no surprise they think magically, meaning they think their thoughts have power and that they are responsible for everything around them. When something good happens, they feel pride. When something bad happens during this stage (divorce, death of a sibling, etc.), they often feel guilt, thinking somehow it was their fault, which may last a lifetime.

Parenting tips: This is an important time for bonding and building trust with your child and an ideal age to begin using the Love and Logic concepts. At about 18 months, it's time to start setting loving limits as a form of discipline (see more about how discipline is really a teaching and training tool in chapter 6). It's also a time to allow little ones to begin experiential learning. This means allowing kids to make small mistakes that come with small consequences and to enjoy the thrill of early successes. Introduce them to the concept of brain health and start teaching them to love their brain. An online course like our Brain Thrive Pre-K–Grade 1 (www.amenuniversity.com) can help.

Elementary years: Once they hit school age, 6 to 11 years old, they develop friendships and ties outside home (e.g., scouts, sports) and identify with the parent of the same sex. Their attention span dramatically increases, and they think more in literal terms, often black or white. They need supervision, rules, and structure to feel comfortable. And then their brains hit the next major stage of development.

Parenting tips: During this period, it's a good idea to empower problem-solving and allow your child to engage in progressively greater challenges. As children learn to ride bikes, ride skateboards, or get involved in other sports, be sure they wear helmets to protect the brain and discourage them from playing brain-damaging sports like football. Encourage school-age kids to start adopting brain-healthy habits (see page 24, principle 6).

Preteens and young teens: At age 11, the brain begins to prune extra connections. The circuits that remain are more specific and efficient. The brain is one of the best examples of the "use it or lose it" principle. Connections that are used repeatedly in the early years become permanent, while those that are not used are pruned. So, if a child does not play sports when they are young, then those nerve tracks get pruned. Or if a child does not learn to play a musical instrument, then the brain cuts those connections. That's what makes it harder to learn new activities later in life.

In everyday life, here's how this new stage of brain development looks. Preteens and young teens from 11 to 14 move toward more independent thinking, struggle with a sense of identity and shyness about their bodies, and realize parents aren't perfect and identify their faults for them. (Perhaps this just helps keep us humble.) Young teens are more heavily influenced by their peers, and close friendships become important. This is when they also begin testing rules and limits.

Parenting tips: Understand that this is when children need to learn to balance autonomy and individualization with safety. Continue to implement limits and focus on modeling brain-healthy habits (see page 24).

Teenagers: Around 14, teens move toward further independence, start complaining about their parents ("I know how to do it myself!" "Mom, really?!") and withdraw emotionally from Mom and Dad. They are extremely concerned about their physical appearance, and their friends are the most important people in their lives, even though they frequently change relationships. During the middle teen years, kids show more interest in specific careers.

Once teens hit 17 to 19, they are getting more secure in their identity and have more stable relationships. They can anticipate consequences for their actions and show the ability to delay needs and wants. Their concern increases for others and about their own future.

Parenting tips: One of the biggest reasons that parents and teenagers struggle with each other is because as children grow, you expect more and more from them, yet teens do not have adult brain capacities. Many teens may, in fact, be "acting their age" when they are struggling to do the right thing. The better you understand the brain and its key functions, the more empathy and support you will be able to offer your child when they are pushing your limits. At this age, you need to help teens understand the difference between acceptance and agreement. Although teens may view themselves as mature enough to make their own decisions, it is still your job to step in as their prefrontal cortex when necessary. Encourage brain-healthy behavior. Our online course Brain Thrive by 25 (www.amenuniversity.com) offers guidelines for teens and young adults to adopt good brain habits.

Early adulthood: During the late teens and into the mid-twenties, the front third of the brain, called the prefrontal cortex (PFC) or executive brain, continues to develop. Myelin continues to be deposited in the PFC until age 25 or 26, making the PFC work at a higher and more efficient level. The car insurance industry knew about maturity and brain development long ago. Typically, automobile insurance rates change at 25 because drivers are more thoughtful and get into significantly fewer accidents because their judgment centers work better.

Parenting tips: Continue encouraging young adults to take ownership of their own brain health.

7 BRAIN PRINCIPLES FOR PARENTS AND KIDS[4]

1. **Your brain is involved in everything you do.** How you think, how you feel, how you act, and how well you get along with your children, spouse, and friends has to do with the moment-by-moment functioning of your brain. Your brain is the organ behind your intelligence, character, personality, and every decision you make.

2. **When your brain works right, you work right. When your brain is troubled, you have trouble in your life.** When your brain is healthy, you tend to be happier, mentally stronger, healthier (due to better decision-making), more successful (also due to better decision-making), and a better parent. When your brain is not healthy, for whatever reason (such as multiple concussions, poor eating habits, or a family history of mental health problems), you tend to be sadder,

sicker, less successful, more vulnerable to mental health issues, and a less effective parent. The same goes for your kids.

3. **Your brain is the most amazing organ in the universe.** Your brain weighs about three pounds and has about 100 billion neurons (nerve cells) and more connections than there are stars in our galaxy.

4. **You need to fall in love with your brain and develop brain envy.** Because your brain runs your life (and your child's life), you have to care for it. Unfortunately, not enough people care about the brain, because they can't see it. You can see the wrinkles on your face or the blubber around your belly and do something about it if it bothers you. Most people, however, never get the chance to see their brains, so they don't know if there are problems or if it's headed for trouble.

5. **Many things hurt the brain. Avoid them.** Based on brain imaging work at Amen Clinics and more than 30 years of clinical practice, we have identified the 11 major risk factors that harm the brain and steal your mind. If you have any of these risk factors, parenting may feel harder than it should. And if your child has any of them, it can rob them of the mental strength, resilience, and focus they need to succeed in life. We developed the mnemonic BRIGHT MINDS to help you remember the 11 major risk factors.[5] I've written about these risk factors in several books, but I have adapted them here to show how they can hurt the brain and impact your life as a parent and your child's life.

- **B is for Blood Flow.** Blood flow supplies the oxygen and important nutrients your brain needs for optimal functioning and carries away waste. Our brain imaging work shows that low blood flow—from hypertension, lack of exercise, or other issues—is associated with many issues that can affect parents or kids at different ages, including problems with focus, moods, addictions, and more.

- **R is for Rational Thinking.** Every thought you have triggers the release of neurochemicals that impact brain function. Thoughts can be positive and beneficial or negative and harmful. If your brain is infested with ANTs (automatic negative thoughts), they can steal your mind and rob you or your child of joy.
- **I is for Inflammation.** Having high levels of inflammation harms the organs in your body, including your brain. Elevated inflammation is associated with mood issues, lack of motivation, and a leaky gut that causes gastrointestinal issues, allergies, and more. Research shows that chronic systemic inflammation at an early age in children has long-term impacts on brain development.[6]
- **G is for Genetics.** Brain health and mental health issues clearly run in families; however, your genes are not your destiny. Your daily habits can influence those genes and either switch them on or off.
- **H is for Head Trauma.** Concussions and head injuries—even mild ones that occur at any age—can contribute to learning problems, trouble with focus, mood issues, anxiousness, a vulnerability for abusing alcohol or drugs, and more.
- **T is for Toxins.** Exposure to environmental toxins found in personal care products, nonorganic produce, mold, paint, alcohol, smoke, pesticides, and other everyday items is harmful to the brain. And research shows that children's developing brains are especially vulnerable to toxic exposure.[7] Brain fog, learning problems, autism, ADHD, and other issues have been linked to toxic exposure.
- **M is for Mental Health.** Having mental health problems makes it much harder to be an effective parent and makes it more challenging for children to do well in school and in life. For example, ADHD can make it difficult to focus or follow through on things. Anxiety can make you overprotective and can interfere with a child's school life, home life, and friendships. Being depressed can rob you or your child of motivation and joy. On average, it is 11 years from the time a person first has a mental health symptom to when they are first evaluated and treated.[8] And research published in 2020 shows that kids up to age 25 experience the longest delay from the onset of symptoms to the time they receive treatment.[9] That is way too long.

- **I is for Immune System Problems and Infections.** If your immune system is out of balance, you may be more vulnerable to infections that increase the risk of brain fog, mental health problems, and memory issues. In some children, some infections—including strep, Lyme disease, COVID, and mononucleosis—have been known to trigger the onset of neuropsychiatric issues.[10]

- **N is for Neurohormone Issues.** When hormones are out of whack, it negatively impacts brain function. For example, thyroid problems can zap energy, lead to fuzzy thinking, and cause trouble concentrating or paying attention. These problems can be mistaken or misdiagnosed as mental health disorders.

- **D is for Diabesity.** The word *diabesity* is a combination of *diabetes* and *obesity*, both of which decrease the size and function of your brain. Diabesity can affect moods, memory, learning, focus, and more.

- **S is for Sleep.** The brain needs sleep to stay healthy. In adults, sleeping less than seven hours a night has been associated with a higher risk of anxiety, depression, dementia, ADHD, and more.[11] Lack of sleep hits teenagers especially hard. A research study involving 27,939 high school students found that getting just one hour less of sleep on weekdays resulted in a 38 percent increase in feeling hopeless, as well as significant increases in the chances of substance abuse, seriously contemplating suicide, and attempting suicide.[12]

6. **Many things help the brain. Engage in regular brain-healthy habits.** The exciting news is that many things are also good for your brain and can boost its function. When you implement them into your daily life, parenting can be less tiring and more fulfilling. Incorporating them into your child's life enhances their ability to live up to their potential. Here are BRIGHT MINDS strategies you can use to minimize your (and your child's) risk factors.

- **B is for Blood Flow.** Engage in physical exercise (30 minutes a day), practice meditation and/or prayer, and eat foods such as pomegranates, citrus fruit, and walnuts (they increase blood flow).
- **R is for Rational Thinking.** You don't need to believe every stupid thought you have. Thoughts come and go and are influenced by what you see, hear, and eat; just because you have a thought doesn't mean you need to pay attention to it. Helping kids learn this at an early age can have a powerful effect on the trajectory of their lives, setting them up for greater confidence, less sensitivity to constructive criticism, and a can-do attitude in the face of obstacles. Learn to kill the ANTs by questioning your thoughts. Teach this simple method to kids of all ages: Whenever you have a thought that makes you feel bad, mad, sad, or out of control, ask yourself if it is true. See chapter 7 for more information on eliminating the ANTs.
- **I is for Inflammation.** Eat an anti-inflammatory diet, including more foods high in omega-3 fatty acids (such as salmon). Take supplements, such as fish oil and probiotics, and give them to your kids too. And floss your teeth (and teach your children to do so) every day.
- **G is for Genetics.** If you have a family history of mental health conditions, behavioral issues, or memory problems in your family, get serious about brain health as soon as possible, get screened early, and look for any signs of trouble in your children. Know your family's risk factors and work to prevent them every day. For example, Dr. Amen has obesity and heart disease in his family, but at the age of 69, he doesn't have either. He is on an obesity and heart disease prevention program every day of his life.
- **H is for Head Trauma.** Protect your (and your child's) head. Wear a helmet when biking, skiing, skateboarding, etc. Don't let kids play contact sports like tackle football, and avoid heading soccer balls. Always wear a seat belt when in a car and hold handrails when going up or down stairs. Avoid climbing ladders, and never text while walking or driving.
- **T is for Toxins.** Avoid toxic exposure. Download one of several apps available to help reduce exposure to chemicals, such as Think Dirty, and find nontoxic alternatives. Don't slather your (or your child's) body with products that contain toxins, such as

oxybenzone in sunscreen, parabens, and phthalates (fragrance) in cosmetics. Eat organic whenever possible and avoid alcohol, marijuana, and cigarettes. Test for mold if you suspect its presence in your home. In addition, support the body's four organs of detoxification:

- Kidneys: Drink more water.
- Gut: Eat more fiber, and choose organic foods.
- Liver: Quit smoking and avoid drugs, limit alcohol, and eat brassicas (cabbage, broccoli, cauliflower, and brussels sprouts).
- Skin: Exercise vigorously enough to sweat.

- **M is for Mental Health.** Adopt brain-healthy habits and eliminate your automatic negative thoughts (see Rational Thinking). Get daily physical exercise, practice stress-management techniques, and increase intake of omega-3 fatty acids.
- **I is for Immune System Problems and Infections.** Check vitamin D levels, and if they are low, get more sun or take a supplement. Eat immune-boosting onions, mushrooms, and garlic. Get screened for common infections and be sure to treat any infections in yourself or your child early.
- **N is for Neurohormone Issues.** Test and optimize your hormone levels as a parent and avoid hormone disruptors (found in pesticides, some food products, and some personal care products) for you and your kids.
- **D is for Diabesity.** Eliminate or limit sugar, eat a brain-healthy diet, and don't eat more calories than needed.
- **S is for Sleep.** Make sleep a priority in your family. Aim for 11–14 hours for toddlers, 10–13 hours for preschoolers, 9–11 hours for elementary and junior high schoolers, 8–10 hours for teenagers, and 7–8 hours for adults. Turn off tech devices 1–2 hours before bedtime.

7. **You can change your brain and change your life.** The most important and hopeful lesson we have learned from over 250,000 brain scans is that you are not stuck with the brain you have—you can make it better at any age. Before you make any decisions, one of the simplest things you can do is ask yourself, "Is this good for my brain or bad for it?" See the box below to learn how to teach this technique to young children. We all need to work hard to improve

our brain health, because with a better brain comes a better mind, better parenting, and a better life.

Getting Kids to Think About Brain Health: Chloe's Game

Getting your children interested in brain health and learning what's good for their brain or bad for it from an early age will have a powerful and positive impact on the rest of their lives. It's actually easy to do. Dr. Amen found the simplest way to begin is to turn it into a game. He started playing this game with his daughter Chloe when she was two. He calls it Chloe's Game. You can use your own child's name.

Is this good for my brain or bad for it?

Here's how to get your kids to start asking themselves, *Is this good for my brain or bad for it?* Dr. Amen would say something like "Walnuts," and Chloe would say, "Good for my brain!" If Dr. Amen said, "Salmon," she'd say, "Yummy, very good!" But if Dr. Amen said, "Skateboarding without a helmet," she would say, "Scary bad!" You might be surprised how well young kids can distinguish what's good for them and what's bad for them.

They continued playing this game as Chloe grew, and the questions evolved as she aged. After she got her driver's license, Dr. Amen would say, "Driving without your seat belt?" and she would shoot him a disapproving look and say, "Ugh, so bad!" When she was about to head off to college, he asked, "Joining a sorority?" and she paused to think about it. She replied, "Well, the social bonding would be great, but if there's a lot of drinking or drugs that would be terrible." What makes this game so great is you can play it anywhere—in the car, at the grocery store, at dinner—and it can be a good conversation starter.

THE PRACTICAL NEUROPSYCHOLOGY APPROACH

Your child needs a healthy brain to be mentally strong. Anything that interferes with brain function can also interfere with character. Damage to the brain from infection, trauma, malnutrition, or toxic exposure (such as from alcohol or other drugs) can damage your child's character. Without healthy brain function, children cannot do the things that are most human, such as make plans, control their instincts, and give and receive love. Character and morality are intertwined.

In a number of studies, poor brain function has been associated with decreased morality.[13] A moral person is someone who does the right thing, is fair in their actions, and avoids doing harm without necessary reasons (such as in war). People with diminished morality are those who don't care if they do the right thing, can be unfair in an interaction without it bothering them, and can hurt others for their own gain.

Who your child becomes, in large part, is shaped by brain function. A healthy brain allows them to act in consistently positive ways. Having a healthy brain allows them to learn from you, their siblings, and their teachers; it allows them to learn from the mistakes they make so they do not have to repeat them; and it allows them to notice the behaviors that make them happy and those that don't.

But having a healthy brain is only part of the equation in raising mentally strong, confident, resilient humans. There is also some basic parenting psychology that needs to happen in the home. Think of the brain as a high-powered computer. You can have the top model, but if all you do is download video games or stream YouTube videos, it's not functioning at its potential. You need the good hardware, but you also need high-quality software.

To raise mentally strong kids, we need a marriage of neuroscience and practical psychology. As parents, we must look after our own brain health as well as the brain development of our children in addition to using proven parenting skills. One without the other will never be enough.

FOUR CIRCLES OF MENTAL STRENGTH

Look at how the four circles of mental strength played a role in Susan's life as the 45-year-old mother of four children (two with ADHD) and a manager at a nonprofit. When Susan came into Dr. Amen's office, she told him, "I'm just not feeling good. I'm tired all the time, whether I sleep in on the weekends or not! I can't remember the simplest things, and it seems like I can't keep my mind on anything for more than a minute before something distracts me. I am feeling very overwhelmed."

FOUR CIRCLES OF MENTAL STRENGTH

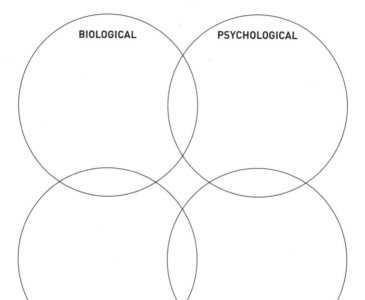

She sighed. "And it's getting worse. Stuff I used to be able to do easily I now really have to struggle through."

Susan was a classic Helicopter mom who had reached the burnout phase. Her kids—especially the two with ADHD—rarely completed their chores, got in trouble at school, and liked to push her buttons to get a rise out of her. Susan felt like she was dropping the ball, was quick to get irritated with the kids, and then felt like a failure as a mom. *What was she doing wrong?* she wondered.

Susan is like so many women who come to Amen Clinics for help. She thought she ate a healthy diet but started most days with coffee and a bagel and had a terrible sweet tooth throughout the day. She wanted to work out but couldn't find the time. At night, she consistently drank two glasses of wine to relax. There was one major part of her body that she never gave any thought to—her brain. The irony is that Susan's brain decides what she eats and how much she sleeps. Her brain decides whether to snap at her children or to take a deep breath and try a more loving, logical approach.

Of course, none of these decisions is necessarily conscious. But Susan's brain makes them nonetheless. If Susan knew how to take care of her brain, how to give it the biological, psychological, social, and spiritual care it required, then she would be more likely to feel great and have the energy she needs to be a more effective parent.

With Susan, Dr. Amen drew four big circles on a whiteboard in his office. In the first circle, he wrote *Biological* and began with a set of questions to look at the biological factors influencing her brain. There was a family history of depression, and her diet was not great, which is a terrible thing to do to your brain. She also tended to eat on the run a lot because she was so busy—also not good for the brain.

Another big biological problem in Susan's profile was the five or fewer hours of sleep she got each night. With four children and a demanding job, it was hard to get everything done in a day. But not getting enough sleep is one of the worst things you can do for your brain (and for your children), so this was a big concern.

In the second circle, he wrote the word *Psychological*. Psychologically, Susan was thinking in undisciplined and negative ways. Her busy brain kept returning to the same worries, anxieties, and self-criticisms: *I should have done that differently. My daughter probably hates me. I'm not doing enough for my kids. What is wrong with me, anyway?* Susan was prone to a kind of perfectionism in which she magnified her flaws and minimized her good points.

In Susan's mind, her children's normal childhood crises were clear evidence that she was not being a good enough mother. Dr. Amen refers to these automatic negative thoughts as ANTs. These psychological issues were both the result of Susan's poor brain health and a contributing factor to it.

In the third circle, Dr. Amen wrote *Social*. There, too, Susan's brain was facing a number of challenges. She felt separated from the most important people in her life, distant from her husband, and irritable with her kids. At work, she felt overwhelmed. The support she might have gotten from friends or from her community at church seemed out of reach, because Susan felt too exhausted to reach out.

In the last circle, he wrote *Spiritual*. As it happened, Susan's brain was in good shape in this area. She had a deep sense of meaning and purpose in her life that sustained her, even in this challenging time. She felt her work mattered to others, and she knew that her presence at home was crucial for her husband and children. She had a deep sense of connection to God, the planet, and the future. Susan's brain definitely benefited from her sense of meaning and purpose.

SUSAN'S FOUR CIRCLES

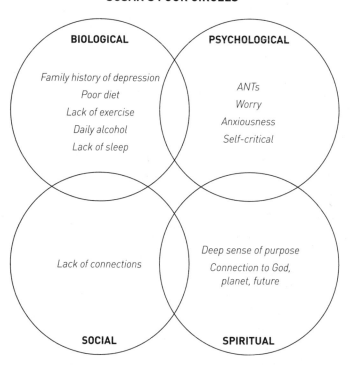

When Susan learned how to optimize the four circles of her life using the same tools and strategies you'll find in this book, she became a much more effective parent and derived far more enjoyment from her four children. Understanding how the four circles impact your own life is the first step in learning how to encourage your children to adopt a four-circle approach in their own lives. When children discover early on to optimize all of these areas, it helps them create a balanced life that promotes brain and mental strength.

Let's do a quick exercise. Think about the four circles in your own life and in your child's life and write down areas that are hurting the brain, making parenting harder, and stealing from your child's mental strength, as well as things that are boosting the brain, making parenting easier, and fortifying your child's mental wellness.

MY FOUR CIRCLES

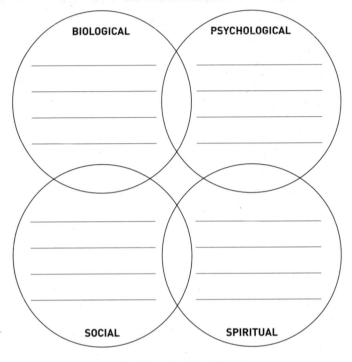

MY CHILD'S FOUR CIRCLES

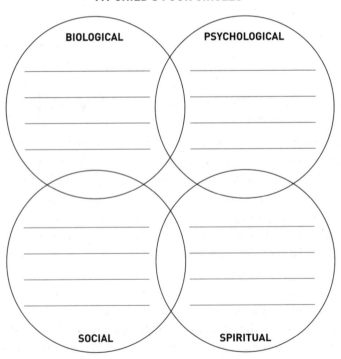

A TALE OF TWO HIGH SCHOOL BASEBALL PITCHERS

To illustrate how brain health and psychology intersect, look at two high school pitchers: Keith and Troy. Keith grew up in a family where both parents were so self-absorbed they didn't pay much attention to him. As a baby, when Keith cried, his parents often took a long time to respond or just let him continue crying. This disrupted some of the most fundamental elements of a child's life: attachment and empathy.

One of the first things babies learn is cause and effect—when I cry, someone comes to hold me, coo at me, or meet my needs. It's a simple "If A, then B" equation. When this occurs on a regular basis, it creates and strengthens neural pathways involved in attachment and empathy. People who grow up without nurturing parents don't develop those neural pathways. This often leads to behavioral problems early in life. In these kids, the "terrible 2s" are beyond terrible.

As Keith grew up, one of his baseball coaches noticed he was left-handed and invited him to try pitching. Keith excelled at hurling a baseball, and all of his attention turned to baseball. His parents were thrilled and desperately hoped pitching might be Keith's ticket to success. He certainly wasn't doing well in academics. Because he lacked empathy and missed out on learning about cause and effect as a baby, he simply didn't think through the consequences of his actions, and he made some really bad decisions. His parents would come to the rescue whenever Keith got into trouble.

Somehow, Keith got a scholarship to play baseball in college. Despite his past troubles, he had everything going for him, and the future looked bright. The night before his first day at college, however, he hopped into a car with a friend and shouted, "Hey, let's steal an ATM!" With that terrible decision, Keith's scholarship and baseball career vanished into thin air.

Now look at Troy. He didn't have the same natural pitching talent that Keith did. However, his parents nurtured him as a baby and provided him with what he needed to develop the four circles of life. With this foundation, Troy was able to apply himself to his training to improve his abilities and eventually earned a college scholarship like Keith. And just like Keith, he got into a car with a buddy the night before going to college. Troy and his friend were bored and thought, "We should have some fun. What should we do?" Instead of hatching a plan like Keith's, Troy backpedaled and said, "Well, I need to leave early for college tomorrow and I don't want to be tired, so we should probably just go home and get some sleep."

A lifetime of building brain-healthy habits and making good decisions helped Troy develop the mental fortitude to do the right thing. He went on to play baseball in college, graduated with honors, and played in the pros for a short time until he got injured. Because he had also paid attention to his studies, he shifted rather seamlessly to another career and became very successful.

IT'S NEVER TOO LATE TO BOOST BRAIN HEALTH AND PARENTING SKILLS

After reading about the importance of early brain development, you may be worried that you didn't instill brain-healthy habits in your children early enough. The good news is, it's never too late to start. Even if you didn't lay the best foundation, you can still turn things around. The brain imaging work at Amen Clinics proves that the brain can change, even if you've been bad to your brain or if your child has developed bad brain habits. And if you've made some parenting mistakes in the past, you can correct them with the strategies in this book.

Think back to the examples of the two drivers at the beginning of this chapter. If you stay focused on the road ahead rather than worrying about what's in the rearview mirror, you can become a better parent and raise kids who are mentally stronger.

Raising Kids with Special Needs or Disabilities

When it comes to parenting, kids who have special needs present unique joys and challenges. If your child has a physical disability, learning disorder, developmental delay, brain/mental health challenge (more on this in chapter 13), or other issue, rest assured that you can use the strategies and techniques in this book.

We encourage you to educate yourself about your child's condition and to explore therapeutic techniques with science-backed benefits. In addition, it's important to know that getting an accurate diagnosis for your child can be the key to finding the most effective treatments. At Amen Clinics, we have found that brain imaging is an important piece of the puzzle when it comes to diagnosis for many conditions. We have seen kids who were unfocused, underachievers, sad, angry, or even aggressive, and when we scanned their brains we discovered that they had previous head injuries, exposure to toxins, or a chronic infection like Lyme disease that was contributing to their symptoms. Knowing what's causing or exacerbating any issues can be so helpful in understanding, loving, and raising your child.

We have met with many parents of kids with special needs, and they are often filled with stress, anxiousness, sadness, grief, and a sense of guilt. This can easily lead to exhaustion or burnout. Remember that taking care of yourself is as important as caring for your child. One of the most important things you can do for yourself as a parent—and for your child regardless of their unique needs—is to adopt brain-healthy habits (see chapter 9). By supporting your (and your child's) brain and emotional well-being, you can develop a more loving relationship and improve mental strength for you both.

Action Steps

- Every day you are modeling health or illness. If you want your kids to live brain-healthy lives, model it.
- Remember to think about where your child's brain is in the development process.
- Know the seven brain principles for a healthy life and implement them into your daily life.
- Encourage your kids to take ownership of their own brain health.
- Incorporate the four circles of mental strength: biological, psychological, social, and spiritual.

For maximum effectiveness, focus on brain health in addition to using proven parenting skills coming in the next chapters.

CHAPTER 2

MENTALLY STRONG KIDS LIVE BY CLEARLY DEFINED GOALS

Goals help us start doing positive things rather than remaining stuck worrying about negative things.

Think back to before your child was born. Did you and your spouse sit on the couch and share your dreams for how your child would turn out some day? We all have. But we doubt that any parent-to-be has ever said anything like the following:

> "Oh, I can't wait until our daughter grows up to be disrespectful and entitled."
>
> "I can't wait for the first time we get called into the principal's office to talk about our son's attitude problem."
>
> "When our kids become young adults, I hope they refuse to move out of the house and won't get a job or pay rent."
>
> "Won't it be great when we have to raise our grandkids because our own adult children are too ill-equipped to parent them on their own?"

Obviously, nobody wants any of these scenarios. We want the best for our kids, and we want them to grow up independent, self-assured, and successful—mentally strong. The love we have for our children drives us to provide for them, protect them, care for them, and teach them all we can. Our children certainly don't want to grow up to be ineffective adults who have to rely on their parents. Yet the trends are showing that teens and young adults today are more likely to experience a "failure to launch," with 56 percent of 18- to 24-year-olds living at home, according to statistics from the U.S. Census Bureau.[1] Sadly, too many parents find themselves concerned that, based on the way they were raised or how things are going in their home or in the homes of other families, there's a strong possibility that the above situations may become reality.

That's what was happening in Gina's life. At 41, she and her husband Tony, 43 (who ran the Italian restaurant Tony's parents had started), were raising 16-year-old Luca. Their lifelong dream was to have Luca join them in the family business and take it over one day. They thought that being hard-working role models would be enough to inspire their son to want to fulfill that dream, but he didn't seem interested in anything other than hiding out in his room drawing cartoons and working on his computer. Even though he was intelligent, Luca procrastinated on his homework, and Gina would jump in and do it for him. And even though she asked him to clean up his room, he just kept adding dirty clothes to the piles on the floor—and eventually Gina would pick up after him.

Gina and Tony had been bringing Luca to work with them since he was a young boy, introducing him to the various aspects of running a restaurant. But their son showed little enthusiasm for following in the family business, much less for applying to college. Gina, who handled the accounting, tried to get Luca interested in numbers. She also had him help out in the kitchen with the cooks, and she put him alongside Tony as he greeted diners and kept the bustling eatery running smoothly. Luca was apathetic about all of it. The pair were worried about Luca's future and tempted to label their son as lazy or unmotivated. Tony began trying to steer Luca away from his cartoons and computers and pushing him to start getting serious about the restaurant business. Gina was starting to worry that Luca would never have the skills to do so, and she was beginning to wonder if he would ever be motivated enough to move out. What could she do?

Do you have similar worries about your child? Do you wish you knew how to better steer your kids in the right direction? Maybe your child is still young, but you're wondering what are the best ways to instill motivation as they grow. What if you could implement some powerful practices right now that could dramatically increase the odds of a very bright future for you, your kids, and your grandchildren? Parenting is one of the toughest and most important jobs. We all want to do right by our kids and set them up for success, not just in careers, but also in relationships, health, money, and spirit. So we'll outline how combining better brain function with Love and Logic's psychology-based child-rearing strategies is the ultimate secret to parenting success. It's the marriage of these two pieces of the parenting puzzle that puts you on the path to raising mentally strong kids and having more fun while doing it.

It is time to start thinking about what you are trying to achieve in your day-to-day interactions with your child. We bet that you are like most parents and want to see certain traits develop in your child, such as being:

- Confident
- Resilient
- Competent
- Responsible
- Respectful
- Kind and caring
- Resourceful
- Self-controlled
- Problem solver
- Generally positive in their attitude
- Able to calm themselves
- Able to tolerate discomfort
- Able to delay gratification
- Able to learn from their mistakes
- Comfortable asking for help when needed
- Have healthy relationships and set good boundaries with others
- Know how to say no to temptations from others
- Have the skills and education to have a job they enjoy that also pays the bills
- Have good relationship skills and spend time with quality people
- Take care of themselves and be physically and emotionally healthy
- Live by clearly defined goals and a sense of purpose

These are the traits of someone who is mentally strong—and you can help your kids develop them. Even though we all want these things for our kids, we may not know how to achieve them or we get so busy that we lose sight of what really matters. It can happen to all of us, even to the authors—a child psychiatrist and a child psychologist!

Do you know what you are trying to accomplish as a parent, or do you feel like some days you are simply "winging it"? Unless we want our children to wander aimlessly through life and unless we want to flip-flop through parenthood, we need to pinpoint a desired destination. As parents, this means envisioning the type of adults we want our kids to become. Instilling mental strength, motivation, and a can-do attitude in your child is easier than you think, and it all starts with goal setting. For yourself and your kids.

After meeting with Dr. Fay, Gina and Tony immersed themselves in the Love and Logic program and began to think deeply about their goals as parents and about the man they wanted Luca to become. Three things jumped out at them almost immediately. These became some initial goals that immediately helped them start moving in a better direction with their son:

- Teach him to take responsibility for his own life and decisions.
- Help him learn to care about others and display good character.
- Help him focus most of his energy on his strengths.

So initially, they stopped doing his homework for him, allowing him to experience the consequences of failing to work hard. They also got him involved in some community service opportunities and began expecting him to help around the house. Finally, they stopped criticizing what he struggled with and focused on noticing and encouraging his love of drawing and design. Although Luca gave some initial pushback, his motivation changed and so did his engagement. This initial work gave them the encouragement they needed to keep using the power of goals.

HOW SETTING PARENTING GOALS HELPS YOU AND YOUR CHILD BECOME MENTALLY STRONGER

When Dr. Amen first mentions goal setting to his patients who are parents, they often look at him with blank stares or mutter something vague about a career or money. Goal setting is not only for some far-off dream. It is for you now as a parent, and it plays a major role in your ability to raise a confident, competent, mentally tough child. Making goals that you can focus on daily will make a big difference in your life. Being goal-directed is crucial for effective parenting. And brain health is essential to goal setting and the behavior to achieve those goals.

We'll guide you toward the best practices and principles based on neuroscience and Love and Logic for goal setting, brain health, and strong parent-child relationships. This is why Gina and Tony achieved success. Their goals helped their brains guide them toward effective behaviors. In other words, their goals pulled them up from the mire and allowed them to start *doing* things rather than *worrying* about things.

Guess what part of the brain controls goal setting. The prefrontal cortex (PFC), the most evolved part of your brain as an adult and the least developed part for kids and young adults. The PFC, which is involved in planning, forethought, judgment, impulse control, and empathy, isn't fully developed until the mid-twenties. Until your child reaches that age, *you* need to step in and act as their PFC. (You will learn more about the brain throughout this book.)

For this part of your brain to be as effective as possible, you need to know what you want and what is important to you. When the PFC functions properly, you can engage in goal-directed behavior and effectively supervise your words and deeds. You are able to think before you say things and tend to say things that improve your chances of achieving your goals. You'll also tend to think before you act, and the rest of the brain helps create the behaviors that are consistent with your goals.

How to Find Your Purpose in Life

For your goals to be meaningful and effective, it's important to understand your purpose and keep it in mind as you raise your kids. To discover your purpose, ask yourself the following questions:

1. What do you love to do? Do you love to cook, write, draw, teach, parent, and so on? What is something you feel qualified to teach others?

2. Who do you do it for? How does your work connect you to others?

3. Are there hurts from your past that you can turn into help for others? Turn your pain into purpose.

4. What do others want or need from you?

5. How do others change as a result of what you do?

6. How do you want to be remembered after you die? What do you want your legacy to be?

Take note that only two of the six questions are about you; four of them are about others. Happiness and meaning is often found in helping others.

Your mind takes what it sees and makes it happen. So it is critical to visualize what you want for yourself as a parent and for your child and then match your behavior over time to get it. Too many parents are thrown around by the whims of the moment (or the whims of their kids), rather than using their PFC to create a strategic plan for themselves and their children of all ages. Is your PFC calling the shots, or have you let your emotions take over?

WHAT DO YOU WANT AS A PARENT? WHAT DO YOU WANT FOR YOUR CHILDREN?

Ultimately, your goals determine your behavior. Being clear with what you are trying to achieve as a parent will take your behavior out of the realm of an unconscious repetition of the past and focus your actions in a positive direction. When you are clear about your goals for yourself as a parent and for your child, you'll be proactive and positive. And you'll instill in your kids the foundation they need to be mentally strong enough to deal with real-world stresses and become responsible adults. Without clarity, you can become reactive, ineffective, and easily frustrated (every parent has experienced those moments). You'll also lack the ability to show your children what it takes to have a purposeful and productive life. This results in raising kids who lack the mental toughness, motivation, and confidence to be successful in all areas of their life. That is why we have each developed written goals to keep ourselves on task as parents.

The word *written* is important here. A 2021 brain-imaging study from Japanese researchers analyzing the effectiveness of writing things on paper versus inputting information into mobile devices strongly suggests that the act of writing something on paper stimulates specific parts of our brain heavily involved in memory.[2] In addition, in a 2015 study analyzing goal setting, a psychology professor at Dominican University divided 149 participants into five groups: unwritten goals; written goals; written goals and action commitments; written goals and action commitments sent to a friend; and written goals, action commitments, and weekly progress reports sent to a friend. After four weeks, it was clear that the group of people who wrote down their goals, developed action steps, and sent weekly progress reports to a pal achieved significantly more of their goals than any of the other groups. The group that didn't write down goals and simply thought about what they wanted to accomplish achieved the least.[3]

On the following pages, we have included our personal goals for parenting and what we each want for our kids—Dr. Amen's adult children, college-age young adult daughter Chloe, and teenage nieces, and Dr. Fay's adult kids and teenage son. We each keep a list of our individual goals where we can look at them every day. Dr. Amen's are in the top drawer of his desk at work, and Dr. Fay's are pinned to the wall in his office. We each start the day by looking at our goals. Starting the day this way helps us to keep our behavior consistent with what we want.

Dr. Amen's Parenting Goals

As a parent, my overall goal is to be a competent, positive force in my child's life.

1. Be involved—I want to be there for my children, so I will ensure that I have enough time for them.

2. Be open—I will talk with them in such a way that will help them talk to me when they need to.

3. Be firm/set limits—I will provide appropriate supervision and limits until they develop their own moral/internal controls.

4. Be together—Whether married or divorced, it is best for the children when both parents agree and support each other in the process.

5. Be kind—I will raise my children in such a way so that they will want to come see me after they leave home. Being a parent is also a selfish job.

6. Be fun—I will joke, clown, and be playful with my kids. Having fun is essential to physical and emotional health.

Dr. Fay's Parenting Goals

1. Be loving—I will be present and demonstrate unconditional acceptance.

2. Be firm—I will provide limits and accountability through natural or logical consequences.

3. Be a good model—I will show kindness, humility, honesty, and resilience.

4. Be dependable and trustworthy—I will follow through on what I say I will do.

5. Be thankful and joyful—I will focus on what is positive and will demonstrate faith.

6. Be generous—I will have a good attitude about sharing my time and resources with others.

7. Be honorable—I will strive to bring glory to God in all that I do.

Dr. Amen's Goals for His Kids

For my children, the overall goal is to enhance development and mental strength.

1. Be relational—We live in a relational world. It is imperative that I teach my children to get along with others.

2. Be responsible—My children need to believe and act as if they have some control over their own life. Their problems are not always someone else's fault. Otherwise, they act like victims.

3. Be independent—I will allow my children to have some choices over their own lives so that they will be able to make good decisions on their own.

4. Be self-confident—I will encourage my children to be involved with different activities where they will feel a sense of competence. Self-confidence often comes from our ability to master tasks and sports.

5. Be self-accepting—I will notice more positives than negatives in my children to teach them to be able to accept themselves.

6. Be adaptable—I will expose my children to different situations so they will be flexible enough to deal with the stresses that come their way.

7. Be emotionally free—I will allow my children the ability to express themselves in an accepting environment. I will also seek help for my children if they show prolonged symptoms of emotional trouble.

8. Be fun—I will teach my children how to have fun and how to laugh.

Dr. Fay's Goals for His Kids

1. Be responsible—I will allow my kids to make plenty of small mistakes when they are younger, so that they will see that every choice they make has consequences. I will allow them to see that blaming others for their problems doesn't work.

2. Be respectful—I will show them respect and expect it from them. I will help them see that disrespectful behavior brings about sad consequences.

3. Be resilient and resourceful—I will allow them to experience adversity and to see that they have the capability to solve problems and to cope with discouragement.

4. Be generous—I will model this for them and give them many opportunities to share what they have with others.

5. Be humble—I will teach them that all good things are gracious gifts from above.

6. Be joyfully relational—I will show them that lasting relationships are more precious than the stuff we own or the circumstances we find ourselves in.

If you like these goals, copy them. Revise them to fit your own goals and desires for your children, adding your own special touches. Then put them up where you can see them every day and ask yourself, "Is my behavior getting me what I want for myself as a parent and what I want for my child as they grow into adulthood?"

We firmly believe that you must look at your goals *every day*. This takes them out of the realm of wishful thinking and places them in the realm of everyday behavior. If you only look at your goals occasionally, they will likely have a fate similar to most New Year's resolutions: disappointment.

When you know what you want, you are more likely to change your behavior to get it. This is because your brain receives and creates reality. In fact, in studying successful children and parents, we have found that what they have in common is a sense of personal responsibility and clear goals.

So Dr. Amen has his patients—whether they are 5 years old or 75 years old—do a goal-setting exercise he developed called the One Page Miracle (OPM). He's written about this exercise in some of his previous books,[4] but it is adapted here specifically for parents and children. This exercise will help you be effective in nearly all of your thoughts, words, and actions. This exercise can quickly focus and change your life and your child's life.

Specify exactly what you want (not what you don't want) in the major areas of your life as a parent—relationships, work, money, and self—to encourage a balanced approach to life. Under self, you'll consider the four circles of mental strength. Spend time developing your OPM, and revise it often. Burnout occurs when we are overextended in one area or neglecting one or more areas.

One Page Miracle
for Parents

What do I want for my life as a parent?
What am I doing to make it happen?

RELATIONSHIPS
Spouse/Partner: _____
Children: _____

WORK
_____
_____

FINANCES
_____
_____

SELF
Physical: _____
Emotional: _____
Mental: _____
Spiritual: _____

Here is an example from Gina, Luca's mom mentioned at the beginning of this chapter. She spent time thinking about her goals as a parent as well as her goals for her teenage son, Luca.

One Page Miracle for Parents: Gina

What do I want for my life as a parent?
What am I doing to make it happen?

RELATIONSHIPS

Spouse/Partner: I want my husband and I to be on the same page in terms of parenting our son, so we provide a united front.
Children: I want to get to know my son Luca better. I want to help him be more self-motivated and to help him develop the mental skills he needs to be independent. I want him to get a job he likes that will pay enough for him to enjoy a certain lifestyle.

WORK/FINANCES

I want to be a good role model for Luca to see how rewarding it can be when you have a good job that you love.

SELF

Physical: I want to be healthy and model a healthy lifestyle for my son.
Emotional: I want to focus more on the positive, so I can feel more at peace.
Mental: I want to change my pattern of criticism.
Spiritual: I want to feel like my life matters.

HOW TO HELP YOUR KIDS SET GOALS

Goal setting is not just for parents, although it starts with you. It is also one of the best ways to develop your child's prefrontal cortex and mental strength to help set them up for success. As with parents, when children know what they want, they are more likely to match their behavior to get it. Usually, though, when we ask young children and adolescents about their goals, they tend to say something about being a firefighter, celebrity, or technology billionaire when they grow up. It's important to teach children of any age to make short-term, right-now goals as well as long-term ones.

Help your child develop their own OPM to boost their own clarity about what they want in life. Rather than approaching this as a task or chore, be sure to explain to them that the OPM is a tool that will help make their dreams come true. That way they will be more inclined to want to participate. The OPM is appropriate for kids at almost any age, starting around the time they go to kindergarten or first grade. Goal setting can also be beneficial for kids with special needs or disabilities, helping them stay focused on realistic, attainable objectives. Think of this as a wonderful opportunity for you to connect with your child and get to know them and their innermost wants and desires. You may be tempted to "tell" your child what their goals should be, but it is critical that you refrain from doing so. To help them identify their goals, be prepared to ask them questions, such as:

- What do you enjoy doing?
- What is something you would like to get better at?
- Is there anything you have never done but would like to try?
- What would make you happy?
- How can you show people that you love them?
- How can you help others who are hurting?
- What do you think is your purpose in life?

Next to each subheading (change "Work" to "School" or "Chores"; include "Money" if they get an allowance or have a job), have your child clearly write out what's important to them in that area. Be sure to have them write what they want, not what they don't want. If they are having a hard time thinking of something, gently coach them with suggestions, such as, "You seem to really enjoy math class" or "I notice that you take great photos." Be positive and have them write in the first person. After you finish with the initial draft (you'll frequently want to update it as they grow up), place this piece of paper where you and your child can see it every day, such as on the refrigerator, by your child's bed, or on the bathroom mirror. That way, every day your child can focus their eyes and their brains on what's important to them. This makes it easier to match their behavior to what they want. Their life will become more intentional, and they will spend their energy on goals that are important to them rather than wasting their efforts on things that don't serve them. This lays the foundation for mental strength, helping them build the willpower to follow through on things of value and say no to unhealthy temptations.

When Gina initially asked Luca to do this exercise with her, he rolled his eyes at her. But when she assured him it was so they could focus on what *he* wanted for his life, not what *she* wanted for him, he agreed. Together they went through the One Page Miracle. Gina had to bite her tongue several times, but she learned so much about her son in this simple exercise. It turned out that Luca didn't lack motivation; he simply had no interest in running a mom-and-pop restaurant. He was passionate about drawing, design, and computers.

Luca went over to his computer, clicked on a file, and showed it to his mom. He had designed a new logo for the restaurant but had been too scared to show his parents. Gina was astounded by how good it was and promised to show it to Tony. Luca also told her he had come up with a plan on how they could start an online store to sell the family's wildly popular marinara sauce, but he didn't think they wanted to hear his ideas. The pressure they put on him to follow in their footsteps had filled him with resentment and demotivated him in other areas of his life. Trying to force him into what they believed was best for him had backfired and was robbing him of the mental strength he deserved.

One Page Miracle
Luca, Age 16

RELATIONSHIPS

Parents: I want to have the kind of relationship with my parents where I can feel like it's okay to be myself and that they will accept me for who I am.
Siblings: I don't have any siblings.
Friends: I want to have friends who have the same interests, so we can encourage each other.

SCHOOL/WORK/CHORES

School: I want to go to a school where I can focus on the things I love—drawing, design, and computers.
Teachers: I want to find teachers who can be mentors to me.

Work/Chores: I want to take our family business in new directions with an online store, a better website, and updated graphics. At home, I want to get a dog, so I will commit to walking it once a day every day.

MYSELF

Physical: To feel good in my body.
Emotional: To wake up feeling excited for the day.
Mental: To focus on doing well in subjects I love.
Spiritual: To feel more connected to something greater than myself and to try meditation.

Here are examples from other children at different ages, so you can see the types of goals that might be appropriate for your child.

One Page Miracle
Allie, Age 6

RELATIONSHIPS

Parents: I want my parents to be proud of me.
Siblings: I want my brother to be nicer to me.
Friends: Make new friends at my new school.

SCHOOL/CHORES

School: To be a good student.
Teachers: I want my teachers to like me.
Chores: I want to learn to help make family dinner.

MYSELF

Physical: To be healthy.
Emotional: To have fun.
Mental: To be kind.
Spiritual: To pay attention better at church.

One Page Miracle
Joe, Age 9

RELATIONSHIPS

Parents: I want to have a kind, loving relationship with my mom and dad. I want them to trust me and be proud of me.
Siblings: I realize that my brother will always be my family. Even though we may fight sometimes, I will treat him the way that I would want him to treat me.
Friends: It is important to have friends. I will treat other people with kindness and respect. I will make new friends with kids who have the same kinds of goals I have.

SCHOOL/CHORES

School: School is for me. It is to help me be the best person I can be. I give school my best effort every day. I want to learn and become a smart person.
Teacher: My teachers are there to help me. I will treat them with respect and kindness.
Chores: When I have work to do, either around the house or at a job someday, I will do my best and feel proud of my effort. I will help around the house and do my chores with a good attitude. I know I need to help my family and do my part.

MYSELF

Physical: To be healthy and to take care of my body.
Emotional: To feel good, happy.
Mental: To be thankful.
Spiritual: To live in a way that makes me feel proud and to live close to God and be the kind of person He would want me to be.

One Page Miracle
Melissa, Age 20

RELATIONSHIPS

Parents: I want to stay connected to my parents even though I now live in my college dorm and not at home anymore.
Siblings: I want to be a good role model for my younger brother and sister.
Friends: I want to have a few close friends I can really count on, and I want to spend more time with my boyfriend.

SCHOOL/WORK

School: I want to do well in my undergraduate work, so I can get accepted to law school.
Teacher: I want to develop a good relationship with the professors from whom I can learn the most.
Work: Although my weekend job isn't in the field I want to go into, it's still important to do my best and learn as much as possible about how to be successful in the workplace.

MYSELF

Physical: I want to improve my volleyball skills so I can move up from the junior varsity to the varsity team.
Emotional: I want to learn ways to cope with the daily stress of going to college, working, being on the volleyball team, and having a boyfriend.
Mental: I want to get enough rest so my focus and attention are as good as they can be while I'm at school and at practice.
Spiritual: I want to get more involved with my church.

One Page Miracle for Kids

What do I want for my life?
What can I do to make it happen?

RELATIONSHIPS

Parents: _____

_____

Siblings: _____

_____

Friends: _____

_____

SCHOOL/WORK

School: _____

_____

Teachers: _____

_____

Work/Chores: _____

_____

MYSELF

Physical: _____

_____

Emotional: _____

_____

Mental: _____

_____

Spiritual: _____

_____

DOES IT FIT?

Three of the most powerful words in the English language are "Does it fit?" When you ask yourself if your behavior fits your parenting goals, it is so much easier to reach those goals. Every time you are going to say something to your children or do something, ask yourself, "Does it fit?" Do your words and actions fit with your goals as a parent? Do they help your child reach their personal goals? Are they fueling their mental strength? If the answer is no, don't do it. When you can answer yes, you will know that you are on the right path.

Equally important is teaching your kids to ask themselves, "Does it fit?" The simple concept of matching behavior to help achieve what they really want is easy to comprehend, even at a young age. This is one of the foundational steps to becoming a mentally strong, competent, responsible, caring human.

Teach kids that to be mentally strong it is critical to have clearly spelled out goals and that the achievement of almost anything they want can be broken down into a series of very small steps. The achievement of any of those small steps is not beyond their capacity, which means that achievement is really about getting clear on what they want and then moving toward their goals daily.

Action Steps

- Spend time thinking about what you want for yourself as a parent and for your child as they grow into adulthood. Use this information to create your own One Page Miracle.
- Spend time with your child brainstorming about what they want in their life and help them create their own OPM.
- Place your OPMs where you and your child can see them every day.
- Ask yourself, "Does it fit?" to see if your behavior fits with your goals and is helping you achieve them.
- Teach your children to ask themselves, "Does it fit?" to make sure their actions are improving their chances of reaching their goals.

CHAPTER 3

IS YOUR PARENTING STYLE BREEDING MENTAL STRENGTH OR WEAKNESS?

The two words firm *and* kind *are the essence of great parents who raise great people.*

Do you love your children and want to be an involved parent? Of course, you do! That's why you're reading this book. But not all parents are alike. Some parenting styles make it harder to achieve the goals you have for yourself and your child—contributing to lack of motivation, neediness, feelings of entitlement, or feelings of anxiety. Other parenting styles facilitate the process of raising young people who are competent, and even better, allow us to enjoy our kids more in the present moment. If you want to get on the fast track to fun times and a brighter future, you need to take an honest look at yourself. You may unknowingly be making parenting harder than it needs to be. What's your parenting style? Take this pop quiz:

- Do you routinely do your child's schoolwork for them?
- Do you frequently solve problems for your child?
- Do you give your kids—regardless of their age—detailed instructions for just about everything they do?
- Do you typically plan your child's day?
- How much time do you spend on your child's needs?
- Do you allow your child to make mistakes and suffer the consequences?
- Do you usually feel like you are working harder on your children's problems than they are?
- Do you find yourself making threats that you can't back up?
- Do you stonewall (not talk to), ignore, belittle, shame, or react with sarcasm when angry?

- Do you give your kids free rein to do whatever they want?
- Does your fear of upsetting your kids often keep you from setting and enforcing limits they really need?
- Are your decisions mostly based on your fears or past hurts, or are they primarily based on what will help your child grow in responsibility and self-confidence?

Based on your answers, you likely fall into one of four main parenting styles, which we will cover in this chapter. Before we dive into the four styles, understand that your parenting style usually comes from several factors: what your parents or caregivers modeled, other parents you admired, cultural influences, and your brain health and mental wellness, to name a few. You may feel comfortable with your current style, or perhaps it isn't working well enough for you. This chapter will help you fine-tune your style to be a more effective parent, so you can raise resilient, responsible, respectful kids.

In Dr. Amen's practice, he frequently sees a variety of parenting styles and a number of problems that come with them. Decades of research beginning with the work of clinical and developmental psychologist Diana Baumrind in the 1960s show that parenting styles can be viewed along two lines: from loving to hostile and from firm to permissive.[1] You've probably heard of these terms.

LOVING I am rooting for my child to succeed and have deep empathy and compassion for them.	**FIRM** When I say something, I mean it, and I will back it up.
HOSTILE I demand you do things my way and will punish you for mistakes.	**PERMISSIVE** I will clean up my child's mistakes.

Jim Fay and Foster Cline, MD, describe three styles:

- Helicopters: This most closely matches the Loving and Permissive style.
- Drill Sergeants: These are the parents who are Firm yet Hostile.
- Consultants: These parents are Loving and Firm. They also empower their children to take responsibility for their decisions.[2]

We also include a fourth style we term Uninvolved. These parents are both Hostile and Permissive.

Before we take a deep dive into these various styles, we want you to know that at Amen Clinics we have a "no jerk" rule. This concept comes from a 2007 book with a mildly obscene name by Robert Sutton.[3] Basically, it means we won't hire anyone who treats people badly because we don't want any toxic waste contaminating our workforce. We firmly believe that this rule starts with us, the people who are at the top, running our companies. We set the tone for the entire enterprise. In the family unit, this means you don't want any family member to be disrespectful or hurtful because that will create dysfunction for everyone. Most important, it all starts with you, the parent. If you act like a jerk, there's a bigger chance your children will too. Don't be a jerk! Instead, follow our rules of how to act in a Love and Logic home.

How We Act in Our Love and Logic Home

- I will treat you with respect so that you know how to treat me.
- Feel free to do anything you want, as long as it does not cause a problem for anyone else.
- If you cause a problem, I will ask you to solve it. Please let me know if you need any ideas for doing so.
- If you can't solve the problem or choose not to, I will do something.
- What I do will depend on the unique person and the unique situation.
- If you ever believe that something I have done is unfair, please let me know by whispering to me, "I'm not sure that's fair."
- We can schedule a time to talk. What you say may or may not change what I decide to do.[4]

Now, let's take a closer look at these common parenting styles to give you a better sense of which one sounds most like you. We will introduce you to the styles that make parenting harder and increase the chances of producing kids who are ineffective, helpless, and entitled. We will also give you a glimpse at the styles that are most likely to help you achieve your goals and help kids of all ages become mentally strong, independent problem solvers who can successfully reach their goals.

HELICOPTER PARENTS (LOVING AND PERMISSIVE)

This parenting style describes those parents who often seem sweet and kind to their children and give them anything they want. They are reluctant to challenge or frustrate their children. Sounds reasonable, doesn't it? Protect your children. Make life as easy and smooth as possible. The problem occurs when these parents give in to their child's every whim. Their overall goal is to create a perfect world for their kids. An example of this parenting style are the parents who constantly criticize their child's teachers, demanding that grades be changed and that their child be given more second chances to succeed. These are the same parents who eventually find themselves hiring lawyers to defend the teen or young adult facing drunk driving, petty theft, or drug use charges. These well-meaning yet confused parents have the wrong idea. They want their kids to like them rather than wanting to raise brain-healthy, mentally strong children. Sadly, this approach doesn't empower kids with the skills and attitudes required for success in the real world and instead creates narcissistic teens and adults.

At Love and Logic, we call them "Helicopter parents," which has become a ubiquitous term that conjures images of parents swooping in to rescue their children from life's slightest challenges. As mentioned earlier, Jim Fay and Foster W. Cline, MD, identified this common style.[5] Jim had recently left an inner-city school where he was working with a lot of students who were facing some major challenges—low-income households, food insecurity, walking to school through high-crime neighborhoods, and so on—and he was excited to start a new administrative position at a new suburban school. Jim naively believed that being at a school where the families had higher incomes meant there would be fewer problems.

Wrong!

Soon after landing on the new campus, Jim realized he was in for a new set of challenges he hadn't encountered. Parents were flooding the campus, toting lunch boxes, socks, and homework their kids had forgotten. Moms and dads would march into a classroom, confront the teacher, and hold the instructor personally responsible for their child's poor academic performance or unacceptable behavior in class. If the kids got into any kind of jam, the parents would fly in, hover over the kid, and drop a metaphorical rope ladder to whisk them away from the harsh land of cause and effect. For Jim and Dr. Cline, the imagery was so clear, the term *Helicopter parent* was born. While the parents think they have their kids' best interests in mind, all of these Helicopter rescues are robbing children of the mental fortitude to fend for themselves in life. (In chapter 4, we'll talk about when it's okay to rescue your child.)

Years later, Dr. Charles Fay (Jim's son) met a woman who was a prime example of this parenting style. Miranda admitted to Dr. Fay that she used to be a high-powered Helicopter parent who hovered nonstop around her daughter, Wanda. She would stand out by the school's playground with binoculars to keep an eye on Wanda, and if she noticed any sort of conflict, she would rush in to smooth it over. In the mornings, she always made sure Wanda was impeccably dressed even if it meant Wanda missed the bus and Miranda had to drive her to school. Miranda also volunteered for numerous school committees, primarily so she could keep an eye on the teachers and make sure they were doing a good job.

Over time, all this rescuing started taking a toll on Wanda's mental well-being. Wanda was becoming depressed, apathetic, incapable of making any decisions, and afraid to try anything new. Miranda, meanwhile, was feeling exhausted, irritable, and burned out. Helicopters burn a lot of fuel, and when they don't refuel, they drop like a rock. Miranda was heading down fast.

Helicopter Parents

Can you relate to being a Helicopter that's running on fumes? Here's why being a Helicopter parent can be so draining. Helicopter parents:

- Rescue children when rescue is not needed
- Send this message to their kids: "You are weak and incapable. That's why I need to protect and rescue you from the world."

- Create kids who are irresponsible, incapable, and often resentful
- Experience massive parenting burnout
- Parent from the limbic system (the brain's emotional centers) rather than from the prefrontal cortex (the brain's CEO in charge of executive functions and logical thinking)
- Fail to consistently support the Four Circles of Mental Strength (biological, psychological, social, and spiritual) in themselves and their children throughout their lifetime
- Make most of their parenting decisions out of fear

By constantly rescuing her daughter, Miranda was sending Wanda the underlying message that she wasn't bright enough, strong enough, or mentally capable enough to navigate life. Miranda believed that she needed to create an ideal environment void of any obstacles because Wanda couldn't handle it on her own. Acting out of fear and a desire to control the outcome, Miranda was trying to engineer the future. Unfortunately, this technique backfires by creating kids who are irresponsible, unprepared, and full of resentment.

It is well-documented that as humans, we grow by facing challenges. Donald Meichenbaum, a psychotherapist and one of the founders of cognitive behavioral therapy, has written extensively about a concept called *stress inoculation training* that involves exposure to minor stressors as a way to build resilience and coping skills to handle bigger stressors.[6] Helicopter parents rob their children of these learning opportunities, effectively leaving them ill-equipped to cope with life.

The good news is, even for extreme Helicopter parents like Miranda, there is hope to adopt a more effective parenting style. Later in this chapter, we will show you how Miranda went from Helicopter mom to letting Wanda take charge of her own life and how they are both happier, healthier, and psychologically stronger because of it. Before we get to that, let's look at another common parenting style.

DRILL SERGEANTS (HOSTILE AND FIRM)

Dr. Amen was a U.S. Army psychiatrist for seven years and knew many parents like this. Military Drill Sergeants play a very valuable role in defending our country, and we are extremely grateful for their service. However, parents who use this style with kids create major heartache. They were either raised this way themselves or feel like it's the best way to raise responsible and respectful children. Though they value the role of authority and rules, Drill Sergeant parents tend to be rigid and inflexible, possibly because their anterior cingulate gyrus (ACG), deep in the front, middle part of the brain, is operating at a high level. The ACG is like the brain's gear shifter. It helps people to be flexible and go from one thought or action to another. When the ACG is too active, however, people can get stuck on worries or behaviors that aren't helpful, and they have a tendency to be argumentative and oppositional. This often causes a child to be anxious or fearful. In addition, children of these parents may inherit an overactive ACG and have the same inclination to be quarrelsome and antagonistic and to have trouble shifting attention.

In a nutshell, Drill Sergeant parents want it done their way, and they get their child's compliance through anger, intimidation, and fear. This style leads to a lot of conflict and unstated messages, such as:

"You do it when I say it, how I say it, without any questions. I hope you got it!"

"I stapled your homework to your mittens, so you won't lose it like you always do."

"I put your daily schedule in your pocket, because I know you can't think for yourself."

"Here's your list of approved friends. Don't lose it."

"Here's a chart showing you what to think, choose, and do."
"You'll be going to the same college I went to and majoring in the same subject, because your interests and desires aren't important to me."

You might suspect that Drill Sergeant parents harshly bark out these orders, but they may use a soft voice while delivering the commands. (A gentle tone doesn't change the dictator approach.) Either way, they are micromanaging their children's lives because deep down they don't believe their kids are capable of making their own decisions. Sadly, this often becomes a self-fulfilling prophecy as these kids are conditioned to second-guess themselves or to wait for approval from their parents. Some research suggests an authoritarian parenting style also interferes with healthy attachment, making it harder to develop a strong parent-child bond.[7] In chapter 4, you'll read about why bonding and relationship are so important in effective parenting.

Take a look at Tara and her son, Chuck. This little guy came out of the womb as a natural people pleaser. Easygoing and mellow, Chuck grew to enjoy art, cooking, and other things that didn't interest his mother at all. Tara, on the other hand, was hard-charging and highly motivated. She firmly believed there wasn't a problem in the world that couldn't be solved with an Excel spreadsheet. According to her, placing checkmarks in those little boxes was the sign of a good life.

In Chuck's view, checkmarks and boxes felt too constraining. For him, life was all about free-flowing creativity, socializing with friends, and hanging out. But as a people pleaser, he generally did what he was told and managed to do fairly well at school. Then came his teenage years, a rush of hormones, and a technical writing class that involved some of those dreaded boxes and checkmarks.

Tara received a call from his teacher.

"We've got a problem," the teacher said.

"What's the problem?" asked Tara.

"Chuck hasn't been doing his science papers."

Tara hit the roof. She assured the teacher that she would take care of it. When Chuck got home that afternoon, the Drill Sergeant in Tara ranted and raved about the missed assignments. Then, feeling guilty, she whipped up an organizational chart and a spreadsheet with all the assignments from the teacher. She presented the materials to Chuck and said, "We're going to get all these assignments done. I'm going to work on them with you every night until they're all completed. Don't worry, Chuck, it's going to be okay."

This is a classic example of the Guilt Cycle we see in Drill Sergeant parents. They get angry when their child makes a mistake or doesn't perform up to their expectations, but then they rush in to rescue them out of guilt. This is a very harmful pattern that perpetuates irresponsibility and resentment in children.

In Chuck's case, Tara came to the rescue by telling her son what to write and how to write it. She practically wrote the science essays herself. And Chuck just seemed to go along with whatever his mom said. Tara thought she was doing an amazing job of navigating the situation to ensure Chuck would be successful and get a good grade in the class. About a month later, however, his teacher called again.

"I still haven't seen those essays," the teacher said.

This time, Tara was so mad she rocketed up through the ceiling tiles and then the roof shingles before coming back down. She demanded to have a meeting to sort things out. In the school office, the teacher, Tara, and Chuck sat uncomfortably. The teacher told Tara that Chuck was a real pleasure, but he wasn't going to pass her class if he didn't turn in his assignments. This is the moment when Chuck came of age. He swiveled his chair and looked his mom straight in the eye and, totally relaxed, said, "Mom, you can make me write those papers, but you can't make me turn them in." Chuck didn't have drugs in his locker; he had a stack of essays in it. Why didn't he turn them in?

Does it surprise you that someone like Chuck would sabotage his own life when he felt like he was being controlled? It's true. In an effort to gain some sense of self-control, children will often rebel and act in ways that don't serve them. This leads to some very intelligent kids, teens, and young adults making poor, self-destructive decisions that don't help them reach their goals.

This also contributes to kids choosing belief systems that are the opposite of their parents' beliefs, often out of spite or as a way to get back at their folks for trying to control them. Research shows that overbearing parents can even play a role in eating disorders in which kids restrict their eating as a way to gain control over at least one thing in their life.[8]

The lesson here is that when Drill Sergeants try to control the outcome, they usually end up disempowering their children. Like Helicopter parents, their actions have lasting consequences that fuel incompetence, unhappiness, and discord.

Drill Sergeant Parents

- Bark orders, deliver orders in a gentle tone, or micromanage
- Send "you-can't-think" messages
- Create kids who are irresponsible, incapable, and often resentful
- Often fall into the Guilt Cycle of berating and then rescuing
- Experience massive parenting burnout
- Parent from the limbic system (the brain's emotional centers) rather than from the prefrontal cortex (the brain's CEO in charge of executive functions and logical thinking)
- Fail to consistently support the Four Circles of Mental Strength (biological, psychological, social, and spiritual) in themselves and their children
- Make most of their parenting decisions out of fear masked as anger or an overly controlling nature

Also similar to Helicopter parents, Drill Sergeants are highly involved because they love their children and want what's best for them. With the strategies in this book, parents falling into both counterproductive styles can shift gears. They can put their energy into a more effective approach that helps create happier, more respectful, more responsible, and far more resilient kids. This is especially important if they are parenting children with special needs of any kind.

UNINVOLVED PARENTS (HOSTILE AND PERMISSIVE)

To put it simply, these are the parents who do not care. They are usually overwhelmed in their own lives—they may have had a head injury, drank too much, or experienced trauma—all of which can negatively impact brain function. They are often angry people and detached from their child. Generally, there is a lack of bonding, caring, and adequate supervision. When Dr. Amen described this type of parent in one of his parenting classes, a police officer gave the following example of the uninvolved parent: "I knew a father who gave his 15-year-old son a $100 bill and told him that he didn't want to see his face all weekend long."

These parents provide no structure and don't supervise their children, meaning no one is acting as their frontal lobes while theirs are still in the development process. In the long run, this type of parenting prevents the brain from maturing because children are making their own decisions without the guidance of a parent helping them make good choices. This throws a wrench into the mental development process too. As kids grow into adulthood, they are more likely to make the same mistakes, be more susceptible to peer pressure, and neglect thinking about the consequences of their actions. Considering that you are reading this book on how to be a better parent, it's clear that you don't likely fit into this category, so we won't delve deeply into this parenting style.

CONSULTANTS (LOVING AND FIRM)

Welcome to the wonderful world of the Consultant parent! Whereas Helicopters and Drill Sergeants expend so much effort that ends up leading to burnout and harmful results, the Consultant parenting style requires less effort but makes it so much easier to reach the goals you have for yourself and your child and smooths your child's transition to being a competent and confident adult. In addition, it lets you all have a lot more fun along the journey.

These parents demonstrate respect to their kids, and they expect it in return. They teach their kids how to mind the first time, and then they expect them to do so. They are also reinforcing, warm, positive, and uplifting to the children. They know how to give options and choices, yet they have high expectations for good behavior. As mentioned earlier, one way to describe these parents is *firm* and *kind*. You can use a gentle tone while still enforcing your answer or instruction. This parenting style is the most advantageous way to exemplify being a child's frontal lobes until theirs finish developing in their mid-twenties. It means you are giving your child the mental training they need to make the best decisions once they are on their own as an adult. It also paves the way to a smoother relationship with your child and helps form secure attachment, according to research.[9]

How Do Children Show Respect?

How will you know when your child is being respectful? Basically, respect is when your child shows they care about others. Here are some examples of how respectful children act:

- Being polite
- Using kind words
- Displaying good manners
- Saying "please," "thank you," and "excuse me"
- Sharing with others
- Waiting patiently until it is their turn
- Being careful with other people's things so they don't break
- Speaking with a quiet voice in public settings
- Being calm in public areas
- Letting others speak without interrupting
- Doing what parents ask them to do without whining

What does respect sound like from a child? It isn't just what they say, it's how they say it. Being respectful means their tone of voice is free of sarcasm, and eye rolls don't accompany their words.

Let's look at how it worked for Wanda's mom, Miranda. By the time Wanda got to junior high, Miranda was still helping her get dressed, driving her to school when she missed the bus, then escorting her to her classroom. Wanda was a good kid who was starting to develop some very unpleasant habits. Have you ever met a child like this?

One morning, the teacher handed Miranda a CD and said she thought it could be helpful for her. Miranda looked at the title: "Helicopters, Drill Sergeants, and Consultants." Curious, she popped it into the CD player and listened to it on the drive home.

When Miranda realized what it was about, she quickly ejected the CD. *How dare that teacher try to tell me how to parent my child*, she thought.

Over the next few days, Miranda would look at the CD in her car every time she drove Wanda to school. One morning, after helping Wanda pick out her clothes, fix her hair, make her breakfast, get her homework ready, and driving her to school, which made her late for her own job, Miranda felt overwhelmed and exhausted. *I can't keep going like this*, she thought. She put the CD back into the player and soon had to admit that she had a problem: She was a Helicopter parent.

She discovered for the first time that she needed to let Wanda make some mistakes so she could learn from them and become more resilient. The next morning, she decided to put it to the test. As usual, Wanda woke up and called out to her mom. "Mom! My hair's a mess. Where's my skirt? I can't find my homework! I'm hungry!" Miranda stifled her typical reaction of racing in to help and simply said, "Oh, Wanda, that's gotta be so hard. If any kid can figure it out, you can. I can help after I'm ready myself."

After a few moments of silence, Miranda heard some whining followed by the distinct sound of cereal being poured into a bowl. An instant later, she heard the bowl crash onto the floor. "Mom, I need you to clean this up," Wanda yelled.

Wanda piped up again, saying, "I need my homework!"

"I'm sure you can find where you left it," Miranda calmly replied, adding, "My car leaves at 7. If you miss the bus, you can pay for gas, and remember, gas prices have gone up."

Wanda missed the bus and paid her mom for gas. The next morning, it was a similar scenario. Wanda whined about her hair, homework, and hunger. Miranda said she would be happy to help *after* she got ready herself. Wanda made it onto the bus that morning, but she looked like a wet cat, and she forgot her homework, which was going to lower her grades.

Miranda realized that raising a confident, self-directed daughter required allowing her to make mistakes and experience the logical or natural consequences. She also discovered that it was better to let Wanda make those mistakes when the consequences were more "affordable." If youngsters don't have the opportunity to make mistakes and learn from them at an early age, the consequences become bigger and more harmful as they get older.

What Are Affordable Consequences?

- Refusing to eat what is served at dinner and feeling hungry until breakfast
- Forgetting their homework assignment and getting a bad grade as a result
- Missing the bus and having to pay Mom for the time and gas spent to get a ride

- Getting angry, breaking their favorite toy, and doing without it
- Eating too much and feeling sick
- Getting a speeding ticket and having to pay the fine
- Spending all of their own money on something that quickly breaks
- Forgetting their sports equipment and having to sit out of a game
- Sassing their parent and experiencing the consequences of not being taken somewhere they want to go
- Being nasty to friends at the playground and immediately being taken home to spend some quiet time in their room

Over time, Wanda grew to enjoy problem-solving and taking charge of her own life. Her confidence soared, her decision-making improved, and she was more cheerful and ready to take on new challenges. Miranda was able to engage in some much-needed self-care, which gave her better energy, a brighter outlook, and a more positive mindset about her daughter.

With practice, it became second nature for Miranda to let Wanda figure out things on her own. That doesn't mean there weren't any setbacks. When it came time for Wanda to apply for college, Miranda found her old fears creeping in and worried that her daughter wouldn't complete her applications in time. She even hopped on Wanda's computer and started filling one out. When Wanda walked in and saw what her mom was doing, she got angry. "You're having a relapse, Mom!" she said. The pair of them broke down laughing, and Miranda admitted she was wrong. Once again, Miranda had to make peace with the idea that it's okay not to be perfect. Just like it was all right for Wanda to make mistakes, it was permissible for her to make them too.

Consultant Parents

- Rescue or micromanage *only* when absolutely necessary (see chapter 4)
- Allow their children to make affordable mistakes
- Send healthy and empowering messages to their kids
- Create adults who are responsible, capable, and optimistic

- Guide their children to own and solve the problems they encounter
- Focus mostly on strengths and successes
- Feel energized and find joy in parenting
- Parent from the prefrontal cortex (the brain's CEO in charge of executive functions, focus, goals, and logical thinking) as well as the limbic system (the brain's emotional centers) in terms of bonding but not out of fear
- Work on attachment with time and listening, and thus create positive lifelong relationships (see chapter 4)
- Support the Four Circles of Mental Strength (biological, psychological, social, and spiritual) in themselves and their children
- Make decisions based on solid science and healthy common sense rather than their own emotional needs

Action Steps

- If you're a Helicopter parent or Drill Sergeant, think of three things you can stop doing tomorrow to decrease micromanagement of your child.
- Examine what's fueling your fears and anxiety about your child's future and address those issues.
- Make a list of mistakes you made as a kid and what you learned from them.
- Write out three mistakes you want your child to make this month, three mistakes this year, and three mistakes by the time they reach adulthood.

CHAPTER 4

NOTHING WORKS WITHOUT RELATIONSHIP

Our kids won't bond with our values unless they first bond with us.

We've emphasized the importance of brain health, goals, and parenting styles and how critical they are for developing and maintaining mental strength in both parents and kids of all ages. Strong relationships are also an essential part of this process. We'll give you five proven strategies, each of which communicates great love to kids. Great love means great bonding. And bonding helps your child's brain and emotional development.

THE SECRET TO YOUR CHILDREN PICKING YOUR VALUES

Do you want your child to share your values? Talk to them and consistently apply the strategies in this chapter. Children pick the values of parents with whom they have a strong bond. So if you're a Republican, a Democrat, or anything else, and you want your children to adopt these same beliefs, spend time with them, listen to them, speak nicely to them, and show them compassion. If for some strange reason you want your kids to adopt values that constantly grate on you like the sound of a jackhammer, then neglect them, don't talk to them, and criticize them constantly. Be indifferent or angry with them, and they will take a position opposite yours. The children who are countercultural (and often try to embarrass their parents) are basically telling off their parents.

Positive bonding provides a host of benefits that contribute to mental strength and ultimately make your job as a parent easier, including:

- *Shared values:* When there is a trusting relationship, kids tend to place their parents' values in the emotional part of their brain. Kids carry those values with them everywhere they go, which is why their parents continue to influence them even when they aren't present. Youngsters who have bonded with their parents follow their example, motivated by respect and love.

- *Healthier brain development:* The science is clear: Healthy relationships form the foundation of healthy brain development. The brain learns best in an environment of love, support, and clear direction.

- *Better ability to cope with stress:* Research shows that babies whose relationships are mostly positive are better able to handle stress compared with infants who have primarily negative relationships.[1]

- *Enhanced learning and life skills:* Children who have a strong sense of attachment with their caregivers also experience the opportunity to learn and grow in a safe environment. When the brain feels safe, parts devoted to language, social-emotional skills, self-control, and academic learning are stimulated to grow and thrive.

- *Reduced risky behaviors:* In a study published in the *Journal of the American Medical Association*, researcher Michael Resnick, PhD, and colleagues at the University of Minnesota reported that teenagers who felt loved and connected to their parents had a significantly lower incidence of teenage pregnancy, drug use, violence, and suicide.[2] So important is the bonding between children and parents that it over-rides other factors traditionally linked to problem behavior. The article concluded that the degree of connection—or "limbic bonding" that occurs in the emotional centers of the brain—that teenagers feel with parents and teachers is the most important factor in whether they will engage in risky sexual activity, substance abuse, violence, or suicidal behavior.

CONSEQUENCES OF UNHEALTHY RELATIONSHIPS

When parents fail to bond with their children, it sets the stage for trouble, robs mental strength, and makes parenting even harder than it already is. Sadly, many kids grow up with neglectful or cold and controlling parents. Let us be clear that we aren't talking about momentary lapses when you lose your cool, react with a harsher tone than you'd like, or make a mistake. As parents, we all make mistakes. And that's actually a good thing. When our kids see us make a mistake, own up to it, and apologize, it helps them know how to behave when they mess up. Unhealthy bonding occurs when parents habitually ignore their little ones or are overcontrolling. In such cases, a dif-ferent type of bond develops that leads to a host of negative consequences, including:

- *Oppositional values:* Without relationship, kids are more likely to be oppositional and to rebel by taking on views that are counter to their parents' values.

- *Lack of independence:* Kids feel shackled to their parents and are unable to break free or feel independent.

- *Poor decision-making:* Youngsters tend to make choices based on unmet needs for affection and control rather than on healthy love and logic.

- *Adopting parents' unhealthy behaviors:* In far too many instances, kids grow up to act just like their parents in ways that are detrimental to their own personal wellness, relationships, and parenting ability. The parents have become lodged in their children's hearts and brains and have hijacked their children's habits.

- *Unhealthy brain development:* Growing up in a home where tension, disappointment, unpredictability, fear, criticism, or lack of encouragement dominate the landscape is detrimental to brain development and mental strength. Not surprisingly, children's brains adapt to survive in such environments, making it far more difficult for them to develop the ability to relate well to others, exhibit self-control, and learn academic subjects.

Even if you grew up in a home with controlling parents or if you haven't done the best job of building a relationship with your children, there is hope to repair your bond.

FIVE MESSAGES OF RELATIONSHIP BUILDING OR REPAIR

As you read the remainder of this chapter, keep in mind that developing or mending relationships with kids depends on consistently sending five essential messages. Sometimes these are conveyed with words. More frequently they're communicated nonverbally, through our tone of voice, facial expressions, and overall emotional tone. It is also important to emphasize that the strategies you're about to learn also help us heal and move past the hurts in our own lives. These messages will work for any child, younger or older, including those with special needs or disabilities.

Message #1: We notice you, you are important to us, and we are committed to meeting your needs.

Ideally, this critical message begins from the moment a baby is born and is especially powerful in the first two years of life. In the first year of a baby's life, it's all about having their basic needs met. According to many experts, including our friend Dr. Foster Cline, this first-year cycle is essential to the development of bonding, pro-social behavior, and the ability to learn cause and effect.[3] For example, let's say your baby daughter is hungry. If she cries and you come, she learns that someone notices her. If you smile, make eye contact, hold her, and feed her, it triggers the release of oxytocin, a neurochemical involved in bonding and trust. She develops a bond that will enable her to relate with love to herself and others, experience a healthy sense of control over her life, and learn from experience—all elements of mental strength.

In the second year of life, this cycle shifts from needs to wants. The little one wants something—a toy, a blanket, a bottle—and will make that desire known through pointing or words. Crawlers and toddlers often want things that aren't good for them or that could put them in danger—touching a hot stove, running into the street, or climbing too high on the furniture. In this phase, youngsters are testing to see if we love them enough to say no. Ultimately, this cycle builds a bond of trust, even though it can bring about some short-term tears and temper tantrums.

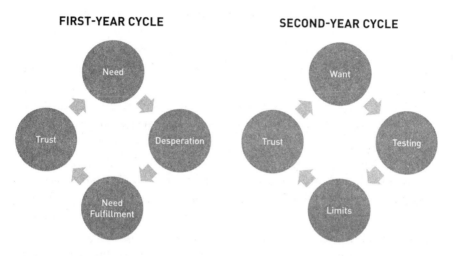

FIRST-YEAR CYCLE

Need → Desperation → Need Fulfillment → Trust

SECOND-YEAR CYCLE

Want → Testing → Limits → Trust

The essential commonality between the first- and second-year cycles is that the parent is aware of the child's needs and displays consistent devotion to meeting them. How can we continue to help our children see that they are valued in this way? Let's take a look.

EFFECTIVE PARENTING STRATEGY: SPECIAL TIME

Relationships require two things: time and a willingness to listen. Unfortunately, too many of us aren't getting enough quality time communicating with our kids. A 2018 survey found that over 70 percent of parents struggle to communicate with their kids in a meaningful way.[4] And 40 percent of those surveyed admit that conversations with their kids typically run shy of the 10-minute mark. It is not possible to bond or have much of a relationship in only a matter of minutes. The brain's limbic system—or emotional center—enables us to connect socially with others. When we are bonded with others in a positive way, it's as if they live within us in our brains.

Here is an exercise Dr. Amen recommends that will improve the quality of your relationship and the limbic bond with your child in a very short period of time. *Special time* works no matter how old your children are. You may think your children are too busy or uninterested in spending time with you. When this happens, I recommend that you nudge the issue with your kids, telling them that they're important to you and that you need time with them. Of course, the way in which you spend time with them is critical.

Too often parents tell children how to think before the parent understands the situation. This behavior cuts off communication and decreases the chances that the child will come to you in the future. By responding in a positive reflective way, you encourage communication. When you respond in a harsh, condescending, or critical way, you decrease communication, which may cause a sense of loneliness and alienation in a child or teen. See the box for instructions on how to put this strategy into daily practice.

Special Time Instructions[5]

1. **Spend 20 minutes a day with your child doing something that they would like to do.** Approach your child in a positive way and say something like, "I feel we have not had enough time together, and you're important to me. Let's spend some special time together every day. What would you like to do?" The purpose of this time is to build the relationship with your child. Keep it positive. When our daughter Chloe was little, my wife, Tana, would read to her every day. As she got older, Chloe began reading to Tana. It was a wonderful bonding time for the two of them.

2. **During special time, do not give any parental commands, questions, or directions.** This is very important. This is a time to build the relationship, not discipline difficult behavior. If, for example, you're playing a game and the child starts to cheat, you can reframe her behavior. You can say something like, "I see you've changed the rules of the game, and I'll play by your rules." Remember, the goal of special time is to improve the relationship between you and your child, not to teach. (Of course, at other times, if the child cheats, deal straightforwardly with it.)

3. **Notice positive behaviors.** Pointing out the good is much more effective in shaping behavior than noticing the bad. (Read the story about Fat Freddy the penguin later in this chapter.)

4. **Listen more than you talk.** Good communication is essential to any relationship. In order to get your child to talk with you, you must first show that you are willing to accept and listen to what they have to say. You must also believe that they have the capacity to solve many of their own problems if they are allowed to talk through them.

Message #2: We value your feelings.

It is so important to let kids know that we value their feelings. This improves their sense of self-worth and self-esteem. Dr. Fay clearly remembers one of the many times his dad, Jim, showed that he valued Dr. Fay's feelings, and it really stuck with him: "I was just 10 years old at the time, and our family was having dinner with Dr. Cline who lived nearby. My dad and Dr. Cline were grousing about how their teachings about limits and accountability only worked in half the kids. They couldn't figure out why the same strategies didn't work for the other half of the kids, who basically ended up just disliking their parents more than they already did. All of a sudden, they turned to me and asked, 'What do you think, Charles?'"

"'Who, me?' I asked. I didn't have an answer for them, but the fact that these two grown men with decades of experience wanted my input made me feel special."

They eventually found the solution they were seeking, and in part, it came from observing the actions of a woman who worked in the school administration office. Mrs. MacLaughlin was a strong but loving woman who was the first person students visited when they had an "emergency" like a forgotten lunch, lost coat, scraped knee, or a hassle with another student. Students in that school believed that all such "crises" required a quick rescue call to one or both of their parents—and these were the days before cell phones.

As they begged to use the office phone, Mrs. MacLaughlin would smile sweetly, look into their eyes as if they were the most precious thing on earth, and say, "Oh honey, what happened?" The kids would describe the problem, she'd listen with great interest, and then she'd respond with empathy by saying:

"Oh, that's gotta feel so bad. It's never any fun to have a problem like that. It's sad, but I can only let you use the phone if there is an emergency. If any kid can handle this, though, you certainly can."

The kids generally figured out how to solve their problems on their own without using the phone, leaving them full of self-confidence and love for Mrs. MacLaughlin. Jim Fay and Dr. Foster Cline soon discovered the key to making the Love and Logic approach really work: empathy.[6] Mrs. MacLaughlin always provided a strong dose of this magic before she set a limit or held a student accountable for their actions. This showed the students that she valued their feelings.

Empathy opens a child's heart and mind to learning, whereas anger shuts the door on learning and relationship.

ANGER VS. THE POWER OF EMPATHY

Empathy, when done correctly, sends a message of love and competence. Some parents think that raising their voice or unleashing ultimatums is the way to get kids to toe the line. It might scare kids into submission, but it comes at a price. Kids whose parents routinely lose their temper or yell at them are vulnerable to a host of consequences that rob mental strength, including:

- Feeling stressed, which has negative implications for brain development
- Blaming themselves for whatever is making their parent mad
- Responding to a parent's anger with aggressive behavior
- Having trouble sleeping
- Physical ailments, such as stomachaches
- Increased risk for mental health issues later in life

Even more concerning, harsh parenting practices also negatively impact how the brain develops and how it functions. A 2021 study found that frequently yelling or getting angry at children is associated with children having a smaller brain in adolescence.[7] When it comes to the brain, size matters.

When a parent gets angry, the child's brain can view it as a threat. This fires up the amygdala, a brain region that is associated with emotions like fear and anxiety and that is linked to the fight, flight, or freeze response. Guess what this does to the thinking regions of the brain in the prefrontal cortex—it shifts activity away from the thinking areas and makes kids more likely to react with heightened emotions.

Of course, all of us lose our temper once in a while, but there are simple strategies you can use to calm anger. For example:

Take a few deep breaths. Gaining control of your breath can help soothe irritability and deliver more oxygen to your brain to help you respond more rationally to a situation. As soon as you begin to feel anger rising, take a deep breath, inhaling for four seconds, hold it for one second, then exhale for eight seconds. Repeat this 10 times, and you'll feel more at peace.

Know your triggers. Keep track of when you get mad. Is it when you haven't eaten for too long? Is it when you've had a stressful day at work? Is it when you haven't gotten enough sleep? When you know your vulnerable times, you can make a plan to circumvent anger before it starts.

Take a time-out. If you feel like you're going to lash out in anger at your kids, simply say, "I need a time-out," and take a few moments for yourself. Going for a quick walk, doing a few stretches, or listening to some happy tunes for just a few minutes can often be enough to defuse anger.

Empathy, on the other hand, is far more powerful and beneficial than anger. Empathy is our ability to sense what others feel. In dealing with your kids, empathy pays great dividends. Findings from a 2020 study show that parental empathy enhances kids' social competence, which is associated with reduced risk of emotional and behavioral problems.[8] Increased empathy also leads to an important side effect: accountability. Research[9] shows that empathy also plays a role in brain function and activates areas involved in cognitive skills,[10] learning, and bonding.

ANGER VS. EMPATHY

ANGER	EMPATHY
Threats or lectures make it easy for kids to blame parents for the consequences they experience.	Empathy makes it harder for kids to blame parents for the consequences of their poor decisions.
Anger and frustration shut the door on learning.	Empathy opens the heart and mind to learning.
Anger leaves parents feeling stressed and leads to a sense of guilt.	Empathy allows parents to be free of stress and guilt.
Anger teaches kids to use anger.	Empathy teaches kids to demonstrate empathy, forgiveness, and problem-solving skills.

EMPATHY VS. SYMPATHY

Empathy is often confused with sympathy. The two couldn't be more different. While empathy is being able to understand and share another person's feelings, sympathy is feeling sorry for someone else. Here are a few examples that show the difference between the two:

Sympathy: "It's too bad you didn't get chosen for the dance squad. Maybe if you take more lessons, you can make the squad next year."

Empathy: "That must feel bad not getting chosen for the dance squad. I'm here for you if you want to talk about it."

Sympathy: "That's terrible that your friend said something mean to you. At least you have other friends."

Empathy: "It's okay to feel bad when someone says something mean. I get it."

Each is largely communicated through subtle yet very powerful factors, such as tone of voice, facial expression, and other forms of nonverbal communication.

Sympathy creates lack of confidence and fear.
Empathy builds confidence and resilience.

SYMPATHY COMMUNICATES

- *You poor thing. I don't know how you're going to make it.*
- *I'm so upset by what happened to you.*
- *This is about my feelings.*
- *You are a victim.*
- *This is my problem to solve.*
- *You need my rescue.*

EMPATHY COMMUNICATES

- *This is really hard, but I know that you will make it.*
- *I see that you're really upset by what happened to you.*
- *This is about your feelings.*
- *You are strong.*
- *This is your problem to solve.*
- *You might need some guidance, but you have what it takes to solve this problem.*

Message #3: We value and accept what you think.

How many times with your kids, and even adults you care about, have you jumped in to solve a problem, soothe their anxiousness or sadness, or help them avoid an uncomfortable situation, just to find that it didn't work very well? What do people really want and need at these times? It's your presence, not your problem-solving.

EFFECTIVE PARENTING STRATEGY: ACTIVE LISTENING

Active listening is a technique therapists use to improve communication. It can help you hear and understand what your child is saying. Active listening is simple and involves three steps:

1. Repeat back what you hear without judgment.
2. Listen for the feeling behind the words.
3. Reflect back what your child is saying and feeling.

Simply saying, "I hear you saying . . . Is that what you meant?" can help you avoid misunderstandings, cool down conflicts, and increase communication.

Active listening with children and teens increases the level of understanding and communication. And when they feel understood and valued, they feel closer to you.

Here's an example of how this might play out:

1. Repeat what is said without judging the content of the words.
Teen: I want to dye my hair blue.
(Could be an inflammatory statement)
Ineffective Parent: Not as long as you live in my house!
(Ends the conversation or starts a fight)
Effective Parent: You want to dye your hair blue?
(Then stays quiet long enough for the teen to explain)

I want to dye my hair blue.

2. Listen for the feelings behind the words.
Teen: All the kids are wearing their hair that way.
(As if she has somehow taken a scientific poll)
Ineffective Parent: I don't care what anyone else does; you're not going to have blue hair. If they are going to jump off a bridge, are you going to do that too?
(Again, this sets up a fight with the teen or causes them to withdraw.)
Effective Parent: Sounds like you want to be like the other kids.
(Encourages understanding and further communication)

3. **Reflect back what you hear the child saying and feeling.**

Your teen might then respond: Sometimes I feel like I don't fit in; maybe changing my appearance will help.

Ineffective Parent: Don't be silly. Of course, you fit in. Your appearance has nothing to do with it!

Effective Parent: You think your appearance prevents you from fitting in?

(Gives them space to expand on their feelings)[11]

Nine Communication Pitfalls to Avoid with Your Kids[12]

1. *Poor attitude.* You expect the conversation to go nowhere and subsequently don't even try to direct it in a positive way.

2. *Negative assumptions about the child.* Up front you don't trust what your child or teen will tell you, and you remain stiff and guarded during your time together.

3. *No reinforcing body language.* Body language is important because it sends conscious and unconscious messages. When a parent and a child are having a discussion and one person fails to make eye contact or acknowledge the other person with facial or body gestures, the person who is talking begins to feel lost, alone, and unenthusiastic about continuing the conversation. Eye contact and physical acknowledgment is essential to good communication.

4. *Competing with distractions.* Distractions frequently doom communication. It's not a good idea, for example, to try to communicate when the child is watching their favorite TV show or when they are in the middle of a video game.

5. *Never asking for feedback on what you're saying.* Many parents assume that they are sending clear messages to their child and become upset when the child doesn't do what was asked. Kids may have poor attention spans or may have trouble listening because of their emotions or thoughts about some issue. It's often important to ask them to repeat back what you said to clarify they really understood your comment.

6. *Kitchen sinking.* This occurs in arguments when you feel backed into a corner and then bring up unrelated issues from the past to protect yourself or intensify the disagreement. Stay on task until an issue is fully discussed.

7. *Mind reading.* You arbitrarily predict what your child or teen is thinking and then react on that "imagined" information. Get curious about their actual thoughts and feelings.

8. *Sparring.* Using put-downs, sarcasm, or discounting your child's ideas erodes meaningful dialogue and creates distance in your relationship.

9. *Lack of persistence.* Often with a child, communication requires your repeated efforts. Don't give up. Remember, kids do not think like adults, and you may need to keep trying.

SHOULD WE EVEN LISTEN TO VIEWS THAT SEEM OUTRAGEOUS? Has your child ever said something outrageous that makes no sense (like wanting blue hair)? Do you tend to tune them out if they start talking nonsense? Are you worried that if you don't vehemently voice your disapproval, they will assume that you are silently giving them approval? It is possible to listen without condoning unwanted behavior.

Take a look at how Dr. Charles Fay, when he was 16, tried to convince his dad, Jim, that Charles should get a sports car even though they lived in a town where it snowed like crazy during the winter and the roads got icy and dangerous. Jim could easily have stifled the conversation by saying rear-wheel-drive vehicles don't handle well in the snow. Instead, Jim let Charles share what he loved about those sports cars, and they bonded over how cool they are. The conversation went something like this:

Charles: Dad, I gotta have a sports car! They're really good in the snow if you get snow tires.

Dad: Wow, I love them. What do you like about them?

Charles: They're really sporty with the two-doors, and you can get a four-speed. And there are all kinds of aftermarket parts you can get.

Dad: That sounds like a super fun car, but I'm not sure that would work for me. I know if I had one, I would slide it right off the driveway where it gets icy. That would be so frustrating.

Charles: Yeah, but they look so cool.

Dad: Well, I'm not financing the car, but I'm sure you'll make the best decision.

After thinking about the reality of driving a sports car on icy roads, Charles didn't end up getting one. However, his dad let Charles feel like he was the one making the final decision. Plus, it was fun to talk about what they liked about them, and they had a great father-son bonding moment.

Sometimes, kids will bring up something outrageous just to see if the parent loves them enough to listen. Imagine if your teen came home one day and said, "It doesn't hurt to experiment with drugs. Ancient cultures used all sorts of hallucinogenic substances. They aren't bad for you. It's just that some people are stupid and overdo it."

As a parent, you might have alarm bells going off inside your head. And you might be thinking, *I've got to nip this in the bud.* However, if you come down hard and start lecturing your teen about the dangers of drugs, it just shuts down the conversation. A different tactic might be to ask them to tell you more about these ancient cultures. After listening to what they have to say, you can let them know why that wouldn't work for you. For example, you might say, "I would be afraid if I tried one of those drugs that I would be so out of it that I would end up in a dumpster."

Don't expect your teen to applaud you for being so wise. What this does is plant a seed about the downsides of what they're contemplating. It makes it clear that you aren't condoning such behavior, but you are listening. When you listen, you have a better relationship, and when you're bonded, odds are your teen will make better choices.

Message #4: You are capable. We believe in you.

For decades Dr. Amen has collected penguins. He now has over 2,500 penguins. His collection started on the island of Oahu at Sea Life Park. He spent the day there once with his 7-year-old son. In the middle of the day, they went to the penguin show. The penguin's name was Fat Freddy. Freddy could jump off a 20-foot board; he could bowl with his nose; he could count. He even jumped through a hoop of fire. They were really impressed with this penguin.

Toward the end of the show, the trainer asked Freddy to get something. Right away Freddy went to get it and brought it back to the trainer. Dr. Amen thought to himself, *I ask my kid to get something for me, and he wants to have a discussion about it for 20 minutes, and then he doesn't want to do it. What's the difference? I know my son is smarter than this penguin.*

I love how you did that. Here's a fish for you.

After the show, Dr. Amen asked the trainer how she got Freddy to do all of those neat tricks. The trainer looked at the father and son, and then she said, "Unlike parents, whenever Freddy does anything like what I want him to do, I notice him, I give him a hug, and then I give him a fish."

The light went on in Dr. Amen's head: Whenever his son did things that Dr. Amen liked, Dr. Amen paid no attention to him. But whenever his son did something Dr. Amen didn't like, Dr. Amen gave his son a ton of attention because he didn't want to raise a bad kid. Well, guess what Dr. Amen was really doing? He was encouraging his son to be a pain in the neck. By misbehaving, he got more and more of his dad's notice.

What do you think Fat Freddy would have done if he was having a bad day and didn't follow the trainer's instructions, and the trainer said, "You stupid penguin. I never met a penguin as dumb as you. We ought to ship you out to Antarctica and get a replacement"? If Freddy could have understood her, he might have bitten her or run to the corner and cried (depending on his temperament). The trainer's response made all the difference.[13]

Dr. Amen's penguin collection reminds us to shape behavior in a positive way and notice what is good more than what is not. After all, don't we all enjoy being noticed and applauded for our behavior?

Reinforce your child's good behavior for following the rules and striving for their goals if you want them to continue. When you think of acceptable behavior, imagine a playing field. When the child's behavior is appropriate, they are within the boundaries. When their behavior becomes inappropriate, they are outside of the boundaries. If you affirm and praise them when they are within the appropriate boundaries, they are more likely to continue doing what you like.

WHEN PRAISE BACKFIRES

Some parents say that whenever they try to praise their child, it's like water off a duck's back. It just doesn't soak in. Their child has low self-esteem, and no matter how often they provide positive reinforcement, it falls flat. Sadly, some kids have preconceived notions about themselves, and they are reluctant to let go of them even if they are negative. Well-meaning compliments can unintentionally stir up self-doubts.

In these cases, it's best to think of the word *love* as a verb and an action. Taking action to help kids prove to themselves that they are capable and valuable can be far more powerful than verbal praise. That's where Jim Fay's *Four Steps to Responsibility* come in (see below).[14]

Effective Parenting Strategy: The Four Steps to Responsibility

Step 1: Give your child a task they can handle.

Step 2: Hope that they make a mistake or misbehave.

Step 3: Provide sincere empathy and allow them to live with the consequences of their mistake or misbehavior.

Step 4: Give them the same task again.

Here's how these four steps worked for a parent of a very inquisitive child: Brian, age 9, struggled in school, but he liked taking stuff apart to see how it worked. His wonderful parents got him an alarm clock so he could get up all by himself in the morning (step 1). It had numbers that flipped down, and he couldn't resist taking the screws off the back and opening the cover so he could peer inside and see how it worked. This wasn't the mistake (step 2) they expected him to make—they thought he wouldn't set it correctly and would wake up late, miss the bus, and have to pay them for a ride to school. Nevertheless, his mother and father showed empathy (step 3) by noticing how excited he was to take the clock apart and saying, "If any kid can put it back together, it's you."

Brian worked hard to put the cover back on, and when he did it, he felt an incredible sense of accomplishment and self-worth. No amount of praise from others could have made him feel that good about himself. He learned to trust that if he made a mistake, his parents weren't going to fly off the handle. Instead, they believed that he could solve his own problems.

That night after Brian fixed the clock, his parents gave him the same task again (step 4) by asking what time he was going to set the alarm to wake him up. The next morning, the alarm went off as planned, and he got up and made it to the bus on time all by himself. What a self-competence builder!

Parents of young kids and children with special needs are often understandably reluctant to apply this strategy. They often wonder, "Will it really work with such a young child?" or "Will it really work with a child with the challenges mine has?"

Notice that the first step involves giving your child a task they can handle. This might be very small—asking a 4-year-old to place their plate next to the kitchen sink after a meal—or much bigger—having your 17-year-old drive to the grocery store and do some shopping for the family. Regardless of the size and complexity of the task, the parent teaches the child how to complete it prior to assigning it. In fact, parents of young children and children with special needs are wise to rehearse the skill and provide visual cues, such as a list of pictures depicting the sequence of steps involved.

It's also fine to provide some suggestions for handling the mistake they have made. Guiding kids toward solutions helps them learn how to brainstorm ideas when other problems arise. It is important to remember that guiding them by providing solutions isn't the same as lecturing them and trying to force them to accept your advice. Simply share some ideas and allow them to decide whether they will use any of your suggestions.

Using the Four Steps to Responsibility is even more important with children who don't value themselves. Here are some additional self-competence builders and stealers.

EFFECTIVE PARENTING STRATEGY:
USE SELF-COMPETENCE BUILDERS NOT STEALERS

SELF-COMPETENCE BUILDERS	SELF-COMPETENCE STEALERS
Allowing kids to make decisions even if they make mistakes	Rescuing the kid from mistakes
Sincere empathy	Sarcasm
Being specific about praise: "Even though you struck out that time, you handled it really calmly."	Saying, "You struck out (but that ump needs glasses)."
Allowing kids to struggle	Making everything easy for kids

Having loving family relationships	Allowing kids to witness adversarial family relationships (kids tend to blame themselves for problems in the family)
Focusing most of your energy on strengths	Focusing most of your energy on weaknesses

Message #5: You are worth protecting.

Dave Sanders was a hero. There's a highway named after him in Colorado. Who was he? He was a teacher who saved countless lives at Columbine High School when two students went on a shooting spree on April 20, 1999. Instead of running to safety, Sanders helped students find cover from the bullets. He ultimately gave his life protecting theirs. That's an example of the truest meaning of love.

Although most of us, thankfully, will never be in a situation like the one Sanders found himself in, we as parents are often in the position of sacrificing our comfort and momentary feelings of well-being to rescue our kids from danger. That danger can come from outside or inside. Outside dangers are things like when a toddler races toward the street when a car is whizzing by. Inside dangers include our kids' own impulses and poor decisions.

Rescuing has gotten a bad rap. Too many parents do far too much rescuing when it isn't necessary. However, Dr. Foster Cline shares some helpful tips on when it's okay, or even required, to rescue kids and teens (see box). When they know that we believe they are worth protecting, it builds relationship. When done appropriately, occasionally rescuing our kids builds a bond of trust. It also increases the odds that they'll be willing to rescue us when we truly need it!

EFFECTIVE PARENTING STRATEGY:
UNDERSTAND THE RULES FOR RESCUE BY FOSTER CLINE, MD

IT'S OKAY TO RESCUE WHEN ...	IT'S NOT OKAY TO RESCUE WHEN ...
Your child is at risk of losing life or limb.	They are facing a hardship from which they can learn and grow.
Your child isn't in the habit of needing rescue.	They constantly rely on it.
Your child is grateful for the rescue.	They demand rescue or feel entitled to it.

Your child is a confident kid.	Your child lacks confidence and needs to see that they are capable of coping with adversity.

When you consistently send these messages of love to your child, they grow up self-confident and assured. With the feelings of security and safety that come from these loving messages, you give your child's brain, sense of self, and mental strength room to develop.

Action Steps

- Spend 20 minutes of special time with your child today.
- The next time your child is struggling with something, try just being present and letting them do the talking.
- Practice active listening with your child.
- Choose two discussion starters that you can use with your kids.
- Think about how you can use "That wouldn't work for me" when your kids say something outrageous.
- Think of a task you can give your child to use the Four Steps to Responsibility.
- Use self-competence builders.
- Understand the rules for rescue.

CHAPTER 5

LIMITS AND RULES BUILD MENTAL FORTITUDE

*Limits and rules let a child know what you expect of them
in a clear way and make them feel safe and secure.*

Kids need limits and rules. That's the bottom line. What do limits and rules have to do with bonding and maintaining positive relationships in developing mental strength? Setting limits sends the following underlying messages to our kids:

- I love you enough to pay attention to your actions.
- I love you enough to keep you safe.
- I love you enough to provide discipline.
- I love you enough to show you how to take care of yourself.
- I love you enough to give you what your brain needs.

Here's an example of the powerful message of love we send when we set limits. When Dr. Amen's daughter Kaitlyn was a teenager, she liked to push back. On one occasion, she wanted to go to a concert with friends. Dr. Amen said no, but she continued to pester him about it. This is often where parents give in out of exasperation; we get it! If Dr. Amen had done that, though, he would have been reinforcing overactivity in the anterior cingulate gyrus of Kaitlyn's brain—the brain region associated with oppositional and defiant behavior. The result wouldn't have been peace for Dr. Amen; Kaitlyn would have become more oppositional and more obsessive the next time around.

So, Dr. Amen gave a very clear response: "Sweetie, I've told you no. And now you've asked me more than once. You know the rule: 'No arguing with parents.' (See Rule No. 4 in this chapter.) So, if you ask me again, the answer will still be no, and there will be a consequence—no phone or internet for the rest of the day. It's up to you if you want the consequence or not." After that, Kaitlyn let it go. By being insistent, firm, and kind, Dr. Amen had actually taught her brain that she could stop the oppositional behavior she was stuck in. In fact, this tactic is part of a behavior therapy that helps people with obsessive-compulsive disorder, but it can also be highly effective for all kids of all ages.

WHY CHILDREN AND PARENTS NEED LIMITS

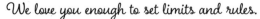

We love you enough to set limits and rules.

Your child's brain needs limits. Rules and limits provide a sense of safety, and research[1] shows it helps with healthy development of the brain's hypothalamus-pituitary-adrenal (HPA) axis, more commonly known as the stress response system. Healthy activity in the HPA axis reduces levels of the stress hormone cortisol in the brain, thus enhancing overall brain function. Healthy brain function fortifies mental strength. Decades of research[2] show that authoritative—not *authoritarian*—parenting that involves setting firm and loving limits helps kids develop:

- Responsibility
- Independence
- Social skills
- Academic performance
- Good behavior

In addition, children and teens who grow up with limits and rules are less likely to experience mental health or behavioral issues, such as anxiety, depression, or substance abuse.

On the flip side, a 2022 study found that unpredictable or inconsistent parenting can interfere with the healthy development of a child's emotional brain circuits.[3] This may contribute to a greater risk for mental health issues and addictions in adulthood. Dr. Amen has seen far too many young adults in Amen Clinics with anxiousness, panic disorders, mood issues, and substance abuse. In many cases, these individuals grew up in permissive homes without limits.

Rules benefit parents too. They allow you to know when a child is following the rules and give you a basis for reinforcing them with clear, unemotional consequences. In particular, written rules have power. Children are often rule-oriented and respond to physical signs (e.g., rules posted at the pool). For example, when Dr. Amen's nephew Andrew was 3 years old, he was afraid of monsters at night. For several weeks, Andrew's parents searched his bedroom with Andrew in an attempt to assure him that there were no monsters in his room. They looked everywhere: under the bed, in the closet, behind the door, and under the covers. Then they realized they were adding to Andrew's fear by looking for the monsters.

At Dr. Amen's suggestion, Andrew's mother decided to make a sign for her son's room. She and Andrew drew a picture of a monster, then put a red circle around it with a slash across it, and wrote, "NO MONSTERS ALLOWED." Surprisingly, Andrew's fear went away because he believed the sign kept monsters away from his bedroom.[4]

NO MONSTERS ALLOWED

LIMITS ARE NONNEGOTIABLE NEEDS

Limits and rules need to be set in stone. They aren't optional desires. However, there's one important thing you need to know: Kids—and adults—often resist limits. And if you don't understand this, it can test your patience and lead to anger and frustration that make you give in when you know you shouldn't.

Look at one couple who had been going out once a week for date night until their daughter was about 3 years old. The parents had hired a babysitter and were just heading out the door to go to the movies when their little girl threw a fit.

"It's not fair you get to see a movie and I don't," she wailed.

When she spiraled into a full temper tantrum, the parents looked at each other with resignation, shut the front door, and stayed home to soothe their daughter. That was their last date night.

Do you see the problem here? The parents gave in to their daughter's short-term reaction rather than staying focused on her long-term development. And it sent a clear message to their daughter that she was in charge. Her parents had successfully modified her behavior, but in a negative way that spelled trouble for the future. The tyke learned that if she acted like a tyrant, she could get her parents to cave and cater to her desires.

This is an example of parenting like a slot machine. Slot machines don't pay off often, but if you keep at it, they will eventually pay out. To kids, this means if they keep pestering you, there's a chance you'll give in. B. F. Skinner,[5] in his groundbreaking research on behaviorism, found that providing intermittent reinforcement was a far more powerful way to train an animal—or a person—compared with constant reinforcement. Variable rewards fuel what every gambler believes: "Next time, I'm going to win big!" Here's how this plays out with kids. Let's say you veer off track from consistent reinforcement of a rule, like allowing your kid to eat dessert *before* dinner while you were on a family vacation. Then that out-of-the-ordinary treat can lead your child to persist in trying to get that variable reward again. It instills this thought: "The next time I act up, my parents might give in and give me dessert before dinner."

This is not a belief you want to plant in your child's brain. It undermines efforts to set limits and sets you up for that Guilt Cycle we wrote about in chapter 3 (blowing up, feeling bad, then rescuing). And it causes kids to get addicted to manipulating their parents' behavior.

SIX STEPS TO SETTING EFFECTIVE LIMITS

Before you dive into the deep water and race through the following steps to set limits for your kids, take time to prepare. If you rush into this, it's possible to run into unforeseen issues. It's like the time Dr. Fay decided to take a rowboat out onto a lake. He hopped into the rowboat and eagerly started rowing, thinking what a glorious day it was. Before long, he noticed that there was only about an inch difference between the water level and the top of the boat. He was sinking—and sinking fast into some icy cold water. It turned out he had forgotten to put a plug in the back of the boat. He managed to make it back to shore in time, but it just goes to show you that we all need to plug the holes in our parenting plans.

Great parents learn and begin to practice skills *before* making big changes. Read through the following steps to setting limits and try to anticipate what might go wrong and how you'll deal with it. Keep in mind that communicating limits to kids with special needs or disabilities may require some finesse. Be sure to use simple terms and incorporate pictures, music, touch, or role-playing to help them understand what you expect of them.

Step 1. Go back to your goals.

When you're trying to set limits, revisit the goals you have for yourself as a parent and for your child. Ask yourself these questions:

- What type of adults do you want your kids to become?
- What must you *consistently* model to achieve these goals?
- How do you set limits that *consistently* allow you to support these goals?
- How do you *consistently* follow your goals rather than your short-term feelings?

When you can answer these questions, you're ready to choose the limits you want to set. In addition, be sure that the limits you're setting are completely enforceable. If you can't enforce them, they will backfire.

Step 2. Be prepared for how your kids may react.

Be aware that setting limits can cause a wide range of reactions—think of that little girl who had a meltdown when her parents wanted to go to a movie for date night. In some cases, rules and limits may make things feel worse before they get better. In psychology and psychiatry circles, we call this an "extinction burst." At Amen Clinics, Dr. Amen has seen kids react to new rules and limits with anger, whining, temper tantrums, crying, yelling, bargaining, and other behavior issues. When faced with such intense reactions, it can make parents think the limits aren't working and consider abandoning them. Don't! Giving up and giving in makes parents look like flip-floppers and fuels manipulative behavior.

Understanding ahead of time that your child may not like new rules and limits and may respond in unwanted ways helps you avoid feeling angry, frustrated, discouraged, or guilty. Knowing that the extinction burst is typically temporary—a few days to a week—can give you the confidence to continue enforcing new limits despite short-term outbursts. Keeping your eye on the long-term outcome is the key to getting through a troublesome transition period. When parents prove that change is here to stay, they soon begin to enjoy more respectful, responsible, and happier kids.

Step 3. Learn to neutralize arguing from your kids.

We love you too much to argue.

As noted in step 2, when you begin setting limits, you may encounter arguing from your kids. Fortunately, Love and Logic has been helping parents neutralize backtalk for decades. (See "Neutralize Arguing" below.) One of the most important tools in the firm and kind parenting toolkit, this simple strategy helps you stick with the limits and rules that will help you achieve the goals you have for yourself and your kids.

Neutralize Arguing

There are few things more damaging than allowing kids to believe arguing, backtalk, or manipulation are good ways to get their way, get you upset, or deflect responsibility. That's why wise parents who raise mentally strong kids use the following two-step process any time this begins to happen. Use this skill as soon as children are old enough to experiment with arguing, usually around the age of 3 or 4.

First, do not overthink. By resisting the temptation to give too much consideration to what the child is saying or doing, we increase the odds of staying calm. It's a lot easier to avoid having our buttons pushed when we aren't paying much attention to the button pusher. It's also far easier to resist launching into an ineffective lecture.

Second, calmly repeat a Love and Logic "one-liner." Rather than trying to reason with your child, which validates their arguments, stick with one of Love and Logic's parent-tested one-liners. Here are some examples:

- "I love you too much to argue."
- "What did I say?"
- "I know."
- "I'll listen when your voice is calm and respectful."

> *Caution! This technique will backfire if delivered with sarcasm, frustration, or anger.*

Step 4. Learn to quiet the arguing in your own mind.

Perhaps even more challenging than stifling arguments with our children is learning to quiet the backtalk in our own minds. Did you know that every single time you have a thought, your brain releases chemicals? Whenever you have an angry, hopeless, depressing, or frightening thought, your brain releases a certain set of chemicals that cause your whole body to react and feel bad. Think about the last time you were really angry with your child. What happened in your body almost immediately? If you're like most people, your muscles probably became tight, your breathing sped up, your hands began to sweat and get colder, and your heart rate rose. (This is the principle behind lie detector tests: Your body reacts to what you think.)

On the other hand, every time you have a positive, happy, hopeful, successful, or pleasant thought, your brain releases different chemicals that make you feel good and relaxed. The opposite physical responses occur: Your heart rate slows down, your hands get warmer and drier, and your muscles relax. Thoughts are powerful. Unless you think about your thoughts, they are automatic. They just happen. So what you think is critical to how you feel and how you parent.

Parenting requires clear thinking. And your thoughts do not always tell the truth. Thoughts lie—a lot. It is your uninvestigated thoughts that can wreak havoc on your parenting. You don't have to believe every crazy, wild, or reactive thought that goes through your head.[6]

It's important to think about your thoughts to see if they help or hurt you. Unfortunately, if you never challenge your automatic negative thoughts (ANTs), they invade your mind like ants at a picnic. ANTs pop up in your brain seemingly out of nowhere, and when left unchallenged, they bite, nibble, torture, and infest your mind. When you're trying to set limits, ANTs can make you doubt yourself or convince you to abandon your new rules. But if you don't remain mentally strong, you can't teach your kids how to be mentally strong.

In chapter 7 we will provide a much deeper view on this subject and give you a time-tested process that will help you stay firm and loving by combating any negative thoughts and their associated feelings of anger, frustration, guilt, or hopelessness. We'll also show you how to help your kids learn to combat their own ANTs so that they, too, can control their thinking and live happily and purposefully.

To get you started, here are some of the most common parenting ANTs and their accurate competing thoughts (ACTs):

ANTs	ACTs
These new rules aren't working, and they're making my child worse.	These new rules are causing a temporary extinction burst, but they will pay off in the long run.
I'm a failure as a parent.	I'm doing the best I can, and I'm learning from my mistakes.
Things would be easier if I just let my kid do what they want.	Being permissive will ultimately make my life and my child's life harder.

What would your parenting life be like if your head was full of ACTs rather than ANTs? What would your children's lives be like if they could learn to do the same? Stay tuned for chapter 7.

Step 5. Make sure that the limits you use are enforceable.

Selecting enforceable limits won't do any good unless you communicate them clearly and effectively to your kids. The way you share the rules determines how effective they will be and how well you are able to follow through with them. Communication experts indicate there are two types of directions: beta (ineffective) and alpha (effective).

BETA DIRECTIONS (INEFFECTIVE)

1. Chain directions: too many directions strung together. Children with short attention spans may only be able to handle one or two directions at a time.

2. Interrupted directions: giving a direction and then having a long discussion before the child is to carry it out.

3. Repeated directions: also known as nagging.

4. Vague directions: unclear directions often lead to nothing being done.

5. Question directions: "Would you please do this?" It's not really a question. Do not present directions as a question or as a favor unless you mean it that way.

6. "Let's do it together" directions: offering to do a chore or task with a child when they have refused. This positively reinforces the child for not complying with your command. Note that suggesting doing a chore together the first time as a way to teach a child something new is an effective directive.

7. "Psycho-twister" directions: these directions have an extremely inappropriate message attached to them. For instance, "If you don't do that, I'm going to leave you, send you away, etc."

ALPHA DIRECTIONS (EFFECTIVE)

1. Mean what you say when you give a chore or a direction and be clear that you are willing to back it up with consequences if the child disobeys.

2. State the direction simply but directly.

3. Give one single direction at a time.

4. Make sure the child is paying attention when you give the direction. Establish eye contact with them first.

5. Be sure you've reduced or removed all distractions in the room.

6. If you're unsure whether your child has understood the direction, tell them to repeat it back to you.

7. If the direction is complex or the child traditionally has trouble doing it the way you like, write down all the steps involved in doing the task. For example, "A clean room means the bed is made, drawers closed, clothes and toys off the floor, and nothing underneath the bed." This makes it easy to check and reward when it's done right.

Alpha directions lead to remarkable improvement in compliance, especially with a child who finds it difficult to comply. Too often, parents believe that children should know how to act without the rules being clearly communicated to them. Establishing clear, written rules and expectations gives direction for your child's behavior. When your child knows what you expect, they are much more likely to be able to give it.

Another key element in communicating limits and rules centers on whether you say, "You will" or "I will." Introducing new rules and limits to kids using phrases that begin with "You will" places the emphasis on *their* behavior. The problem here is that we can't always control their actions; the only thing we can consistently control is our own behavior. Ultimately, starting with "You will" sets up unwinnable power struggles.

On the flip side, sharing limits and rules by saying, "I will" focuses on our behavior—something that is within our control. These are what Love and Logic calls "enforceable statements" that turn our words into gold rather than Monopoly money. Look at the following "You will" and "I will" statements for examples.[7]

"YOU WILL" VS. "I WILL" STATEMENTS

You will not talk to me like that!	I will listen when your voice is calm like mine.
You need to take out the trash.	I will drive you to baseball practice when I see that you have taken out the trash.
I'm sick and tired of cleaning up after you. You will put those toys away . . . now!	I allow kids to keep the toys they pick up.
You will show me some respect. All I'm trying to do is help you.	I will help you with your homework as long as I feel that I am being treated nicely.

Step 6. Remember that empathy opens the heart and mind to learning.

As with all parenting endeavors, setting and enforcing limits with empathy enhances a child's brain development, encourages bonding, and builds mental strength. As we learned in the previous chapter, empathy is associated with function in regions of the brain involved in learning and executive functions. Anger and frustration, however, can activate the fight-flight-or-freeze response in the brain, which can increase stress and interfere with healthy brain development.

Here's how a parent might apply empathy with a 4-year-old. While shopping, the little one spots a Matchbox car on one of the shelves. He races over to the toy, grabs it, and shows it to the parent, saying, "I want this!" Of course, effective parents never give in to demands, but they also remain firm in a loving way. Instead of lecturing, "No, you don't need that car. You are not getting it!" they provide a caring message of empathy as they say something like, "If I was your age, I would want one of those cars too. Won't it be great one day when you have the money to buy it?" Then the parent quickly returns to shopping, signaling to the child that they are moving on. If the child drops to the floor in a fit of rage, the parent may need to buy themselves some time to think of a consequence by calmly replying, "Oh, this is sad. I'm going to have to do something about this when we get home."

While it's always possible that your child may throw a fit even if you handle it this way, you might be amazed by how a quick dose of empathy and acknowledgment can prevent, or at least minimize, many tantrums and power struggles. A little empathy goes a long way. It helps kids adhere to the limits we set and guards against falling into the Guilt Cycle of reacting harshly, feeling guilty, and resorting to rescue because you feel bad about your response.

HOW MANY LIMITS SHOULD YOU SET?

There is no magic number when it comes to setting rules, but some of us can get carried away and set too many. Take conscientious Camilla, for instance. She had a rule for just about everything. Her list of limits was so long that she and her spouse and kids were overwhelmed trying to implement them all. She came to Dr. Fay and said all these limits were making her a nervous wreck. Dr. Fay let her know that having a few all-encompassing limits can be less overwhelming for everyone. Eventually, he helped her whittle her list down to just two foundational limits to start:

- "Feel free to do whatever you like as long as it doesn't cause a problem for anyone in the universe."
- "If you cause a problem, I will ask you to solve it."

These worked well in her family, but in other families, a few more concrete rules can be helpful. Remember that every family—and every child—is different and it is best to tailor the rules accordingly. You may need to go through some trial and error to find what works best for your situation. Or start with some proven essentials and then go from there.

DR. AMEN'S EIGHT ESSENTIAL RULES FOR KIDS

After more than three decades of working with parents and their kids, Dr. Amen has found that all families are unique. However, some foundational rules are beneficial for all parents and kids.

Rule No. 1: Tell the truth. Honesty is an important value in our family. If you break that rule, you not only get in trouble for doing what you shouldn't have done, but you also get in trouble for lying. The rule is very clear: Tell the truth!

This rule applies to little lies and big ones. When you allow a child or teen to get away with the little lies, the bigger ones are easier to do. One of the best gifts you can give a child is to teach them to be honest. If they can be honest with the world, they are more likely to be honest with themselves. Of course, this means if you want children to follow this rule, you cannot tell lies. Children do what you do, not what you tell them to do. So, when you're with your child and someone calls to invite you to an event and your phone is on speaker, *do not* lie about why you can't make it.

Rule No. 2: Treat others with respect. This means no yelling, hitting, kicking, name-calling, or put-downs. Relating to others in a positive way is a skill many children (and adults) lack. Disrespect breeds conflict, social isolation, and loneliness. Respect is crucial to good relationships with others. When you relate to others in a positive, respectful manner, you will attract many more positive people and situations. Teaching this lesson to children early will save them years of frustration.

Rule No. 3: Do what Mom or Dad says the first time. Authority is good, necessary, and actually makes kids feel secure. Yet more and more parents are leery about exercising their authority. They're not quite sure if it's a good thing, so it's easy to lean toward being permissive. What is worse is becoming ambivalent—sometimes we're tough, and sometimes we're not—leading to confusion for children. As mentioned earlier, research has shown that parents who are permissive have the most problems with their children. Parents often come into Dr. Amen's office and say they have to tell their child to do something 10 to 12 times. That leaves him wondering, *Who's in charge of whom in this situation?* If you tell the child to do something 10 times, and then you get upset, what are you teaching the child? You're teaching them that it's okay to disobey until you go nuts.

When Dr. Amen would tell his son, Antony, to take out the trash, if he didn't start moving within a reasonable period of time, say 10 seconds, Dr. Amen would give him a warning. "Son, I asked you to take out the trash. You can do it now, or you can take this consequence, and then you'll still have to do it. It's up to you." Dr. Amen trained his son that he was serious the first time. When you communicate the expectation that your child must obey you and you're willing to back it up, they'll get the message and start to do what you ask *the first time you ask.*

Rule No. 4: No arguing with parents. Many children—especially when they become teenagers—continually argue with their parents. Now, it does come with the qualifier to remind your child, "I want to hear what you have to say, but I only want to hear it *once.*" One patient of mine had the nickname of "Argueman" because he would say the opposite of whatever his parents said to him. Some children are born to argue—often due to overactivity in the brain's anterior cingulate gyrus, which we discussed in chapter 3. They will just go after you and after you and after you and after you. If you let them continually argue with you, guess who else they go after—their teachers and other people in authority.

Rule No. 5: Respect each other's property. This means we ask permission to use something that does not belong to us and encompasses prolonged borrowing and stealing. So a child is not allowed to take things out of a sibling's room. This rule prevents a lot of fights. If you catch your child stealing from a store, take the child back to the store and have them confess to the store manager. Then have the child return the item *and* pay the value of the item to compensate the store for the trouble. This technique will get your child's attention and decrease the chances that stealing will be a problem in the future. When a child steals or breaks something of someone else's at home, hold the child accountable for that item and pay (in money or work) for the item to be replaced.

Rule No. 6: Put away things that you take out. I believe in building account-ability and responsibility in children. Often, mothers do way too much for their children and have trouble delegating. Parents who do everything end up angry, burned out, frustrated, and depressed. Teach children how to work by getting them to help around the house and pick up after themselves.

A large, ongoing 50-year-old study at Harvard University has been look-ing at 450 inner-city Boston school kids, who are now in their sixties, for the social causes of depression, alcoholism, anxiety disorders, and a variety of other mental health–related illnesses.[8] The study is also looking at self-esteem. The only factor out of 400 variables that correlated with self-esteem was whether the children worked as teenagers—whether at home, caring for other children, caring for the house, or outside of the house. If you do every-thing for your child, they will not develop self-esteem. So, start this principle early. If you do everything for them and then ask them to help at the age of 12, they may throw a tantrum because they're not used to helping.

The payoff of establishing chores as a daily part of Dr. Amen's family life came when his wife, Tana, was picking up their daughter Chloe and one of her friends. They were riding in the back of the car and were visibly exhausted after a full day of play. Chloe had been doing extra chores each day to earn extra money so she could buy a toy she wanted—and she was very deter-mined. But this day she was very tired.

"Mom, I'm supposed to help make dinner today, but I'm really tired," she said. "Do I have to do it?" Tana explained that Chloe didn't have to do any-thing extra if she didn't want to since she had already done her regular chores.

At this point Chloe's friend looked at her and said, "I'm sure glad my mom doesn't make me do chores!"

"What do you mean you don't have to do chores?" Chloe replied. "Everyone has to do chores! I'm doing extra chores so I can earn more money."

"Nope! My mom and dad just give me money because they love me."

Chloe gave her friend a look that only she can give and said, "That makes *no sense*! Money has nothing to do with love!"

Her friend argued, "Yes it does. My mom and dad give me money because they love me *so much*. My mom gives me money every day, and my dad gives me money every week."

At this point Tana was sweating, thinking that she was going to have to come up with a good explanation when Chloe asked why other kids don't do chores. Instead, Chloe rolled her eyes and said, "Chores are part of being a family. It's how families work together . . . and I'm good at it. I like learning how to cook and do other things."

Tana felt tremendous pride in their daughter at that moment. Plus, the clear rules about chores help keep harmony in our home.

Rule No. 7: Ask for permission before you go somewhere. Even though many kids complain about it, parents need to check where their children are, whom they are with, and what they are doing. Periodically, physically check that a child, teen, or young adult is where they said that they would be. Proper supervision is essential to a child's emotional well-being, as it reinforces bonding and helps them feel secure.

Rule No. 8: Look for ways to be kind and helpful to each other. Any parent knows this is not a natural state of being for siblings. In fact, if you have two children or more, sibling rivalry is most likely alive and well in your household. It's not clear why siblings have so much trouble, but if you look at the first Bible story about siblings, it didn't turn out so well. When you make this rule a part of the family culture, kindness and helpfulness will happen more often. To make it a habit, praise or reward a child for going out of their way to be kind and helpful to others. The affirmation will build those traits in them.

When you tell your child what you expect, you're much more likely to get it. Rules set the tone and values for your family. They clearly state that there is a line of authority at home and that you expect children to follow the rules. Not to mention that these are simply good social expectations and etiquette.

Clear Rules for Kids with ADHD

In establishing expectations at home, it's important to use visual clues, such as pictures or short printed directions. Try to minimize verbal directions since children with ADHD may have trouble processing verbal input, especially in a noisy environment. Writing expectations down also has the advantage of being able to refer to them later if the child forgets or denies that you ever told them about it. You can find many more tips for kids with this common condition in Dr. Amen's book *Healing ADD*.

SETTING LIMITS WHEN BEHAVIOR HAS GOTTEN OUT OF CONTROL

The idea of setting limits may make perfect sense to you. But how does it work when your child's behavior seems unmanageable? Here are three important tips.

- **Get solid professional help.** When any of us is facing a crisis, it's normal to become fearful. When fear floods the brain, it becomes difficult to see the big picture, identify and accurately evaluate solutions, and respond effectively. Fear also increases the odds that you will move from one ineffective solution to the next, creating more problems as you do. A caring and competent professional can help you develop a plan for keeping your child safe while implementing solutions that get at the root causes of the problem.

- **Take care of your own physical, mental, social, and spiritual health.** Your child needs you to be healthy. Too frequently, parents try to address their children's overall health without working on their own. Out of love you must go first, so that you can maintain the strength and perspective required to lead your child toward the health and hope you want them to have. We want to emphasize that self-care is not selfish. It's what you need to maintain the optimism and strength your kids need you to display.

- **Nurture your relationships with others.** If you are parenting as a married couple, your marriage is part of the treatment plan. Too often, couples place their relationship way down the list of priorities, thinking that they must place all their focus on their child's problems. This is a big mistake. Ensuring that you honor each other with love and respect, take comfort in each other, and parent as a team is essential. Like taking care of yourself, taking care of your marriage is a supreme act of love toward your child.

  If you're a single parent, build and nurture mutually caring and supportive relationships with other adults. Obviously, this doesn't mean spending so much time doing so that you neglect your child's needs, but it does mean that you spend some time each week demonstrating care for others and accepting their care for you. This is also a gift of love toward your child, as it provides the encouragement and strength you need to love them well.

SETTING LIMITS WITH YOUNG CHILDREN

What about little kids, including ones who are barely verbal? How do we set limits with them? Dr. Cline simplifies it for us by likening it to the value of real estate. It comes down to three factors: location, location, location.

1. **Change your location.** Let's look at a youngster who starts screaming uncontrollably or hitting. This is the time to walk away and give no attention to the child. If your little one protests, respond with, "We'll try again when you're calm."

2. **Change an object's location.** If your child is misusing a toy or you're playing a board game and your child throws a fit because they're losing, quietly take the toy from them or put the game back in its box. Experiment with saying, "Oh, how sad. Time for this to go away." Use your judgment to determine when the object can be reintroduced.

3. **Change the child's location.** In some cases, the best approach for a misbehaving toddler is to say in a singsong voice, "Uh-oh! Looks like it's time for you to be in the playpen (or stroller or shopping cart or bedroom)." You simply move the child to that location until they have calmed down. (See "The Uh-Oh Song" on the next page.)

When you do this consistently with children, they begin to understand immediately that their parents are in control. Simply singing "uh-oh" in a loving way can alert the child and prompt a change in behavior.[9]

The "Uh-Oh Song": A Strategy for Toddlers

- When your child begins to misbehave, sing, "Uh-oh!" and gently lead or carry them to their room or playpen. Just sing this one phrase without adding any anger, lectures, threats, or frustration.
- Resist the urge to talk too much. The more words you use when your kids are misbehaving, the less effective you become.
- If you use their bedroom, give them a choice about the door. Ask, "Do you want to have your door open or shut?" But shut the door if your child tries to come out.
- Say, "Feel free to come out when you're acting sweet." Allow your child to come out only after they have been calm for at least three to five consecutive minutes.
- Don't lecture your child or remind them to come out when they're ready. Just give them a hug and say, "I love you."
- Have fun with them when they are behaving well, and repeat as needed. When our kids love to be around us, the "Uh-Oh Song" has far more power.

Firm and loving limits are like guardrails on a winding mountain road. They provide the direction and security our kids need to explore and find their own special path toward good character and joy.

Action Steps

- Accept the fact that kids of all ages need limits and that limits are nonnegotiable needs.
- Get prepared before you start setting limits.
- Review your goals to ensure limits will help you achieve them.
- Understand that when introducing new limits, kids may initially react negatively.
- Practice how to neutralize arguing.

- Learn to quiet the arguing in your own mind.
- Communicate limits clearly and effectively.
- When setting and enforcing limits, use empathy.
- Consider implementing the eight essential rules for all kids.
- Remember that you can still set limits after behavior has gotten out of control.
- Learn the three simple location rules of setting limits for younger kids.

CHAPTER 6

LOVING DISCIPLINE LEADS TO MENTAL STRENGTH

The cost of our children's mistakes goes up every day. Help them learn when the consequences are small, not later when they may be life and death.

Matt was an elementary school principal. Rene, his wife, was a middle school teacher in the same district. Every year, both were seeing more students struggling with self-discipline, self-esteem, and accepting responsibility for their actions. That's why they didn't hesitate to sign up when they were invited to attend a weeklong conference titled *Love and Logic Solutions for Reaching Challenging Students*. Besides, it was summer, the conference was at a nice spot in Colorado, and they could take turns attending the conference while the other spent time with their 5-year-old, Amelia.

Rene attended the first day, taking furious notes so she could share them with Matt afterward. Dr. Fay started by asking the audience, "How many of your students—and your own children—are making enough mistakes?"

Rene laughed at the question, as did most of the other participants. The woman behind her responded out loud, "Mine make way too many!"

Jim Fay continued, "Is it possible that any of you are stealing from them by trying too hard to ensure that they don't make mistakes? Is it also possible that some of you might be robbing them of responsibility and self-esteem by rescuing them from the consequences of their mistakes?"

Surprised, Rene thought, *I see parents who do this every year.* Then a more sobering thought entered her mind, *Sometimes Matt and I are both of those types on a single day.*

Rene's anxiety gradually lifted as she heard a variety of simple classroom management techniques and positive discipline strategies, many of which she could also apply at home. Most revolutionary to her was the concept that we ought to hope and pray that kids make enough small and affordable mistakes when they are young, so they will have the skills required to avoid making life-threatening or deadly mistakes when they are older. She'd never thought about it that way.

After the conference, she was excited to see her family, and she couldn't wait to share what she had learned. Opening the door to their hotel room, her excitement turned to concern as she saw the tears running down their daughter's face and Matt looking exceptionally frustrated.

"I told her three times to stop jumping on the bed, and she wouldn't listen," he blurted, dangling the broken table lamp by its cord. "Fortunately, she isn't hurt, but she knocked this off of the table, and now we have to pay for it."

Rene had a strange thought, *Isn't this great?* It felt strange to her because her thought was sincere, not sarcastic. Knowing that both her husband and her daughter needed time to calm down, she waited until late in the evening to share her thoughts with Matt. "Honey, I think that this could be a great learning experience for her if we handle it calmly and ask her how she plans to help pay for the lamp."

"She's just 5," Matt initially replied with a bit of irritation.

Rene continued by describing her plan: She'd ask Amelia how she planned to help pay for the lamp. Then she'd share some options, such as using money she'd saved, doing extra chores, or selling some of her toys.

Matt began to soften, grinned, and added, "It's great that she is just 5. If more parents of students at my school held their kids accountable like this, their kids would be happier, and we'd have a lot less stress in our jobs. Besides, she doesn't have to pay all of the cost—just enough so that it helps her see that choices have consequences."

When Rene and Matt shared this story with us, they described how Amelia had worked on and off for a month to replace a portion of the money they had "loaned" her to pay for the lamp. She shared how they even held some of her toys as collateral on the loan.

They learned how important it is to handle situations like that as teaching experiences rather than punishments and remembered it when she started to drive at 16 and shredded a tire when she ran over a curb. "By that age, she'd made enough mistakes and solved enough problems on her own that she was prepared for us even before we had a chance to speak," Matt recalls. "'I know, Mom, Dad, I already have a plan. I called the tire store right away. Those are so expensive! I have some money saved, and I think I can make up the rest by selling my old soccer stuff.' When she said that, it reminded me of what we learned from that conference. It made it so much easier for us as parents, and now she's a generally happy kid who's fun to be around most of the time."

WHAT IS DISCIPLINE?

Ultimately, discipline is about teaching. In fact, the word *discipline* is derived from the Latin word *disciplina*, which means instruction or training. It is also derived from the word *discere*, which means "to learn." Basically, discipline centers on providing instruction and training for learning how to discern right from wrong, good behaviors from bad behaviors, and healthy decisions from unhealthy decisions.

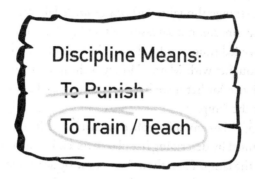

Discipline Means:

~~To Punish~~

To Train / Teach

Somewhere along the way, however, the meaning of discipline got twisted in our collective consciousness. That confusion is evident in these conflicting definitions for the verb *discipline*:

1. To punish or penalize for the sake of enforcing obedience and perfecting moral character
2. To train or develop by instruction and exercise especially in self-control

Many parents believe the first definition, the one that involves punishing or penalizing kids to force them into obedience and to perfect their moral character. But there's a problem with that definition. Nobody has perfect moral character. Sure, there are lots of people we trust enough to watch our kids, borrow our car, or handle our finances, but none of them is perfect. As parents, we need to realize that if we are using discipline in an attempt to make our kids perfect, then we're setting up ourselves and our kids for a lose-lose situation. Perfection isn't an achievable goal.

Let's consider for a moment what history teaches us about putting the thumb on other people and trying to force them to obey. It's not a pretty picture. We can thank psychologists Kurt Lewin, Ronald Lippitt, and Ralph

White for their foundational research on leadership styles that began in the 1930s.[1] Ultimately, Lewin, who is considered the founder of "social psychology," was trying to comprehend a concept that was personal for him. As a Jewish man who had escaped Nazi Germany, he wanted to understand how an entire society of people could allow the Holocaust to happen. How a group of people could believe that everything was okay in spite of glaring evidence to the contrary.

So, Lewin and his fellow psychologists devised a series of fascinating experiments. They looked at how groups of 10-year-old boys behaved when teachers taught using three styles of leadership:

- *Authoritarian*—when the teacher dictated behavior and the group had no say. This is like the Drill Sergeant parent who says, "When I tell you to jump, you ask, 'How high?'"

- *Laissez-faire*—when the teacher was hands-off and the group made all decisions on their own. This is similar to the passive parents who put an iPad in their kid's hands to keep them quiet.

- *Democratic*—when the teacher acted as a facilitator and the group contributed to decision-making. These are similar to the Consultant parents who allow their kids to make most of their own decisions, but who step in when necessary to maintain safety.

The results? The authoritarian group had the highest level of productivity (70 percent), which isn't surprising when you consider that dictators can be very intimidating, especially when they tell you to do something *or else!* But Lewin and the other psychologists were more interested in what happened when the teacher wasn't around. When the authoritarian teacher left, productivity plummeted to nearly 30 percent. It's like it was party time for the kids. The kids with the laissez-faire teacher had the lowest level of productivity (33 percent) regardless of whether the teacher was present or not, which was no surprise since they were basically out of control all the time. What about the kids with the democratic teacher? They chalked up 50 percent productivity, but that number barely dropped to 46 percent when the teacher left the room. These kids had experimented with decision-making and had developed enough self-control and self-motivation—key elements of mental strength—to be productive in the absence of the teacher.

WHICH LEADERSHIP STYLE TEACHES SELF-CONTROL?

LEADERSHIP STYLE	PRODUCTIVITY WHEN TEACHER IS PRESENT	PRODUCTIVITY WHEN TEACHER IS ABSENT
Authoritarian	70%	29%
Laissez-Faire	33%	33%
Democratic	50%	46%

Lewin summarized the experiments, concluding that humans are like physical springs, like the ones we find in cars or inside a mattress. What does this mean? Just imagine that a child is like a coil spring that can be pushed down. As a parent, you might be able to temporarily compress a powerful spring, but sooner or later, you'll get tired, go on a business trip, or send that "spring" off to college. Suddenly, there's no more parental pressure on that spring, and it's going to rebound with a force that's equal to the force that compressed it. The kid is going to be out of control.

As parents, we need to ask ourselves if we have been tricked into believing that first definition of discipline and raising our kids in an authoritarian style. If so, our kids may be behaving in our presence, but they may be unprepared to self-manage as they become older, spend more time away from home, and face more difficult decisions and temptations. Wouldn't it be better to help them learn to behave from the inside out rather than spending much of our time trying to control them from the outside in?

We also need to be honest with ourselves about whether our parenting falls on the other side of the spectrum, and we are failing to set and enforce enough limits. Are we being too permissive or laissez-faire? As parents ourselves, we know that finding the right balance is rarely easy. So keep in mind what we mentioned earlier:

Effective parents are both loving and firm at the same time.

WHICH DISCIPLINE DEFINITION DO YOU BELIEVE?

Take a good look in the mirror and ask yourself, which one of those dictionary definitions of discipline do you believe? There's no shame in your answer. Many of us repeat what we saw our parents do. Others veer to the opposite extreme. Wherever you fall on the discipline spectrum, it's important to recognize which philosophy you've adopted so you can make adjustments if needed.

1. Do you think discipline is mostly about enforcing rules and punishing?
This is often the case in people who were raised by dictatorial parents and who had more of a fear-based relationship rather than a loving bond with them. This could be you if you relate to any of the following statements:

- I was raised by cold and demanding parents.
- My parents were very rigid.
- I never felt loved.
- I always felt like I was in trouble.
- I felt like I was walking on eggshells to avoid getting in trouble.
- I felt like I had no say in my own life.

If this sounds like you, we feel for you. Being raised in that kind of environment presents a lot of challenges. It can also make you want to parent your own children very differently, leading to a desire to avoid anything that hints of punishment or that could cause even mild distress. We see this frequently in our work—a pendulum swing to the other side. This occurs not only on an individual basis but also on a societal level. We call this the Wave of Permissiveness.

If you look back to the late 1960s and early 1970s, there was a movement that likely began with people who had been hurt as children by authoritarian parents. They rebelled by dismissing the dictatorial style of their own parents and adopting a laissez-faire attitude that allowed kids total freedom without limits or rules. The movement gave birth to a slew of parenting books embracing this free-for-all, never-say-no philosophy, making this leadership style more commonplace.

Unfortunately, the Wave of Permissiveness was a total train wreck. And those kids who grew up with permissive parents vowed never to let their kids run amok without supervision, and the pendulum swung back to the other side again, giving way to a new set of books promising to teach you how to stop taking flack from your kids, how to control and punish your kids, and so on.

It's a societal Guilt Cycle that keeps circling back around every few decades.

SOCIETAL GUILT CYCLE

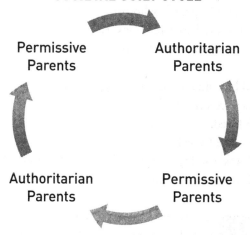

Permissive Parents

Authoritarian Parents

Authoritarian Parents

Permissive Parents

2. Do you believe that it is your job to make your kids feel bad and experience significant distress when they make poor decisions? This is another common belief among parents that has troublesome consequences. If your discipline style involves yelling, threatening, or spanking, it's even worse. Decades of research show that corporal punishment—in particular, spanking—results in detrimental effects on cognitive function, social and emotional development, and self-control.[2] It robs kids of mental strength. Adding to this body of evidence is a 2021 brain-imaging study reported in *Child Development*, which shows that spanking causes changes to the brain in children, activating areas involved in fear and threat responses.[3] Alarmingly, these same neural changes, which raise the perception of threats, are also seen in kids who experience severe maltreatment. So, a child's brain interprets that swat on the behind in a similar way to more extreme forms of mistreatment.

Time Out

Even animal trainers know how harmful corporal punishment can be. Years ago, Dr. Amen went to Marine World, an aquatic animal theme park that used to be in Northern California. He was watching the whale show, and one whale was performing amazing tricks while the other one basically blew off the trainer. When the trainer noticed the whale wasn't behaving the way she wanted, she directed the giant mammal to a different area of the pool for a time-out. At the end of the show, the trainer asked if anyone had any questions. Dr. Amen did. He wanted to know about the whale that was not behaving and why the trainer didn't spank it or swat it with a stick; that's what so many parents do when their children misbehave. The trainer shot a horrified look at him, but then she realized he was being facetious. She said, "If I would have beaten him, he would have never performed for me again. That's because he wouldn't trust me, and I would become a source of stress for him." We can all learn a lot from animal trainers.

Why don't all parents understand this concept? Physical punishment or extreme consequences may have been modeled for you. Or they may have been taught from the pulpit so you think this is the "right" way to discipline. You may not want to parent that way, but you may feel obligated to do so, as if it's your duty to be a punisher. This may be you if you answer yes to any of the following questions:

- Do you ever feel guilty and stressed about this, but feel like you would be letting your kids down if you didn't operate this way?
- Do you ever wish that you had better relationships with your kids?
- Do you ever worry about rebellion . . . particularly when they leave home as young adults?
- Would you like a better way?

3. Do you believe discipline *is a dirty word that infringes on a child's creativity and freedom?* Does the word *discipline* rub you the wrong way? Perhaps you grew up in a home with an authoritarian parent who disciplined harshly and you vowed never to inflict the same treatment on your own children. Or maybe you think it's an outdated concept that has no place in modern child-rearing. People who think this way tend to have a laissez-faire parenting style and are inclined to:

- Allow children to live without rules
- Avoid enforcing limits
- Steer clear of sharing their expectations for the child

- Allow children to behave badly without correcting the behavior
- Encourage individualism over the good of the collective family unit

In general, people who have a disdain for the word *discipline* act in these ways out of love. They have a strong desire to promote creativity and freedom, but the lack of instructional discipline can backfire and lead to problems with self-esteem, selfishness, and unhappiness.

4. Do you believe discipline is not about punishment, but rather a way to teach your children how to develop self-control? If you view discipline as an instructional tool rather than a punishment, you've just made parenting so much easier. Congratulations! Count yourself among these lucky parents if you can answer yes to these questions:

- Do you believe you can discipline in ways that maintain the love and respect of your children?
- Are you reading this book because you know that repetition is the key to learning and staying on track?

If this is a new perspective for you, the good news is that we will show you a better way that helps you and your children. The pendulum doesn't have to swing to the extremes. When we stop being reactive parents and start being proactive parents who use a democratic or Consultant leadership style, we can have the best of both worlds. We can provide discipline while still being loving—it's the firm and loving style we wrote about earlier that fuels mental strength. And it's the cornerstone of the practical neuropsychology approach to parenting.

LOVING DISCIPLINE SHOULD BEGIN EARLY

Jim Fay often shares a touching story about how a kindergarten teacher used effective discipline with one of her students. As you read, remember that discipline is not about punishing—it's about discipleship, or teaching. Many of the skills we teach work well in a variety of settings, including homes, classrooms, and daycare settings. The child in this example, Max, was 6 years old and sometimes displayed anger outbursts because of a severe case of perfectionism. He wanted everything to go just right all the time, even when he was coloring. Max was determined to stay within the lines. When he made a few mistakes with his crayons that he couldn't erase, he got so frustrated he grabbed his crayons and broke them into pieces.

His teacher walked over to him and realized that in that moment she didn't need to be an instructor; she just needed to be empathetic and allow the situation to do the teaching. She told Max, "Oh, Max, you must be having such a hard day."

Max replied, "I hate these stupid crayons."

The teacher gently asked, "What do you think you're going to do about those crayons?"

Max's lower lip started to tremble as he wailed, "I don't know," and put his head down on his desk and cried.

Then the bell rang for recess, and Max jumped up. But the teacher stopped him from joining the other kids and said, "You still haven't solved the problem of your broken crayons. Would you like some ideas on how to fix it?"

Max shouted, "No!" and put his head back down on the table.

The teacher felt awful, but she bit her tongue and waited. A few moments later, Max looked up and asked, "Do we have any tape?"

"Well, yes, we do," she said, handing him the tape. In her mind she was thinking, *This is never going to work.* But how do kids learn? They learn by trying a lot of things that don't work. So, she gave him the Scotch tape. Just imagine a 6-year-old with Scotch tape—it got stuck on his fingers, and there were little balls of it all over the floor. He got mad again, and the tears started flowing again. The teacher said, "Oh, that's frustrating, but if anybody can do this, you can."

Pretty soon, he got the hang of the tape and managed to piece together one of the crayons with it. That brought a big smile to his face. After he fixed one crayon, he moved on to the next one and then another. Eventually, he had them all taped up and put them back into the box. He was so excited to finish so he could go out to recess. But then the bell rang, and all the kids came rushing back into the classroom.

The teacher thought Max might really lose it then, but he didn't look dejected. In fact, he looked very pleased with himself. Still, she couldn't help but feel bad the rest of the day that he'd missed recess. To her surprise, at the end of the day, Max raced out of the classroom, but then he came charging back in and gave her a big hug. He'd never done that before.

When we can step back and let kids work through their problems and simply coach them along rather than solving the problem for them, we let them be the hero. And we get to be co-heroes because we allowed them to do it. It's a win-win for everyone that helps us teach responsibility beginning when children are about 4 or 5 years of age. It's even effective with teens, young adults, and our aging parents.

THE FIVE GOALS OF DISCIPLINE

If discipline is about teaching, what do we hope kids will learn from it? Before we describe the five goals of discipline, let's go back to the importance of goals, which we discussed in chapter 2. To see how discipline can help you achieve your objectives, we encourage you to revisit your goals now. Go back to pages 47 and 54 and copy them in the space below.

One Page Miracle for Parents

What do I want for my life as a parent? What am I doing to make it happen?

RELATIONSHIPS

Spouse/Partner: _____

_____

Children: _____

_____

_____

WORK/FINANCES

_____

_____

_____

SELF

Physical: _____

_____

_____

Emotional: _____

_____

_____

Mental: _____

_____

_____

Spiritual: _____

_____

_____

One Page Miracle
for Kids

What do I want for my life? What can I do to make it happen?

RELATIONSHIPS

Parents: _____

_____

Siblings: _____

_____

Friends: _____

_____

SCHOOL/WORK

School: _____

_____

Teachers: _____
Work/Chores: _____

MYSELF

Physical: _____
Emotional: _____

*Mental:*_____

_____

*Spiritual:*_____

Most parents find that their goals for themselves and their children dove-tail nicely with the following Five Goals of Discipline. Keep your goals in mind as you explore the five goals.

Discipline Goal #1. To help children discern what is wise and kind from what is foolish and uncaring. The first goal of discipline is to help kids learn right from wrong, good from bad. It's basic common sense. It's the MAP of Love and Logic:

- *Model healthy behavior:* In a counseling session with a couple, the dad apologized to his wife for taking his teenage sons hunting with some of his buddies. The other adults were drinking alcohol and swearing the whole time, and the dad felt bad for putting his sons in that environment. But the therapist pointed out that the dad didn't drink or cuss, so it provided a great opportunity for the teens to see their dad as a role model. That's the essence of discipline: teaching by modeling good behavior.

- *Allow safe mistakes:* Allowing kids to have experiences, live with the consequences of their actions, and solve their own problems—the way little Max did with his broken crayons—is a critical component of discipline.

- *Provide empathy:* Showing kids you care about their feelings, just as Max's teacher did, makes them feel respected. And that increases the likelihood that they will listen to you when you discipline them.

Discipline Goal #2. To help children learn when they are young and when the price tags are small. We apologize, dear reader, for sounding like a broken record on this one, but this concept is fundamental to successful parenting. Helping kids learn when the consequences are small—like broken crayons, missing out on recess, or even getting a poor grade on an assignment—is the key. At its core, discipline helps our children have less self-inflicted pain in their lives as they grow into adulthood. Think of it as a path to peace. Providing discipline early allows them to enjoy more peace and productivity.

Remind yourself of this any time your child is bawling, having a melt-down, or calling you the worst parent in the world. Tell yourself that what you're doing is providing a teaching moment that will pay off in the future. A little short-term discomfort can lead to a lot more peace later on.

Unfortunately, if you tend toward being a Helicopter or Drill Sergeant parent, it can be easy to miss out on this concept. Those parenting styles operate in ways that are centered on avoiding short-term discomfort rather than staying focused on our long-term goals. And to be honest, it's usually *your* discomfort you're trying to circumvent in these instances. If your child is throwing a fit in the grocery store, you may shove an iPad in their hands to soothe them rather than use that time for teaching, aka discipline. Much of this avoidance boils down to the fact that many parents want to keep appearances clean rather than messy. Here's what we mean.

Sanitary Approach: Are you the kind of person who wants everything to be clean and orderly? Do you wish you could clean up life's messes with a nifty packet of hand wipes? That's what Benny's parents were like. They both worked, so 3-year-old Benny went to daycare every day. Getting him off to daycare proved challenging. Kids are like airplanes; it's the takeoffs and landings that tend to cause problems. For kids, that means mornings and bedtimes. Takeoffs were particularly rough for Benny. In the mornings, he would dawdle, throw fits, and collapse into a crying heap on the floor. His parents would pick him up, wrangle some clothes on him, give him some food, and put him in the car. Benny did nothing. Do you see a problem here? Benny's parents were teaching him that if he throws a fit, they will do everything for him to make things right. How do you think that approach is going to work for Benny when he's a young adult in the workforce?

Messy Approach: Parents who use practical neuropsychology accept that discipline can be messy. Instead of aiming for perfection that requires parental interference, they aim for personal responsibility. When Benny's parents decided to try the messy approach, they told the little guy, "Good morning, Benny! We sure hope you're going to be able to get yourself dressed by the time you go off to school. But it's no problem if you can't. You can either go to school with your clothes on your body or your clothes in a bag. And by the way, I wonder if your tummy's going to be full or empty. I guess you get to decide about that."

Guess what? Like usual, Benny didn't do anything. So, off he went in his pajamas to Little Precious Ones Daycare (by the way, have you ever noticed that daycares always have these wonderful names, never anything like Little Tyrants or Tantrum Central?). The parents had called ahead to give the daycare a heads-up about their plans, and when they arrived, they handed off Benny's clothes and said a quick "Good luck today!" Benny was mighty upset for about 30 seconds before turning to the teacher and asking, "What's for lunch? I'm hungry!" Over the next few weeks, Benny started making some decisions on his own—like having something to eat and putting on his clothes before leaving the house. His parents didn't have to punish him or nag him, but they did have to be willing to let things get a little messy for a while.

Ask yourself if you're willing to deal with a little messiness now, so you and your children can have less mess later?

Discipline Goal #3. To help children develop self-discipline, so they can experience freedom. One of the most common things we hear from tweens and teens is that they would like more freedom. Most of them think freedom should just be handed to them. What they don't realize is that freedom comes at a cost. On a societal level, it comes at the cost of many brave men and women who defend our country. On a more personal level, it requires self-control and responsibility. As we tell the adolescents and teens we counsel, the secret to gaining more freedom is to become the kind of person that does not need to be micromanaged. When a kid proves that they can be responsible, respectful, and resilient, the doors to freedom open wide.

Discipline Goal #4. To help them learn how to remain mentally strong in the face of hardship. Discipline helps kids learn how to deal with tough situations. Later in this book, we will devote chapter 8 to this topic, but we will briefly introduce you to the concept here. In thinking about raising mentally strong kids, think about a simple pod of coffee that is vacuum-sealed for freshness. This may be ideal for coffee, but we don't want to vacuum-seal our children's lives so that they have no experience dealing with disappointments, difficult decisions, or discipline. If our children are protected from hardships, they won't become the courageous, capable, and character-filled people we hope they will. Instead, they may become adults without the common sense or grit to wrestle themselves out of a wet paper bag.

Discipline Goal #5. To preserve our sanity and our relationships with our children. The final goal of discipline is to strengthen our relationships and make life easier for ourselves. Typically, kids who grow up without loving discipline come to resent their parents, and their parents find themselves counting the days until their offspring become adults and leave home. Unfortunately, many of these kids never fully mature, and they don't become independent. As such, the resentment and chaos often continue for a lifetime.

Healthy relationships always require the healthy development of good limits and healthy accountability, which are two fundamental aspects of practical neuropsychology.

CREATE A DISCIPLINE GPS FOR YOUR FAMILY

When it comes to discipline, we need to create a good GPS that will help us navigate challenging situations. There are two basic approaches you can take: a system-based approach or a principle-based approach. Let's explore the differences between these two systems.

- *System-Based Approach:* This approach involves an iron-clad procedure that you follow every time. For example:

  - Step 1: Kid does this.
  - Step 2: You do this.
  - Step 3: Kid reacts.
  - Step 4: You do that.

  How well do you think this approach will work? Take it from us, it doesn't! One of the problems with this approach is that it forces us to treat each child in exactly the same way despite differences in personality, learning styles, mental health issues, brain development stages, and more. In our experience, we've found that kids will test this system, parents will start blaming each other, and ultimately, kids don't get what they need.

- *Principle-Based Approach:* A better way is to come up with a core set of principles that guide your decision-making about discipline. This allows you to handle things differently based on each child's personality, provided your children adhere to the core principles. It also allows you to tailor discipline to each child based on their unique needs and on each situation. The outcome is a calmer family, in which the kids are less capable of testing and manipulating the adults, there is far less angst among parents, and the kids learn how to become flexible problem-solvers rather than system followers. It's like a car GPS that is dialed in for each driver and knows your preferred routes and driving habits. Wouldn't you prefer that?

THE FIVE NONNEGOTIABLE CORE PRINCIPLES OF DISCIPLINE

To create a principle-based system for discipline, include the following principles.

1. **Model and teach the behavior you desire.** Our kids learn not only by making their own mistakes and dealing with the consequences, but they also gain insights by watching how we behave when things go wrong. One man described how he remembered his father modeling how to be gracious and forgiving with others. He and his father were leaving the grocery store. Just as they got into the car, another driver backed into them, giving their car a rather hard bump. "I was so mad," the man said as he recalled the incident. "I was fit to be tied and wanted my dad to let the other driver have it. But my dad got out and calmly said, 'Hey, it's not a big deal. Nobody's hurt. It's just a little scratch. It's not even worth worrying about.'"

2. **Allow your child to make plenty of affordable mistakes.** Letting kids make mistakes when the price tag is small pays off in the long run. A grandmother was raising her 13-year-old granddaughter who said she needed money to buy clothes for the new school year. The grandmother gave her some money with the caveat "This money needs to cover all your school supplies, extra activity fees, and clothing." The teen went to the store and bought two expensive outfits that burned up all the money. At school, the kids started teasing her by saying, "Hey, how come you always wear the same two outfits?" The girl went to her grandmother and asked for more money, but she didn't get a handout. Instead, her grandmother said, "How do you think you could earn it?" That teenager had to do a lot of chores to earn more money so she could buy some different clothes. That's a lesson she won't forget.

    Learning this lesson as a teen ensures that she'll handle her money more wisely as a young adult. For example, she'll be less likely to blow her paycheck on something superfluous and not be able to pay her rent—a much bigger consequence that could result in getting evicted or having to move back home.

3. **When your child makes a mistake, demonstrate empathy rather than anger, lectures, threats, or sarcasm.** Keeping your cool and empathizing with your child is a must. Look at how Dr. Fay handled a problem in his own home. His son Cody loved toy pirates, but he had a habit of leaving them scattered all over the floor. Dr. Fay nagged him about it, but he eventually realized that wasn't helping. So, one day, Dr. Fay just picked them all up and put them in a place

he called the "Toy Bermuda Triangle" (a place every home should have). When his son came home, he asked where his pirates were. Dr. Fay explained that he's always happy to pick up any toys that his son leaves out, but the only problem is that they don't come back. The next time his son left his toys out, Dr. Fay asked him if he would like his dad to pick them up for him, and his son rushed to put them away, saying, "No, I want to keep these!"

Sometimes, the fewer words, the better. Actions can speak louder than words. This limits the number of warnings you have to give and eliminates the need for lectures or threats.

4. **When possible, give your child an opportunity to solve the problem.** It is always a good idea to let your child try to solve a problem before jumping in to the rescue. Take a cue from a dad whose 15-year-old son was having a difficult time with one of his teachers:

Teen: "Mr. Conrad's always on my case. He's never happy with anything I do."

Parent (with empathy): "That sounds discouraging."

Teen: "Well, he just makes me mad. None of the other teachers give us homework on Fridays."

Parent: "Do you have any ideas about what you might do?"

Teen: "What do you mean? Me?"

Parent: "Yeah. What might you do to work things out with Mr. Conrad?"

Teen: "Oh, man."

Parent: "These sorts of things are never easy. Please let me know if you'd like to hear what I've seen other people do."

What can you learn from this brief example? When a child, particularly a teen, faces a challenge, they learn and grow only when they are required to put their fair share of energy into overcoming that challenge. Letting them come up with solutions also boosts their self-esteem, which helps them develop independence and resilience.

5. **When consequences are necessary, choose one that has some form of logical connection with the child's misbehavior or poor decision.** As you've seen in these examples, the consequences typically have some connection to the poor behavior: breaking a lamp and having

to pay for it, leaving toys on the floor and losing access to those toys, for instance. But what happens when you can't think of a logical consequence? Rather than blurt out the first thing that pops into your head, turn to a time-tested consequence that our friend Foster Cline, MD, originally developed. He calls it the "energy drain"; use his strategy when you find yourself stumped.[4] Look at how an energy drain helped a mom named Tracy.

When you're fighting, it really drains my energy.

Tracy was driving down the road while her two boys were in the back seat fighting, shoving each other, and carrying on like crazy. It was driving her nuts. She couldn't think of a logical consequence, so she said in a sad and exhausted tone of voice, "Wow, when you're fighting, it really drains my energy."

Without using a tone that might send a guilt trip message, she explained that she loved them but that their squabbling had become draining. Is this true? Is it accurate and sometimes appropriate to say that many forms of misbehavior have this effect on us?

After they had gotten home and Tracy had some time to rest and think, she continued by adding, "What do you think you might do to replace the energy you drained from me by arguing and fighting in the car?" They had no clue, but she was happy to provide some ideas. "Some kids put energy back into their parents by staying home from one of their activities. This allows their parents to rest. Other kids replace this energy by doing some of their parents' chores around the house. Others do volunteer work, which makes the parents feel good because their kids are helping make the world a better place."

Her two boys complained like crazy, but they helped each other clean the toilets because they knew if they didn't, it would cause an even greater energy drain. And who knows what consequence their mom would come up with then? Weeks later, Tracy was driving the boys somewhere, and when they started fighting, she lifted her hand and started to say, "I'm feeling really drained . . ." But before she could get the words out, they both interrupted her. "We'd better stop fighting, or she's going to be tired, and we're gonna have to do chores."

Use the energy drain whenever you can't think of something in the moment. It buys you some time so you can come up with an appropriate consequence that has a logical connection to their misbehavior. As most of us can agree, misbehavior does drain our energy. Another great quality of this skill is that you can adapt it to use with kids ages 5 through 105.

By putting these core principles into action, you can learn to discipline your children in a loving and empathetic way that strengthens your relationship while helping them develop better self-control.

Action Steps

- Remind yourself that every mistake your kids make when they are younger is an opportunity for them to develop skills that will help them make fewer larger ones later.
- Send at least one email or text to yourself per week with the following message: "Every mistake handled with love and firmness is an opportunity for learning."
- Practice the five goals of discipline:
  > To help children discern what is wise and kind from what is foolish and uncaring
  > To help children learn when they are young and when the price tags are small
  > To help children develop self-discipline, so they can experience freedom

> To help them learn how to remain strong in the face of hardship

> To preserve our sanity and our relationships with them

• Create a principle-based approach to discipline with these five nonnegotiables:

> Model and teach the behavior you desire.

> Allow your child to make plenty of affordable mistakes.

> When children make a mistake, demonstrate empathy rather than anger, lectures, threats, or sarcasm.

> When possible, give your child an opportunity to solve the problem.

> When consequences are necessary, choose one with some form of logical connection with the child's misbehavior or poor decision. When you're stuck and can't think of a logical consequence, mention an "energy drain" and come up with a consequence later.

CHAPTER 7

MENTAL HYGIENE IS CRITICAL FOR PARENTS AND KIDS

Disinfect your thoughts, and teach your kids how to do it too.

Your thoughts are very powerful. And if you let automatic negative thoughts (ANTs) infest your mind, they can fuel anxiousness, doubt, and inconsistent parenting. The same goes for kids of all ages. Dr. Amen coined the term ANTs in the early 1990s after a tough day in the clinic, when his patients had included four who were suicidal, a pair of teenage runaways, and two spiteful couples with major marital conflict. After getting home that night, Dr. Amen went to the kitchen, flipped on the light switch, and gasped. Ants had infested the kitchen. The tiny critters were everywhere—on the countertops, in the sink, in the food in the cabinets.

The acronym ANTs—automatic negative thoughts—crossed his mind. He realized that the same way ants had invaded his kitchen, ANTs had infested the minds of his patients, stealing their happiness and ruining their day. He realized that ANTs could affect anyone at any age, including young children and their parents.[1] He has written about ANTs in several of his books, but in this chapter, we will show you how they impact your ability to be an effective parent and how they can steal your child's mental strength. More important, we will show you how to disinfect your mind for greater mental strength.

Take Allison, for example. A young mom with three kids under the age of 5, Allison had been overrun by ANTs but had never considered questioning her thoughts. "I don't measure up," she told Dr. Amen. "I can't keep my house clean. I'm always running behind. And I never have enough time to give my children everything they need." She couldn't see anything good about her skills as a mother, and it was clear that it was hurting her relationship with her kids.

Allison needed to start thinking about her thinking. Like her, all parents—and kids—can benefit from practicing mental hygiene and disinfecting our thoughts.

KNOW THE NINE MOST COMMON ANTs

When you don't question the negative thoughts that travel through your brain, your unconscious mind automatically believes them—and they could ruin your day. One negative thought, like one ant at a picnic, is not a big deal. Two or three negative thoughts, like two or three ants at a picnic, become more irritating. And 10 or 20 negative thoughts can cause real problems.[2] That's why it's necessary to recognize the thoughts that go through your head and correct them. Then you'll be able to think logically and clearly as a parent, and you'll be able to teach your children how to spot and kill their own ANTs, so they can become mentally stronger.

Here are nine ANTs that distort situations and can affect you and your children.

1. *Just-the-Bad ANTs:* A negative filter sees only what's bad in situations. Dr. Amen once had a patient who had recently moved his family. He had 80 percent of the household goods put away from the move. But that's not what he focused on. The only part he could think about was the 20 percent that wasn't put away. He told Dr. Amen that he was 100 percent inadequate, 100 percent inferior, and 100 percent disorganized. Even though he was caring for three small children, while his wife was finishing her old job in a town 100 miles away, he could only see what he had *not* done rather than what he had done.

When you have a negative filter, you often discount any successes or positive experiences. Often, when kids who have been difficult to manage have a good day, their parents discount the experience and predict things will quickly turn sour again. Most people and most experiences are a blend of positive and negative. A disciplined mind can focus on the positive while at the same time finding what is valuable in the negative.

Dr. Fay sees a very common theme in the thinking of many parents who are frustrated with their child's lack of motivation or skill in various areas. These well-meaning parents dwell on the idea that it is their responsibility to continually point out what their child is doing wrong. Their rationale goes something like this: "If I don't put my energy into helping my child correct their weaknesses, then they will never become successful." The worry is that without constant correction their kids will become failures, irresponsible, disrespectful, etc. So these parents make sure to provide constant critical feedback, thinking it helps their kids.

This ANT often dominates the thinking of parents who have adopted the Drill Sergeant style. Many of them actually believe their focus on the negative will help their children become better people. Is this truly the case?

Imagine having a supervisor, coworker, or spouse who believes this and only gives you feedback when something is wrong. Sadly, some of you may experience this on a daily basis. This approach does not inspire growth; instead, it leaves people feeling angry, frustrated, and often hopeless. Rather than improving relationships, it can destroy them. And a continual focus on negative behavior sets the stage for small children, teens, and young adults to develop an ANT colony within their head, which then breeds self-doubt, anxiousness, depression, and more.

People of all ages are far more likely to grow and learn when they find themselves around others who focus mostly on what they have done well. They're also far more likely to do the hard work required to address their areas of weakness when they feel valued for their strengths.

Parenting tip: Helping your child develop healthy beliefs about their ability to handle struggles hinges on this time-tested truth: Build them up in their areas of strength so that they will have the mental strength to overcome their areas of weakness.

2. Blaming ANTs: Blaming others starts early. When Dr. Amen's daughter Kaitlyn was 18 months old, she would blame her brother, who was 11, for any trouble she might be in. Her nickname for him was Didi, and she would say, "Didi did it," even if he wasn't home. One day she spilled a drink at the table while her mother's back was turned. When Mom turned around and saw the mess, Kaitlyn told her, "Didi spilled my drink." When her mother told her that her brother was at a friend's house, Kaitlyn still insisted her brother had done it.[3]

Blame is just as easy when you're an adult. Even when another person takes an action that hurts you, blame is harmful to you. When you say, "If only you hadn't done x, I would have been all right," you are really saying, "You have all the power over my life, and I have none." Whenever you blame someone else for problems you're having, you become powerless to do anything about it. And guess who's listening in—your children. Instead, take personal responsibility and focus on what you can do about a situation and on what you want to do next.

While completing doctoral research in psychology, Dr. Fay was fortunate to study the academic work of two incredibly intelligent people: Dr. Bernard Weiner and Dr. Carol Dweck.[4] From their writings, Dr. Fay discovered a form of blame that strongly contributes to lack of responsibility and low motivation. In essence, we are all fascinated with the reasons behind our own actions and the behaviors of others. Interestingly, we tend to attribute our mistakes and misdeeds to factors beyond our control (e.g., we blame bad luck, the faulty genes we've inherited, lack of support from others, etc.). In contrast, we blame the mistakes of others on factors within their control, such as lack of preparation, laziness, chronic irresponsibility, or general poor character. Social psychologists call this the fundamental attribution error,[5] and it represents a very pervasive type of ANT.

Its nastiness stems from the fact that it leaves us feeling stuck: "How can I improve anything about my life when everything about it falls beyond my control?" It also leads us to lack empathy for others. When we fall into the mental habit of ignoring the struggles of others, we find ourselves far more stressed and intolerant.

Exterminating this ANT and helping your kids do the same can lead them to learning to take responsibility, especially for their own happiness.

There's another side to the Blaming ANTs—it involves blaming yourself for other people's problems. Women often have the hardest time with self-blame. "My husband didn't call; he must not love me anymore" is a classic example. Maybe the reason he didn't call has nothing to do with you: He's stressed, distracted, or dealing with a crisis. Another example: "My daughter at college failed her math exam. I should have spent more time helping with her homework in high school." Blaming yourself for your daughter's failure is the act of an undisciplined mind, because by the time she's in college, your daughter's study habits should be her own responsibility, not yours. Neither blaming yourself for everything that goes wrong nor assuming that other people's actions are all about you are accurate reflections of reality. They're just ANTs.

Dr. Fay has worked with countless families where constant conflict and tension were the rule. At the root of this heartbreak was often an insidious ANT called Negative Interpretation. For over three decades, the Center for Marital and Family Studies at the University of Denver has studied this extremely damaging thought pattern, identifying it as one of the top five factors contributing to divorce and family instability.[6] Negative Interpretation, a combo of several ANTs, is when we make a mental habit of automatically thinking that the intent of others is negative and personally directed toward us.

Parenting tip: Here's the solution: Make a commitment with each other and your kids to turn on your sonar. Turning on your sonar means making a habit of assuming that most of the less-than-pleasant behavior of others is rooted in personal hurt, not planned efforts to rob us of joy. It means searching our own hearts for our tendency to ignore the hearts of others. Will your children have far healthier relationships if you teach them that people are like icebergs? The depth of who they are is hidden below the surface. If we aren't aware of it, we'll sink in our interactions with others. After all, which part of an iceberg slashed a fatal hole in the Titanic? Modern vessels traveling the North Atlantic are warned by sonar pings of such hazards.

A Story about Sonar

As Dr. Fay and his siblings rode in the back seat of their family car, they overheard their parents discussing what was going on in their lives. Most of it helped them view others in healthier ways. Is this a powerful way of helping our children learn to think in healthy ways?

One story their father shared had a particularly huge impact on Dr. Fay's view of others.

"We had a meeting today at work," he said to my mother. "One of the people just sat there, stared at the floor, and huffed every time I said anything. During a break, I decided to confront him. I was about to let him have it, then I thought, *Something must be going on in his life that's making him act that way.* Instead of saying something nasty, I asked, 'It looks like you are having a hard morning. Is there anything I can do to help?'

"Looking embarrassed, the guy replied, 'No, Jim. I like your ideas. It's just that my dog died last night. I'd had her for 13 years, and it's hitting me hard. I really appreciate you asking.'"

Shaping Your Child's Beliefs about Success

When children come to believe that success is the result of factors beyond their control, they are far less likely to exert the effort, perseverance, and practice required to earn it.

Use this process to help them see that hard work is the key to achievement.

1. When they do something well, describe it without praising.
   - "You got problem number nine correct on your math worksheet."

2. Ask them:
   - "How did you do that?"

3. Give them three options:
   - "Did you work hard?"
   - "Did you keep trying even though it was difficult?"
   - "Have you been practicing?"

Each of these represents an accurate thought that will help your child exterminate helplessness ANTS.

4. Make sure they say the words out loud because what we say is often our reality. What our child says is more likely to become theirs.

5. If your child struggles with answering or says they don't know, smile and ask this question:
   - "If you did know, which one would it be?"

3. All-or-Nothing ANTs: Any time you think in absolutes, character-ized by words such as *always, never, no one, everyone, every time,* or *everything,* your negative thinking makes a temporary situation look like a permanent reality. These thoughts also make situations to be all good or all bad—with nothing in between. You see everything in black-or-white terms.

You've probably heard this type of thought from your children when they say, "There's nothing to do!" When children say that, they feel down, bored, or unmotivated. Some other all-or-nothing examples: "He never listens to me." "I always have to do what she wants." If your child talks back to you, you might think, *He's always got a smart mouth!* Or if the child doesn't do her chores, you think, *She never does what I tell her to do!* But the thought is not a rational one; it's just a thought. Rarely is any situation that cut and dry.

Celeste, 48, was a divorced mother of five children. She came to Dr. Amen after being unable to shake feelings of depression and inadequacy. Since her divorce five years prior, she had felt sad, lonely, and unlovable. She loved being in a close relationship, so the divorce had really thrown her off emotionally. She told Dr. Amen, "No one would ever want an 'older' woman with five children!"

This ANT closes your mind to other possibilities and keeps you focused on the negative, which will make you feel more anxious and/ or depressed. Then you act from your thought beliefs rather than the truth of the situation. If you really believe that your child *always* has a smart mouth, you're likely to go into a rage when they talk back, when in reality they may only do that 5 to 10 percent of the time.

Parenting tip: Combat this ANT in your children by asking, "When was the last time you [insert whatever absolute they are complaining about]?" or "Do you remember when . . . ?" For instance, if they say, "I always have to sit in the back seat of the car. I never get to sit in the front seat," you would ask, "When was the last time you sat in the front seat? Do you remember when . . .?"

4. *Fortune-Telling ANTs:* When you engage in fortune-telling, you arbitrarily predict the worst—even though you have no definite evidence. Fortune-telling thoughts instantly increase your stress: Your heart beats faster, your breathing speeds up and gets shallow, and your adrenal glands start pumping out cortisol and adrenaline. An example in parenting is when you predict that your child won't obey you in a situation and you become angry with them even before you leave home. No one can predict the future. And unless you're a contract lawyer, there is no good reason to focus on predicting the worst.

What's worse: predicting bad things can actually help them come true. For example, if you predict that your child will not do the dishes properly, you might start to nag him to the point where he gets angry and doesn't clean them well just to spite you. If you're sure that it's going to be a rough day with the kids, you'll be in a terrible mood as soon as anything bad happens, and your day will certainly go downhill from there.

Parenting tip: Teach your kids to talk back to their ANTs when they start to predict the future. Have them write or say phrases that are more rational and realistic. For example, if your child is convinced they are going to fail their next test even though they have studied for it, help them write or say, "I am prepared for this test, so I will probably do just fine. If I don't, I'll ask my teacher or mom for help studying for the next one."

5. **Guilt-Beating ANTs:** Guilt thinking occurs when you beat yourself up with words like *should, must, ought to,* and *have to.* This thinking is prevalent among many parents, and it is uniformly destructive. These words are not helpful in making you feel more positive or connected to your child. It is much better to replace the *shoulds* with phrases such as "It would be helpful for me . . . ," "It is in my child's best interest to do this . . . ," "It fits my goals of having a better relationship to do this . . . ," etc.

Moms especially are often taught to put other people's needs first, so they feel guilty when they stand up for themselves or take time to de-stress. These ANTs also play a role in the Guilt Cycle trap—losing your cool, feeling badly about it, swooping in to rescue—that we mentioned earlier. Reframe the guilt beatings into statements of what you truly want. Instead of "I should volunteer at my kids' school," ask yourself if the behavior fits your goals and time. If the answer is no, move on. Having a process to free yourself from the guilt-beating ANTs will help settle down the noise in your head so you can make better choices.

Parenting tip: Guilt is not a helpful emotion. When you hear your kids saying, "I should . . ." then help them rephrase it by saying, "I want to . . ." or "It fits my goals to . . ." For example, if your child says, "I should eat my vegetables," help them flip that to "I want to eat my vegetables because they make me healthy." Or if they say, "I ought to do my homework," coach them to say, "It fits my goals to do my homework because I want to do well in school."

6. Labeling ANTs: This is very harmful to children. Often parents give negative labels to children who have high energy, low attention, ADHD, etc., without realizing they are unconsciously programming the child to become more "difficult." For example, if you call your child a spoiled brat or a slob, you lump them with all the "spoiled brats" and "slobs" that you've ever known. It inhibits your ability to have a realistic view of your child. Stay away from negative labels. Plus, if the child is a "spoiled brat," it is probably not their fault; it was the parent who did the spoiling. Labeling won't help you deal with a particular issue or to make accurate judgments about yourself or your kids.

Parenting tip: If you catch your kids labeling themselves or other kids, gently remind them that just because someone makes a mistake or does something harmful, that doesn't make them bad or dumb. You might then brainstorm reasons why that person might be acting a certain way; this can also help build empathy in you and your children.

7. Mind-Reading ANTs: Similar to fortune telling, this is when you arbitrarily predict what your child is thinking before you have checked it out. Children often do not know why they do what they do. Yet, when they misbehave, parents often attribute negative motives to the child. For example, "My son is trying to embarrass me. He knows what he's doing, and he likes it when I'm upset." You cannot read another person's mind; children have enough trouble reading their own minds.

Drawing the line between your helpful intuition and the poisonous mind-reading ANT isn't always easy. But once you learn to kill this ANT, your relationships and mood will likely improve.

Parenting tip: This one can show up often in sibling rivalry, which we'll address in chapter 15. For now, teach your child that making assumptions about others is an easy way to miscommunicate and misunderstand. Make a fun rule to help avoid this ANT by teaching the phrase, "If I don't know, say so." This simply means that if you aren't sure what someone else is thinking or why they did something, speak up and ask in an inquisitive, not accusing tone. We like to say it's better to be curious, not furious.

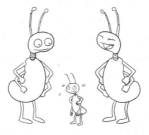

8. Less-Than ANTs: Whenever you compare yourself to others in a negative way, you're letting these ANTs infest your mind and damage your self-esteem. With the rise of social media, our society is experiencing a veritable ANT invasion. People of all ages are spending hours comparing themselves to others' highly curated, digitally enhanced images, making them feel like they don't measure up. It's contributing to unrealistic expectations and crushing pressure, especially in tweens and teens. But these ANTs can hit parents hard too.

Look at Marley. She was a 52-year-old single mother with a high-level job in the banking industry. Although she was successful at work and her children were doing fine, Marley worried constantly that she wasn't good enough. She was a prime example of an intelligent, accomplished woman who had an undisciplined mind and a busy brain. She always felt like an imposter or a fraud, so she drove herself relentlessly to perfection, hoping that would prevent others from "seeing through her" and somehow undermining her position.

Marley's worst ANTs were Mind-Reading and Less-Than. She was constantly assuming that she wasn't worthy of socializing with the other neighborhood moms, believing that they didn't like her, that they talked behind her back, and that they wished she would move to another part of town. She convinced herself that the other moms were intentionally excluding her and her kids from play dates at the park, when in reality, the other moms mistakenly believed that Marley wasn't interested in organizing play dates because she seemed so busy all the time. Her ANTs brought her a great deal of needless unhappiness, anxiety, and agitation.

Parenting tip: No one has a perfect life. Stop comparing yourself to others and help your kids do the same when they feel envious or left out. There's always more to everyone's story that you do not know, and envy only breeds other ANTs such as resentment and self-pity. To help your kids stop comparing themselves to others, make sure you aren't in the habit of comparing them to their friends and classmates. Remind kids that instead of trying to be "the best," it's healthier to "be their best."

I'll be happy when . . .

9. If-Only and I'll-Be-Happy-When ANTs: These ANTs involve arguing with the past or longing for an imaginary future. Dwelling on regrets for things that happened in the past breeds frustration. Spending time contemplating ways your life could be better if things were different without having a plan to make positive changes is a self-defeating mindset. It also fuels dissatisfaction with the present and is demotivating.

Parenting tip: Gratitude is a surefire antidote to this ANT—and thankfulness combats so many negative thoughts and feelings. Practice it on a daily basis and make gratitude a habit in your home.

ANTs IN POPULAR CULTURE . . . AND HOW TO PROTECT AND PREPARE OUR KIDS

We've all heard the term *computer bug*. In today's world, just about everything we use has at least one chip—particularly our televisions, phones, and other digital devices. When operating well, these devices are full of bugs—or better said, ANTs.

Much of today's music, social media, games, movies, and other media are riddled with ANT hills. This infestation has nothing to do with their circuits. Rather, the circuits simply serve as windows into the emotional and spiritual battles fought by humanity since the beginning of time. While protecting our kids by limiting exposure, providing good supervision, and employing safeguards is wise, too much protection without *preparation* will leave them unequipped to protect themselves.

As parents we can prepare our kids to resist these ANTs by recognizing what they are and involving our kids in discussing them. These discussions don't need to be lectures; instead, treat them as opportunities to explore how these ANTs affect all of us. As such, they give our children the opportunity to choose their own positive path, rather than believing that they must stumble along the one that is so frequently laid out by the following ANTs. Here are four more ANTs Dr. Fay has identified; we're sure you can think of more.

1. ***Trust your heart ANT:*** This ANT encourages us to believe what we feel. Our feelings can be just as misleading as our thoughts, so it's important to pay attention to what they're saying and if it's true.

    Parenting tip: Acknowledge feelings, but then encourage yourself and your child to question whether the feeling is telling you something true or misleading you.

2. ***Want What You Don't Have ANT:*** More than ever, messages that contentment can only be found in a multitude of new and expensive possessions daily bombard parents and children.

    Parenting tip: If you practice contentment and enjoy what you have, your kids will pick up on your example.

3. Get Even ANT: Sometimes Dr. Fay finds himself nurturing this ANT by treating someone just as badly, or worse, than they've treated him. This theme makes for exciting movies, endless social media drama, and temporary feelings of power. In real life, it operates like alcohol. The hangover isn't worth it.

Parenting tip: Quote this truth: "Do not be overcome by evil, but overcome evil with good" (Romans 12:21, ESV). Aim to create a home where you treat others better *than they treat you.*

4. If It Feels Good, Do It—Now! ANT: Self-control, perseverance, selflessness, and service are antiquated, prudish concepts developed to make people miserable. That is the lie our children too frequently hear as they interact with popular culture. As we all know, the truth is the opposite. These character qualities, when placed into action, are essential for feelings of well-being, particularly when the focus is on helping others. Research is also beginning to identify the neurological effects of such helping: increased levels of dopamine, serotonin, and oxytocin, which are associated with elevated mood and increased feelings of social connectedness.[7]

Parenting tip: Ask the question, "Then what?" and ask it a few more times to see if the choice that seems to feel good now will also feel good later and be good for your brain.

ELIMINATE THE ANTs

You do not have to believe every thought that goes through your brain. If you want to keep your mind healthy, it's important to focus on the good parts of your life more than the bad parts. Eliminating the ANTs is not hard. The first step to changing your perceptions or thinking patterns is to identify the way you *do* think. The following exercise is so simple that you may have trouble believing how powerful it is, but Dr. Amen has seen it change many people's lives, including his own. Learn first how to use it for yourself and then with your children when you notice them being overtaken by ANTs. Your suffering will diminish, and your health and happiness will improve. We'll also show you a version to use with your kids. A number of research studies have found this technique to be as effective and as powerful as antidepressant medication for anxiety, depression, and eating disorders.

Step 1. Whenever you notice a self-critical or distorted thought entering your mind or when you feel sad, mad, nervous, or out of control, identify it and write it down. The act of writing down thoughts helps to get the pesky invaders out of your head.

Step 2. Use the ANTs Cheat Sheet to identify the type of ANT or negative thought and write it down.

ANT	TYPE
My child will never obey me.	Fortune-Telling
I am a failure as a parent.	Labeling
It is my child's fault!	Blame
I should be a better parent.	Guilt-Beating
My child never does anything right.	All-or-Nothing

Step 3. Talk back to your ANTs. If you were anything like Dr. Amen, you were good at talking back to your parents when you were a teenager. And if you have teens, encourage them to use their back-talking skills with ANTs. In the same way, you need to learn to be good at talking back to the lies you tell yourself. Ask yourself if the thoughts make sense and if they are really true. To do this, you'll need to answer four questions and one turnaround statement, which come from my friend and author Byron Katie.[8] The goal is accurate thinking.

Question #1: Is it true? (Is the stressful or negative thought true?)
Question #2: Is it absolutely true? How do I know with 100 percent certainty?
Question #3: How do I feel when I believe this thought?
Question #4: How would I feel if I didn't have the thought?
Turnaround: Take the original thought and completely turn it around to its opposite, then tell yourself this new version may be true or truer than the original thought.

Look at how young mom Allison did this exercise.

ANT: I don't measure up.
ANT Type: Just-the-Bad

1. **Is it true?** Yes.
2. **Is it absolutely true with 100 percent certainty?** Well, there's no way I can actually know if I truly don't measure up to the "standards" for being a mother.
3. **How do I feel when I believe this thought?** I feel depressed, anxious, stressed, and frustrated.
4. **How would I feel if I didn't have the thought?** I would be relieved and much calmer throughout the day. I'd probably enjoy my kids more and not be so worried about getting my to-do list done.
5. **Take the original thought and completely turn it around to its opposite, then tell yourself this new version may be true or truer than the original thought.** I do measure up. I'm like all the other moms who are simply doing the best they can.

This final thought brought tears to Allison's eyes. She realized that if she kept repeating that she never measured up, then, of course, she would always feel defeated. But if she believed that she did measure up and it was truer than her original thought, she would act and live like a confident, self-assured mom. The power in this method will not only help you correct distorted perception, but it will also help your mood, your self-esteem, and your ability to deal with your child in a more rational and effective way.

TEACHING YOUNGER KIDS ABOUT ANTs

Children as young as 4 can struggle with ANT infestations the same way parents and teens can be filled with negativity. Little kids may have fearful or anxious thoughts about their family, schoolwork, friendships, appearance, and more.

Here are some common ANTs kids may have:

ANT	TYPE
Nobody likes me.	All-or-Nothing
I got one wrong on our quiz out of 10. This is terrible.	Just-the-Bad
I'm stupid.	Labeling
My mommy didn't smile at me. She must be mad at me.	Mind-Reading
It's not my fault. She started it!	Blame

It is so important to train youngsters as young as 4 to challenge their thoughts. Turn it into a game to see who can identify the ANTs that are ruining things. It will create a habit for your children to question every thought that enters their brain.

Eliminating the ANTs is so easy even little kids can do it. Dr. Amen sees children do it all the time. He once helped a child who was depressed. In the beginning, the boy could only think about negatives that happened to him. His family had just moved, so he said he would never make new friends (even though he already had several). He thought he would do poorly in his new school (even though he got mostly good grades) and that he would never have any fun (even though his new house was near a bay and an amusement park). By focusing on the negatives in his new situation, he was making it hard to adjust. He would have been much better off if he had looked at all the positives in the situation rather than the negatives. After three weeks of ANT therapy, he said, "It's an ANT ghost town in my head."[9]

Typically, with smaller children, it's best to whittle down the five questions to just two superpower questions:

1. Is it true?
2. Are you 100 percent sure that [insert negative statement] is true? How do you know?

Here are a few examples of how to work through ANTs with youngsters:

ANT: Nobody ever plays with me.
1. **Is it true?** Well, maybe. Nobody wants to play with me right now.
2. **Are you 100 percent sure that thought is true and nobody ever plays with you?** Well, of course not. I played with my friends just this morning at recess and had lots of fun.

ANT: I'm bored. I have nothing to do.
1. **Is it true?** Yes! I really feel bored. I can't think of anything to do!
2. **Are you 100 percent sure that thought is true and there is *nothing* you can do?** Well, of course not. I have an entire box of toys in my closet, Play-Doh, paper and pens to draw with, and much more. I guess I can find something to do.

Teaching younger kids how to investigate their thoughts will create new neural pathways in their developing brains that will help them manage their minds for the rest of their life. However, it is never too late to start learning this important skill. Learning to disinfect your thoughts at any age can have a dramatic effect on your mindset and a positive impact on your parenting and family life.

CHALLENGE YOUR WORST THOUGHTS

One of the first exercises Dr. Amen gives to his patients—whether they are 8 or 80 years old—is to write down 100 of their worst ANTs. For each ANT, he has them go through the steps to eliminate them. Doing this diligently reduces emotional distress and ends self-defeating thoughts.

Since the brain learns by repetition, doing this exercise 100 times helps eliminate undisciplined thinking so you can develop better mental hygiene. Routines form through a process called long-term potentiation, which is when neurons that fire together wire together to create automatic habits. By taking the time to investigate and eliminate 100 ANTs, you can break your old negative thinking habits and develop more rational thinking patterns.

Use the ANT Eliminator Form on the next page to get started.

ANT Eliminator Form

ANT:_____
_____

ANT Type: _____
_____

1. Is it true?_____
_____

2. Is it 100 percent true?_____
_____

3. How do I feel when I believe this thought?_____
_____

4. How do I feel without the thought?_____
_____

5. Opposite: Could it be true or truer than the original thought?_____

New thought on which to meditate:_____
_____

Dr. Amen often reminds people that when your brain works right, you work right. But when your brain is troubled, you are much more likely to have trouble in your life. When our children know how to combat the trouble-making ANTs seeking to infest their minds, their brains grow stronger, their behavior becomes more positive toward others, and they enjoy neurochemical benefits. Encourage your kids—and yourself—to start thinking about their thought patterns and learning how to manage their minds. Daily mental hygiene is a requirement for mental strength.

Action Steps

- Start questioning your thoughts, and teach your children to do the same.
- Identify the most common ANTs that infest your mind.
- Learn the three steps that can help you eliminate ANTs.
- Begin writing down and challenging your worst 100 thoughts.
- Teach your children about ANTs and how to eliminate them.

CHAPTER 8

RAISING STRONG AND CAPABLE KIDS

Children learn to cope with trials and tribulations
when they are allowed to have them.
With wisdom we provide love, encouragement, and suggestions.
We rescue only when needed.

The classic story *The Three Little Pigs* provides a powerful metaphor for raising strong kids. One little pig built his house of twigs, one built it of straw, and the other built it of bricks. The Big Bad Wolf made quick work of the first two houses, simply because they were built in haste with very weak materials. The first two piglets were poor builders because they placed their priority on short-term happiness instead of long-term stability. The wolf merely blew their houses down with his big bad breath. Only the third house, which required far more time and expense to construct, survived to protect its builder—and the two other piggies who fled to it.

Building something strong takes a lot more work and sacrifice than building something weak. To raise strong, capable kids, we have to put aside our desire to always make our kids happy and comfortable. It means preparing them for the real world, one that isn't always a rose garden.

As an employer, Dr. Fay has even had parents appear in his office, expecting that their "children" be afforded improved opportunities and better pay. No parent sets out to raise children who become entitled, selfish, lazy, or weak in the face of hardships. Yet real societal and family trends have been contributing to larger percentages of people who are blown about by even the slightest breeze and melt in the presence of any difficulty. Sadly, these are the adults who were not allowed to develop the confidence, character, and skills required to weather life's storms when they were younger. In 2010, psychology researchers Kenneth Stewart and Paul Bernhardt observed significant declines in the psychological health, academic skills, impulse control, and self-assuredness of the young adults they studied at that time compared to ones they examined years earlier.[1] They also recorded significantly higher rates of narcissism. Simine Vazire and David C. Funder, another pair of psychology researchers and college professors, observed a similar trend.[2] Today, college professors are routinely seeing parents appear on campus, demanding that their children's grades be changed.

When this many parents are doing this much rescuing, many kids believe they are entitled to it. Therefore, they become self-centered, immediately take offense to anyone who disagrees with them, and melt when they encounter struggles.

Houston, we have a problem!

It's not just our imagination. In fact, Denver, Elephant Butte, Elk Springs, the Big Apple, Bemidji, Boston, Pierre, Mt. Pleasant, Grant, Grand Rapids, and every other sprawling metropolis or tiny town across America has this same problem. So how do we keep it from getting worse?

Don't lose hope; scores of extremely talented, mature, and committed young people work across our great nation. The next time you see one of them, remember that it's possible to raise kids like that. Let their strength bolster your determination to give your children the roots to become young adults possessing the grit to handle a world full of temptations, tough times, and difficult people. Let their maturity remind you that your kids will have an immense advantage in the world if you give them the gifts of resilience, purpose, a good work ethic, resourcefulness, solid problem-solving skills, self-control, and empathy.

STRONG KIDS OR WEAK ONES? WE CHOOSE.

Erica's parents believed that nothing was too good for their little girl. So they ensured that she always had the best clothes, the best toys, the best private coaches, and the best parenting they could provide. This type of parenting, according to her mother, Debbie, meant constant involvement in stimulating and fun activities. It meant making sure that Erica was the center of attention and always felt special. It meant ensuring that she never had a demanding teacher or coach. It simply meant preparing the world for Erica rather than preparing Erica for the world.

Steven, Erica's father, wasn't sure about that approach. At one point he'd suggested to Debbie that their daughter should be responsible for talking to one of her seventh-grade teachers about her struggles with homework. Debbie agreed but informed him that she lacked time that week to be in the meeting to help. Steven lost it: "She's 13, for crying out loud. I think she can handle it without you being there!"

Steven felt guilty for his outburst and quickly agreed that he'd take time off from work to make sure that the meeting went well.

When teenage Erica was arrested for shoplifting, Mom promptly hired the finest attorney. Although this was a significant burden to the family, Debbie reminded Steven that nothing was too good for their little girl. Steven felt a mixture of anger and guilt as he reluctantly agreed to help smooth over Erica's latest mess.

Are you guessing that Erica grew in strength and good character, or do you suppose that she continued to become increasingly out of control and unhappy?

During her freshman year of college, Erica quickly burned through tens of thousands of her parents' dollars and earned a 1.7 grade point average. When it was clear that she'd become addicted to heroin, Steven finally refused to be part of the problem. "We've rescued her so much that now she really needs it," he lamented. "We should have gotten some professional help a long time ago!"

It didn't take long for the therapist to see the pattern and to address Steven and Debbie in a rather blunt manner. "You've been working way harder on your daughter's life than she has. If she's going to beat this addiction and develop a sense of dignity, you must stop the rescuing. She needs to see that she is capable of living life without you trying to make it easier for her. When and if that happens, she'll have an opportunity to develop the self-confidence and strength she needs to rebuild her life. I'll consider continuing to work with you if I see you make a sincere commitment to stop this behavior."

While Debbie shared this story she admitted, "I began to wake up, realizing that we'd crippled our daughter through our overprotection. It took years of hard work on our part and much harder work on Erica's. As she started to see her own strength, and that the only way to feel good is to do something good, she began to heal. She will struggle with this for the rest of her life. I'm sharing our story so that others don't make the same mistakes."

Jim Fay's Five Steps for Guiding Kids to Own and Solve Their Problems

Step 1: Provide a strong dose of empathy.
Say, "This has got to be so hard."

Step 2: Hand the problem back in a loving way.
Ask, "What do you think you are going to do?"

Step 3: When they reply, "I don't know," ask permission to share what "some kids" decide to do.
Ask, "Would you like to hear what some kids decide to do?"

Step 4: Share two or three options.
Say, "Some kids decide to _____. Other kids try _____ or _____. How would one of those options work for you?"

Step 5: Allow your child to solve the problem as they see fit, remembering to use this process only when problems do not have life-or-death consequences.
Say, "I can't wait to hear what you decide. I believe in you!"

STRUGGLES, SUPPORT, AND SKILLS BUILD STRENGTH

Dr. Fay was fortunate to have strong parents. Because they were strong, they naturally remained firm and loving at the same time. Around the time he turned 10, he experienced a sad event that forever etched on his mind the value of resilience. This event often reminds Dr. Fay of the science showing that we develop strength when we encounter trials *and* have someone who guides us by modeling skills, strength, and compassion.[3]

"The event involved a rather ratty-looking dog my family had found and adopted. We children felt sorry for the homely guy and decided that he needed a name. 'Buster' was it. Sweet and loyal, Buster was likely the result of an impromptu encounter between a border collie and another type of herding dog, and he chased everything that moved, attempting to ensure that it stayed with the flock. Cars were no exception.

"One afternoon my father and I were preparing to embark on what Dad consistently referred to as a 'character-building experience.' This one involved me playing a trombone solo at the local Elks Club dinner. According to Dad (and supported by solid psychological research), doing difficult things that help others builds character. As I reluctantly placed my trombone in the trunk, something flashed in my peripheral vision.

"It was Buster blasting down the road, heading straight for a car. The car swerved but the dog didn't. Hurt badly, he managed to stumble my way. He died at my feet.

"Dad and I cried together. Dad held me in his strong arms and told me that he loved me. I was convinced that he did and sure that Dad also loved Buster. Then he said, 'Charlie, we need to get going. We'll take care of Buster when we get back.'

"Yes, Dad expected me to fulfill the commitment we'd made to entertain the Elks. As I played my solo, I focused on Dad's face, full of love and compassion. This wasn't the first time Dad had faced a trial, and it certainly was not the last. With wisdom and strength, tempered with great empathy, Dad gradually taught me how to live amid unpredictable and often challenging events. Are your children learning the same, or do they believe that everything must come to a crashing end when bad things happen?

"The old phrase 'the show must go on' originated in the circus business of the late nineteenth century, meaning that even if something went wrong during a show, the show must immediately continue. Since that time, its application and meaning has expanded to many areas of entertainment, business, and life, eventually meaning that we can't let hardships completely derail our responsibilities, relationships, or hope. The key is support and empathy for hard situations while continuing to meet expectations when possible. At the same time, we need to understand that sometimes plans will need to change because of emergencies or the fallout of a hardship (for example, a broken leg will mean an end to a sports season, but the child could still sit on the bench and support his team).

"Learning music is a good example of this principle. My dad was originally a professional musician. During the 1950s and 1960s one of his steady 'gigs' involved playing for the circus and the professional rodeo circuit. He also gave music lessons, and I was one of his primary students. He believed that music builds intelligence and resilience, and research has shown that his gut was right. The late Dr. Peter Benson of the Search Institute, considered a leading expert on positive human development, identified music as a critical developmental asset, playing a powerful role in helping young people succeed.[4]

"'If you hit a hard spot or make a mistake while playing with the band, don't stop,' Dad would say. 'Just pick up as quickly as you can, and keep playing. If you put more focus on what you are playing well, your brain will automatically help you learn from your mistakes and the tough spots.' This basic rule served me well in third-grade band. It also serves people well in life. If we let our trials and errors stop us and cause us to ruminate, they will derail our lives. If we keep playing, we'll learn, grow, and become stronger."

STRUGGLES, SUPPORT, AND SKILLS BUILD AN ATTITUDE OF SERVICE

We have many hard workers in America: men and women who serve in the military, police force, fire departments, and hospitals; truck drivers, plumbers, electricians, electric line workers, heating and air-conditioning technicians; those who stock shelves in our grocery stores, keep the streets plowed, drive garbage trucks, put tires on our cars, and do the many other hard jobs that keep us and our economy alive. The common thread is that these people have an attitude of service that motivates them to get the job done even under difficult or dangerous conditions.

As we write this book, we've witnessed a severe shortage of strong men and women who are willing to do these critical jobs. This is one of the reasons we are so passionate about parents raising strong and capable kids with "the show must go on" attitudes. Another reason for our passion is that people are lost without purpose. While the good life may appear to some as a place where they encounter no responsibilities, demands, or derailments, the truth is that the human brain needs the challenges, struggles, social connections, and dignity associated with working toward the welfare of others. When people lack this purpose, they fall into patterns of despair, disconnection, and hopelessness. They are more likely to feel depressed and anxious and to lack motivation and focus. Rates of drug abuse, petty theft, violent crime, and general unrest also rise.[5]

Many of the people struggling with mental health issues who come to see Dr. Amen lack a sense of purpose. He lets them know that finding meaning in their life (the fourth circle of mental strength) can have a powerful impact on their well-being. One important study on the effects of having a sense of purpose followed nearly 1,000 individuals for close to seven years.[6] The team of researchers concluded that having a strong sense of purpose made people:

- Less depressed
- Happier
- More self-accepting
- More satisfied with their lives
- More open to personal growth
- Healthier mentally and emotionally
- Able to sleep better
- Likely to live longer

Having a strong sense of purpose also decreases the odds that self-esteem will be affected by negative social media issues, including getting negative comments on your posts or not getting enough "likes" or followers.[7] Whenever Dr. Amen discusses purpose with his patients, he mentions Viktor Frankl, a psychiatrist, Holocaust survivor, and author of *Man's Search for Meaning*.[8] Frankl is credited with saying, "Life is never made unbearable by circumstances, but only by lack of meaning and purpose." He points to three sources of purpose:

- Being productive or doing purposeful work. This involves asking yourself questions such as "Why is the world a better place because I am here?" or "What do I contribute?"
- Loving and caring about other people.
- Having courage in the face of challenges. Coping with life's difficulties and helping others cope with theirs.

It's critical to help your kids find meaning in their own lives by learning to work hard, identifying their gifts, and finding ways to use those gifts to help others. This means you need to know your own purpose first, then you can help your kids discover theirs. Refer back to the One Page Miracle exercise in chapter 2.

How to Help Kids Find Their Purpose

Similar to how you can help kids identify their goals (chapter 2), you can also encourage them to find purpose. This exercise is most suitable for adolescents and young adults, although you can begin conversations about the concept of a purposeful life with younger kids. Here are five steps:

1. **Talk about what gives you a sense of purpose.** Kids learn from parents, so it's important for you to openly talk about your own work and volunteer efforts and how they give your life meaning.

2. **Ask questions.** Ask your child about what's important to them.

3. **Provide support.** Share your child's enthusiasm for their passions and help them develop those interests by introducing them to other adults who may become mentors.

4. **Emphasize their impact.** Help preteens, teens, and young adults understand how their efforts impact others. Ask them who benefits from what they enjoy doing.

5. **Create a purpose chart.** Have your child map out their purpose on a sheet of paper so they can look at it every day along with their One Page Miracle. For this purpose chart, draw a circle and four additional circles surrounding it. In each of the four circles, write responses to these questions:

- What do I care about?
- What are my talents/gifts?
- How do these talents/gifts help others?
- How do I want to change society/the world?

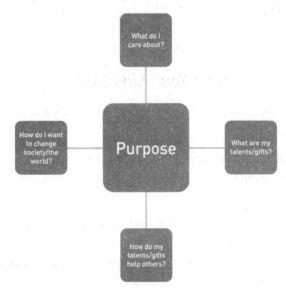

BUILDING A STRONG HOUSE: BRICKS NOT STRAW

The building blocks of strength come down to simple actions you can take, starting when your children are young (although it's never too late to start as long as children are still under your roof). These bricks will build kids who have the intestinal fortitude (guts) to keep going when things get tough. And once you've laid them, parenting will be easier.

Brick #1: Teach them how to do stuff. "Stuff" is a psychological term for mundane things that help kids feel strong when they do them. It's also a term for skill sets that will enable them to become competent and free instead of dependent upon others for fixing everything that goes wrong with their homes, cars, work relationships, and other responsibilities. People who know how to repair stuff have much happier lives than those who don't.

"I was 13 and didn't know how to use a can opener to make a can of soup," admitted a mother in one of our seminars. "My mom did everything for us kids and our father. When she died in a car accident, we were completely lost. I decided right then that, if I ever had children of my own, they would learn to be independent as early in life as possible."

Great parents are great leaders: They are always trying to work themselves out of a job. They're obsessed with teaching and empowering those under their care so that they, themselves, are no longer needed. When leaders do this, they rise to higher levels of leadership. When parents do this, their children become leaders, not helpless followers.

We've created an exercise for becoming more intentional about teaching these intestinal fortitude skills. We call it the Great Under Trials and Stress exercise (GUTS).

Give Your Kids GUTS

To give your kids GUTS, start by asking yourself the following questions:

- **What are the specific things I do to keep my family running?** Examples include cooking, cleaning, washing clothes, paying bills, etc.

- **Can my children learn to do these things?** Yes. Even children can help you pay bills, as long as you are there to ensure that they are doing it correctly. As soon as Dr. Fay's boys could write, they began to help write checks. Dr. Fay often found himself thinking, *I wonder if anyone is noticing that the signature looks a lot different from the rest of the writing?* They probably did, but no one complained.

- **How will I teach them?** Visualize yourself doing the task. What are the steps required? Write these down and follow them with your child. For example, an 18-month-old can easily follow instructions to put small items into a trash can.

- **How can I make much of the learning spontaneous and memorable?** Lessons often cement in our psyches when they come at unexpected times. They also adhere to our brains when we are silly or whimsical rather than too serious. A friend of ours described how her father taught her to change a not-so-flat tire:

I'll never forget it. We were on our way home from the store on a warm summer afternoon. My father got a wild smile on his face and said, "Oh goody! Find a safe spot and pull over. I think we need to change a tire." I was just learning to drive and felt quite confused by the fact that the car seemed to be handling fine. We hopped out and changed a completely good tire. There was nothing wrong with it. It had plenty of tread and plenty of air, so I asked him why we were doing such a crazy thing. He just smiled and said, "So you will know you can."

Make sure to affirm their efforts and contribution to helping.

- **How will I remind myself that the time and effort this requires is well worth it?** Watch your kids and take note of the satisfaction and pride they have when they succeed with the stuff you have taught them. Lock this image into your head. Visualize it often. Also imagine how great it will be to see them as teenagers and young adults who are capable of doing things that their peers cannot even imagine. It's also helpful to remember that if a kid can do it, a kid should do it.

Brick #2: Expect them to spend more time creating than skating. On a related note, as a business owner, Dr. Fay noticed two types of employees. Both types were bright. Both types were capable. One type spent most of their time moving around things that someone else had created. They moved around boxes, products, computer programs, vendor contracts, papers, and even ideas. They seemed to be working hard, but it dawned on Dr. Fay that they never created much that was tangible and didn't try new tasks.

The other type of employee created new and actionable procedures, products, systems, and other stuff that allowed the company to move forward. From this experience, Dr. Fay came to believe that some people have learned to be skaters and others have developed skills and attitudes that lead them to become creators and unafraid of learning new skills. Yes, we do need people to move things around, making sure that they are placed where they need to be. But the sophistication and value of their work pales in comparison to the value that those who are oriented toward creating and getting out of their comfort zones provide.

Around the time Dr. Fay was first discovering these differences, he ran into an extremely esteemed professor of education at a small and rather swanky private college. She'd also created a business that helped younger students improve their odds for admission to highly demanding universities. Dr. Fay asked her, "What's the single most important thing parents can do to help their kids prepare themselves for admission to college? What can they do to prepare their kids for success once they get there?"

She answered with no hesitation: "Have them learn to do as many hard things as possible." She continued, "I remember working with an extremely bright sixth-grade student and her parents. The girl was struggling in some of her classes, and she seemed to lack the work ethic required to handle more advanced academics. When I asked her parents whether she helped her parents by learning to cook, assisting others in the community, creating art projects, discovering how to fix things around the house, learning some vehicle maintenance, challenging herself physically, or anything else demanding or new, they looked confused. Apparently, she was spending all her time reading, and they felt guilty setting limits over an activity typically considered extremely important."

Let's be clear: everyone needs time to relax. Everyone needs time to recharge their mental, emotional, and physical batteries by skating. Reading is a wonderful activity that can be purely for fun. We even need a bit of time to enjoy mindless movies or other entertainment. Skating only becomes a problem when a young person's life has become so unbalanced that they lack sufficient opportunities to exercise their creativity and grit neurons.

When we stop learning or doing anything new, our brains get in a rut. It takes action outside of our comfort zones to create and strengthen new neural pathways. Learning increases the connections within the brain. More connections equal a stronger brain, and research shows that lifelong learning keeps the brain strong no matter the age.[9] It can take as little as 15 minutes of new learning each day. We'll tell you more of the brain benefits for new learning in the next chapter.

Are They Skating, or Are They Creating?

Five questions to ask on a weekly basis:

- **Have our kids made any sacrifices of time, energy, or other resources to help someone else in a meaningful way?** This might include volunteering in the community, going to a younger sibling's activity and cheering them on, carrying the neighbor's newspaper to their door, etc.

- **Have our kids created something that takes thought and creativity, not just a Google search?** Parents can ask their children questions like, "How would you make this item work better?" or "What sort of tool might work quicker to clean up after the dog? Sketch out some plans."

- **In what ways have our kids exercised their large muscles?** Exercise is good for brain health, and kids who are expected to play outside, run, ride bikes (while wearing a helmet to protect their brain), or play sports are more likely to become creative problem solvers than those who sit around staring at devices. Physical exercise produces new brain cells and increases levels of dopamine (a brain chemical that sends messages of pleasure).

- **Did our kids try anything new this week that they didn't believe they'd be good at?** Kids who are encouraged to get out of their comfort zone and try new things are more likely to grow up to be flexible and adaptable.

- **Did the kids exert a reasonable level of effort when attempting something new, or did they give up right away?** Youngsters who continue to make efforts in the face of challenges develop self-confidence and persistence, while kids who give up easily when the going gets tough are more likely to develop anxiety, fear of rejection, perfectionism, and difficulty accepting constructive criticism.

Brick #3: Expect them to complete chores. Kids who complete chores without having to be nagged or paid off become far happier and more successful in school than those who don't. One teacher commented, "If a parent cannot get their child to take dirty dishes from the dinner table to the dishwasher, what are the odds that the teacher will be able to get the same child to complete assignments at school?" Kids who do chores are more likely to succeed in school.[10] That's a scientific fact.

Chores are not punishments. They are opportunities for young people to contribute to the family in real and meaningful ways. It's part of connecting to their purpose as a member of the family. When you expect chores, kids learn grit and develop a sense of being bonded to the family and its values. That's right. When treated as needed and valued members of any team, we internalize the values of that team. Therefore, kids who are allowed to skate at home often lack the roots required to help them resist peer pressure. Rather than gaining their values from their parents and family, they pull them from peers, popular music, and other less-than-reliable sources.

For decades, the Love and Logic approach has encouraged parents to use the term "contributions to the family" rather than "chores." When the focus is placed on contributing, young people are less likely to view helping out as an arbitrary punishment. They're also more likely to eventually understand that one of the primary joys of life is to contribute to the welfare of others. Here are six ways to help kids learn to contribute to the family:

1. *Model contributions.* Let your kids see you completing tasks. Of course, it's wise to remember that they will quickly pick up on whether you are happy about it. When they see you enjoying tasks, they'll be more likely to help out.

2. *Work together.* When you do so with humor and joy, your children are more likely to associate contributing with good feelings. Plus working together is a great opportunity to bond. Note that this is different from the directions in chapter 5 saying to avoid offering to do a chore together when a child has refused to do it. There's a difference between saying, "Hey, let's make a salad together for dinner" and "Since you refused to make the salad, I'll do it with you."

3. *Create a list including all of the things required to keep the family running.* Do this with your children and include the responsibilities only adults can fulfill. Kids need to see the big picture including working jobs, driving, paying bills, dusting the furniture, feeding the cat, vacuuming Cheerios off the floor, mowing the lawn, shoveling the walk, etc.

4. *Go first.* This means saying, "These are the things that I am proud to do for our family." Place your name next to these responsibilities.

5. *Within reason, allow them to choose the responsibilities they are going to complete.* Of course, if they fail to choose, place their names next to a few responsibilities and include a deadline for each. Note: Kids can trade tasks from time to time, as long as it doesn't cause a problem for anyone in the family.

6. *Allow them to forget, and let empathy and consequences do the teaching.* Do not nag, remind, or give repeated warnings. When you nag and remind, your kids come to rely on nagging and reminding. Then you'll find yourself having to do it more. Don't fall into

this trap. Give them an advantage in life by learning to complete tasks without needing nagging and other forms of hand-holding. Hold them accountable if they forget. Do so by providing sincere empathy and some form of reasonable consequence. This might involve doing some of your chores, staying home instead of going somewhere they desire, paying someone outside of the home to do their chores, etc.

A parent recently shared how her 6-year-old completely forgot to rake the leaves in their yard. Being a rather small area, it was completely reasonable to expect him to get them cleaned up. "I didn't say a word to him when he forgot. Instead, I paid the teenager next door to get it done. When my son asked why that big kid was doing his job, I replied with all the empathy I could muster, 'Oh, this is so sad. You forgot to make this contribution, and I love you too much to nag or fight with you about doing this. I paid Theo to do it, instead. It's going to be about $20. How do you think you might repay me?' He cried, screamed, and accused me of being mean. This was hard to take, but it's sure better than him growing up lacking the responsibility to succeed."

It is important to remember that the "price tags" of mistakes increase every day. It is far less painful for our children to learn these lessons when they are young.

Dealing with Defiance over Chores

When a child of any age becomes passive resistant or even says something like, "I'm not doing that! You can't make me!" experiment with these steps:

Step 1: Say, "No problem. I love you too much to fight with you about this. I will take care of it." Use a calm and laid-back tone. Let your child believe they have gotten away with being resistant or defiant. This buys you time to put together a plan.

Step 2: Consider the consequences you might apply. Examples include staying home instead of being driven to some favorite activity, paying someone else to complete the chore, doing without some other treasured privilege.

Step 3: Let sincere empathy and the consequence do the teaching. Say something like, "This is so sad. You refused to clean the bathrooms, so I had to do it. Now I'm too tired to drive you to basketball practice."

Brick #4: Quit your job as entertainment director. In days gone by, very few parents were entertainment directors, feeling responsible for ensuring that their children never became bored. Today, far too many well-meaning parents jump through hoops making sure that their children never experience a lull in the action. Many factors have led to this behavior. Some parents were raised by cold and uninvolved parents who failed to meet their needs. Understandably, they find themselves gravitating toward overindulgence to avoid repeating this hurtful pattern with their own children. Others are captivated by guilt, feeling horrible about something that their child has gone through. Because they love their children and feel badly for them, they want to make up for it by assuming this role. Some parents are simply surrounded by so many other parents raising their children in this way that they assume their behavior is normal and healthy. Regardless of the cause, entertainment director parents are unaware that they are setting the stage for their children to develop a sense of entitlement and chronic unhappiness by overscheduling them and making them the center of attention. Fortunately, it's never too late to change.

Boredom Training Session in Progress

Parents are wise, instead, to allow their children to grapple with the discomfort of occasionally having nothing to do. How many of humankind's greatest works of art, scientific discoveries, and inventions have happened because people had the time to think and to wonder and to imagine something better? In boredom lie the seeds of creativity. When disturbed, this fertile ground fails to yield fruit. This is why Dr. Fay recommends that parents intentionally provide an occasional Boredom Training Session (BTS). To make the most of a BTS, use these steps:

- Provide plenty of items that don't require batteries or power cords, such as paper, pens, crayons, scrap wood and woodworking tools, clay, broken toasters, old coffee pots, etc. Yes, junk can be educational.

- Plan some no-entertainment times for at least one hour once a week, when you do not allow digital devices, TVs, play dates, and other exciting items or activities.

- When the children complain about being bored, parents reply with, "It sounds like you are pretty unhappy. What do you think you can do about it?" Notice how the parents hand the problem to the child rather than feeling responsible to solve it.

- When the child says, "I don't know. I'm booooooooored," reply with something like, "When some kids feel that way, they experiment with making something or seeing what an old coffee pot looks like inside. I can't wait to hear what you decide to do."

- If the child misbehaves or throws a fit, pay very little attention to it and don't give in. Instead provide a quick dose of empathy and offer to help them explore some ideas when they are ready.

We certainly do not condone being cold, mean, or neglectful, but we're also concerned with the number of adults who believe that the best strategy to alleviate boredom is to act out or create drama. How sad their lives become when they run out of people willing to put up with this unhealthy coping strategy. Instead, we hope that your children grow into adults with such active imaginations and resourcefulness that they never feel bored.

Brick #5. Teach kids to say no to themselves. Mentally strong kids need self-control. One of the most difficult things in life—whether your child is 5, 15, or 25—is making a short-term sacrifice in favor of long-term gain. A series of experiments that began over half a century ago reveal that the concept of delayed gratification is a critical component of mental fortitude. Psychologist Walter Mischel conducted one of the most famous trials that involved hundreds of preschoolers at Stanford University and a yummy treat: a marshmallow (or in some cases, a mini-pretzel, mint, cookie, or other snack).[11]

Each child entered a room and sat at a desk facing a delectable marshmallow. The researcher told the child they had to make a tough choice—eat one marshmallow now or wait 20 minutes alone and earn two marshmallows. Many of the youngsters gobbled up the single marshmallow immediately, while approximately one-third of the kids found creative ways to distract themselves from the tempting treat. For example, some clapped their hands, others turned their chair around so they couldn't see the marshmallow, and some whispered no repeatedly.

About a dozen years later, Mischel checked in with the kids, who were now teenagers. The ones who had instantly gulped down the marshmallow were more indecisive, easily frustrated, and disorganized. The tykes who had managed to delay gratification were less easily distracted, better able to concentrate, and less likely to give up on their goals in the face of obstacles. In addition, they scored an average of 210 points higher on the SAT compared to their peers who couldn't wait. By the time the kids reached the ages of 25 to 30, the ones who showed self-control with that marshmallow were more resilient, successful in achieving their goals, and less likely to use drugs, and they had lower body mass index and stronger relationships. The differences continued through middle age when functional brain scans of the two groups found that the prefrontal cortex—involved with judgment, forethought, and impulse control—was more active in the delayers. In the gobblers, however, reward and pleasure centers of the brain associated with obesity and addictions were more active.

These results may seem dire for the little ones who couldn't control their urge to nibble the marshmallow; however, Mischel did do some follow-up tests that showed there is hope for them. The psychologist recruited adults to show some of the preschoolers a variety of strategies to distract themselves from the desire to gobble the marshmallow. After seeing these techniques demonstrated, some of the kids who had previously failed to wait for the bigger reward were able to withstand the temptation and earn the extra marshmallow. To help your child learn to say no to themselves, teach them some of these distraction techniques:

- Sing a song
- Look the other way
- Talk to yourself and remind yourself why it's better to wait
- Take a walk
- Think about pleasant memories
- Play a game

In addition, every time your child asks *you* to do something that isn't good for them—swimming without a life jacket, skateboarding without a helmet, eating an entire container of ice cream—and you say no it teaches them to say no to themselves. By helping your kids resist temptations at an early age, you are reinforcing their mental fortitude, which will pay off bigger dividends throughout their lifetime.

* * *

All living things need manageable struggle to grow and reach their potential. Dr. Fay witnessed an example of this when the rural power company replaced the electrical power lines. The original lines had experienced well over 60 years of extreme winds and temperature variations. Living over 10,000 feet above sea level, Dr. Fay's community often experiences wintertime gusts of over 80 miles per hour. During dry summers the area is also prone to wildfires because of the dense forest and hazards like lightning, unattended campfires, and broken electrical lines.

To replace the lines, crews used helicopters to remove the large old-growth trees, pluck the old power poles out of the rocky ground, and replace them with new and stronger ones. To avoid leaving the entire area barren, they left the younger, smaller trees in place. It wasn't long, however, before winter returned along with its fierce winds. The first round uprooted nearly all of the smaller trees, exposing the fact that they had almost no root structure. In fact, their roots were so underdeveloped that they could barely support their own weight.

The community there learned that the shelter of the larger trees provided support for the newer, smaller ones while also letting them be exposed to some adverse conditions. Adversity without support can overwhelm your children (that's what often happens in trauma) and leave them uprooted. Adversity with support allows them to grow tall and strong. The key is the right amount of support that doesn't overshadow the young trees nor leave them overexposed. The choice is yours as their parent. If you remain committed to supporting your children as you allow them to struggle, they can develop the strength of those capable of resisting the gale force winds of this life.

Action Steps

- Practice the five steps for guiding kids to own and solve their problems.
- Let kids experience the struggles, support, and skills that build strength and an attitude of service.
- Teach them how to do stuff.
- Expect them to spend more time creating than skating.
- Expect them to complete chores as contributions to the family.
- Quit your job as entertainment director and let kids engage in a Boredom Training Session.
- Teach your kids to say no to themselves.

CHAPTER 9

HELPING KIDS DEVELOP AND MAINTAIN HEALTHY BODIES FOR STRONGER MINDS

Do everything to protect your child's future.

If you want your kids to be respectful, responsible, and resilient—*don't we all want that?*—not only do your parenting techniques matter, but so do your biological choices for a healthy brain and body. To help kids get the healthy foundation they need, teach your kids three things:

- Love their brain and body.
- Avoid things that hurt the brain and body.
- Do things that help the brain and body.

In chapter 1, we briefly introduced you to the 11 major risk factors—BRIGHT MINDS—that harm the brain and body and can lead to health issues. We also gave you a sneak peek at some of the simple strategies you can use to minimize those risk factors to improve brain and body health. We will delve now into a few of those factors that can have the biggest impact on your child's life and some practical daily strategies.

In many ways, the best thing you can do for your child is to have them spend time with healthy people. Dr. Amen often says the fastest way to get healthy is to find the healthiest people you can and then spend as much time around them as possible. Encourage your kids to think about choosing their friends the same way. What do they want to be like? What do they want in life?

Use your goals to facilitate healthy activities in your day-to-day routines. Do you want your children to have good focus, energy, attention, and decision-making? Do you want them to be successful in school? Do you want them to have good relationships? Then help them get there with good food choices, physical activity, adequate sleep, brain games, and stress management.

NINE FOOD RULES FOR MENTALLY STRONG KIDS

Did you know that the foods you serve are either making your kids mentally and physically stronger or weaker? Food can help your family feel relaxed, happy, and focused—or tired, sad, and inattentive. The exciting news is that eating right consistently over time is the best way to keep the brain and body healthy. Eat right to think right.

I need to eat right to think right.

One study found that the number of fruits and vegetables you eat affects your happiness. The more fruits and vegetables you eat, the happier you are (up to eight servings a day, and it happens within 24 hours).[1] No antidepressant works that quickly!

Take an active role in teaching your kids how to eat. Help them understand just because they "love" a certain food doesn't mean it's good for them. So find foods your family loves that love you back. Stay away from anything that abuses you. Portray your relationship to food like other relationships in your life. Dr. Amen's experience with four teenagers and hordes of their friends is that if you educate them, give them tasty, healthy options, and gently nudge them in the right direction, they make better choices. Granted, it can take time to get them on board, so exercise persistence.

Several years ago, his daughter Chloe told him, "I'm never going to be as serious as you." She thought Dr. Amen was over the top about health and nutrition. But when puberty hit, and her skin started to break out and her weight changed, she came straight to her dad. "What do I do?" she asked.

"We're going to the health food store, and I'm going to teach you to read labels," he replied. "Your job on this treasure hunt is to find 10 foods that you like that like you back." Ever since then Chloe reads labels and is thoughtful about what she eats. She knew where to turn because her parents had been training her to love her brain (and her body) from an early age.

Here are the top food rules[2] for mentally strong kids:

1. **Mentally strong kids get adequate protein.** Protein fuels mental and physical strength. It enhances focus and provides the necessary biological building blocks for brain and body health. Great sources of protein include fish, skinless poultry, beans, nuts, and high-protein veggies like broccoli and spinach. Include small amounts with each meal. If your family eats grilled or baked fish once a week, everyone will have more gray matter (brain cells) in their brains.

2. **Mentally strong kids go for high-quality calories.** The quality of food you and your children eat matters, perhaps even more than the quantity. Think of a 500-calorie slice of cheesecake compared with a 500-calorie spinach salad with chicken, mushrooms, beets, and walnuts. The cheesecake will make you or your kids feel happy for a short time, but then it will zap energy and focus. Meanwhile, that nutrient-dense salad will keep you feeling full longer, will enhance brainpower, and will fuel the body for school, work, family responsibilities, and fun.

3. **Mentally strong kids eat often to balance blood sugar levels.** Mentally strong kids need balanced blood sugar levels throughout the day. Why? Low blood sugar levels are associated with anxiousness, irritability, inability to focus, and trouble making good decisions. Research also shows that low blood sugar levels are associated with self-control failures.[3] On the flip side, chronically high levels of blood sugar are linked to increased risk for type 2 diabetes, a condition that is skyrocketing in young people. According to the CDC, the rates of this condition in people under the age of 20 have risen 95 percent from 2001 to 2017.[4] To help keep blood sugar balanced, encourage kids to eat protein with each meal and use protein snacks, such as a hard-boiled egg or nuts, before homework or chores. In general, feed your kids three small meals and at least two snacks a day.

Great Snacks for Kids

Sweet potatoes

Hummus

Guacamole

Apples and pears

Peaches

Berries

Frozen bananas

Trail mix of nuts, dried fruits, coconut, seeds

Hard-boiled eggs

Figs

Mangoes and pineapple

Oranges and tangerines

Chicken wings or chicken tenders (grilled or baked)

Grapes

Nuts and nut butters

4. **Mentally strong kids steer clear of sugar and artificial sweeteners.**
The sweet stuff isn't so sweet when it comes to raising mentally
strong kids. Homework, chores, and everyday life will go so much
better if you reduce or eliminate foods with added sugar. All forms
of sugar spike blood sugar, which as you saw in the previous rule
negatively impacts the brain, mind, and physical health. Some sugars are unprocessed and less toxic. Raw honey and raw sugar forgo
the chemical and bleaching process. Raw, unfiltered honey contains
trace amounts of minerals and vitamins and has shown some promise in treating environmental allergies (in small amounts). (Note:
Never give honey—especially raw and unfiltered—to a child under
the age of one. The bacteria could cause botulism.)

A good natural alternative to sugar is stevia. Dr. Amen likes stevia
because it has the least reported problems and the greatest reported
health claims. Stevia extract is 200 to 300 times sweeter than sugar,
so if you use too much, you may find that it tastes bitter. Stevia does
not impact blood sugar levels the way sugar does. Only use stevia
in limited amounts, as it keeps the taste buds hooked on sweetness.

It may seem logical to replace sugar with artificial sweeteners. But artificial sweeteners have turned out to be an unhealthy substitution. Artificial sweeteners tell the brain that "sweetness is coming." So, although they don't spike blood sugar, artificial sweeteners consistently raise insulin, which also raises the risk for heart disease, diabetes, metabolic syndrome, Alzheimer's disease, and other health problems. Plus manufacturers create most artificial sweeteners with chemicals that are unsafe for the body and have unknown long-term effects.

5. **Mentally strong kids stay hydrated.** The brain is 80 percent water. Hydrating it optimizes mental strength. Being just slightly dehydrated can increase anxiousness, sadness, and irritability and zaps energy and concentration.[5] When children drink enough water, they think better, feel better, and are physically stronger. A general rule is that everyone in your home should drink half their weight in ounces per day. When your kids sweat through exercise or play, make sure they rehydrate. Staying hydrated also helps prevent overeating. Often when children think they're hungry, they're actually thirsty.

Dr. Amen's favorite drink is water mixed with a little lemon juice and a little bit of stevia extract. It tastes like lemonade and has virtually no calories. Many of his patients make "spa water": water with a few cucumber, lemon, or strawberry slices in it.

6. **Mentally strong kids eat healthy fats.** Children need fat in their diet for their brain, mind, and body to function well. After all, the weight of the brain is 60 percent fat (if all the water were removed). Omega-3 fatty acids are especially important for physical, brain, and mental health, as deficiencies have been associated with depression, ADHD, obesity, and more.[6] However, bad fats, such as trans fats (look for the word *hydrogenated* on labels) should be eliminated.

Good Fats

Avocados
Cocoa butter
Coconut
Fish: anchovies, arctic char, catfish, herring, king crab, mackerel, wild salmon, sardines, sea bass, snapper, sole, trout, and tuna
Seafood: clams, mussels, oysters, and scallops
Meats: grass-fed beef, bison, lamb, and organic poultry
Nuts
Olives
Seeds

HEALTHY OILS (LOOK FOR ORGANIC, UNREFINED, EXPELLER-PRESSED, OR COLD-PRESSED)
Olive oil
Coconut oil
Avocado oil
Flax oil
Macadamia nut oil
Sesame oil
Walnut oil

7. **Mentally strong kids take their vitamins.** Children are highly active both physically and mentally. Their developing minds and growing bodies require a host of essential nutrients, which *might* be obtained *if* they were eating a perfect diet. Imagine saying, "Kids, I've made your favorite dinner: sardines, beets, brussels sprouts, and sweet potatoes. Time to chow down!" Because most kids aren't eating the healthiest diet possible, there's a good chance they aren't getting the nutrients they need. And even if you are doing your best to prepare healthy meals for your family, good eating habits can go out the window at birthday parties, sleepovers, sporting events, and other kid-friendly activities.

Adding a multivitamin to their sometimes picky or rushed diet is important for their brains and bodies. Give them a multivitamin that provides 100 percent daily allowances of vitamins and minerals. Dr. Amen also suggests adding an omega-3 supplement that has a balance between EPA and DHA. He recommends 1,000 to 2,000 mg per day for children. The third supplement he recommends for all his patients is vitamin D (so look for a multivitamin with D). Most Americans are deficient in vitamin D, and it is essential for brain health, mood, memory, and weight.

8. **Mentally strong kids eat smart carbs.** Carbs are not an enemy. They are essential to your child's life. Their body needs them. But bad carbs, stripped of any nutritional value, are the enemy. So, make sure to eat from the rainbow. This does not mean Skittles, jelly beans, or M&Ms. Colorful plant foods provide an enormous array of nutrients, enzymes, vitamins, and minerals necessary for good health. Vegetables, fruits, and legumes (beans and peas) are high in good-for-you fiber. When it comes to carbs, eat low-glycemic, high-fiber foods, which don't raise blood sugar too much or too fast. Think of a bowl of rice or pasta as the equivalent of eating a bowl of sugar, and teach your kids to see them that way. This doesn't mean you'll never eat those, but make them rare and consider choosing options that contain protein and fiber such as chickpea pasta or black rice.

9. **Mentally strong kids don't eat pesticides or food additives.** Eat organically grown or raised foods when possible. Pesticides used in commercial farming can accumulate in the brain and body, even though the levels in each food may be low. The Environmental Working Group produces an annual list of foods that are high in pesticides and those that are low. Stay updated at ewg.org. Also eat meat that is hormone free, antibiotic free, free-range, or grass fed. You are what you eat, but you are also what those animals ate. When you shop, start reading labels. Turn it into a game with your kids to search for the best brain-healthy food choices in the store, and avoid buying anything with food additives, preservatives, artificial dyes, added sugars, and artificial sweeteners.

Can Red Dye 40 Steal Your Child's Mental Strength, and Maybe Yours Too?

One of Dr. Amen's nurses told him that when her son was about 7 years old, she and her husband began to notice various tics and strange neurological affectations in him. Whenever he ate something bright red or drank a red Slurpee, his behavior became more aggressive and hostile. He would cry easily and storm off in a huff or throw things. She tried to minimize these foods in his diet, but he would often get them at school: Cheetos, Doritos, fruit punch, Red Vines, lollipops, etc.

What she didn't realize was that the strawberry yogurt, whole-grain strawberry bars, and even the canned pasta sauce and ketchup she was giving him at home contained an ingredient common to those other snack foods: a dye called Red 40.

When their son was 14 years old, they brought him to Amen Clinics to confirm their suspicion that he was reacting to this food additive. This teen's brain SPECT scan showed remarkable overall increased activity with exposure to Red Dye 40. After seeing his scan, his parents made it a habit to read every food label and taught their teen how to read food labels so they could avoid the artificial coloring. By eliminating the dye from his diet, the teen's moods and behaviors improved, and he made much better decisions.

OVERCOMING FOOD FIGHTS

You may be thinking this all sounds fine and good, but you might be wondering about the resistance over food that your kids pull at the dinner table. Many parents are frustrated over the eating habits of their children. All their kids want to eat is junk food, and mealtimes are frequently tense when they engage in repetitive battles over food. Parents often find themselves saying, "Eat this. Try that. Eat your vegetables. Try a little bit more. You can't leave the table until you clean your plate!" The child often responds, "No! I don't like it. It'll make me throw up! I'm full (after two bites). I want something else." Everyone at the table feels upset, and no one enjoys eating together.

Dr. Amen, too, has had those dinnertime wars. When his oldest son, Antony, was a toddler, there was a constant battle at the dinner table because he refused to eat all his food. Mealtime was awful, and it affected everyone's mood for the rest of the evening. He says,

> During my child psychiatry training, however, one of my supervisors helped get us out of the struggle. She told us that our son wasn't going to starve to death. He was going through a normal oppositional period, and if we continued to struggle around food, he may end up with some form of an eating disorder. She recommended the following mealtime rules to help children develop healthy habits:
>
> 1. The parents decide what's for meals—with liberal input from the child.
> 2. A child should decide how much or how little they eat from their plate.
> 3. If the child is a picky eater, only put a small portion of food on their plate.
> 4. If the child does not eat at all, do not make arrangements for a "special menu."
> 5. Keep healthy food in the house.
>
> The basic message was to get out of the struggle around food. To our amazement, when we followed her rules and allowed our son to control how much or how little he ate at mealtime, the struggles ended. He actually gained weight, and mealtime became enjoyable.

What you choose to eat and the food you provide at home teaches your kids what to like and, therefore, what to choose. Expose your kids to a wide variety of healthy options so they will learn to like the right food and make good choices when they are away from you.

Eating in a brain-healthy way is one of the strongest forms of love for yourself and for your kids. If you truly love and care for your family, be diligent about putting healthy fuel inside your bodies. In the long run, it will make everyone in your family happier and healthier and better able to choose other brain-healthy activities.

MENTALLY STRONG KIDS PLAY HARD AND REST WELL

Two of the other big needs for mentally strong kids are exercise and sleep. Your children need both. Their bodies are made to move, and they need their rest.

If your child has trouble falling asleep, make it easier to drift off to dreamland. Create a regular sleep schedule, even on the weekends. Put them to bed at the same time every night and get them up at the same time every day. Set up their room to be cool, dark, and noise-free when they go to bed. Allow your children to sleep 7 to 10 hours a night. Do your best to let them wake up naturally, which may mean adjusting their bedtime. Each child is unique, so what works for one may not work for another. Keep trying new techniques until you find the best routine.

Sleep Enhancers

1. Turn off electronic devices and TV at least an hour before bed.
2. Solve emotional or relational problems before sending kids to bed.
3. Create a soothing nighttime routine: A warm bath or shower, meditation, prayer, or gentle massage fosters relaxation and encourages sleep.
4. Read a book or short story (make sure it isn't action-packed) before bed (don't let the child read from a screen at this point in the night; it stimulates their brain to stay awake). *Captain Snout and the Super Power Questions*[7] is a favorite.

5. Play soothing sounds, which can induce a peaceful mood and lull your child to sleep. Consider nature sounds, wind chimes, a fan, or soft music. Studies have shown that slower classical music, or any music that has a slow rhythm of 60 to 80 beats per minute, can help with sleep.[8]
6. Hypnosis or guided imagery, which helps kids achieve a more relaxed state of mind. *Time for Bed, Sleepyheads* is a hypnotic bedtime story for kids 3 to 8.
7. Put a drop of lavender oil under their nose.
8. Have your child wear socks to bed.
9. Look into a supplement such as 5HTP or saffron for kids who worry a lot.

When your kids are awake during the day, make sure they are moving and playing. After all, physical activity uses up their energy and makes them easier to put to bed at night.

Exercise has many other benefits too. Physical activity on a daily basis boosts metabolism, increases blood flow, and gets all the good-feeling neurotransmitters going for a happy brain. Growing up, Dr. Amen's daughter Chloe loved going on long walks and taking spin and boxing classes. She actually told her dad, "I get my work done faster [after I've exercised]." She's onto something: the brain-fitness connection. In fact, research shows that physical fitness improves brain function and enhances academic performance.[9] It also boosts moods, focus, and self-confidence, all elements of mental strength. One study even found that boys who exercise make more money as working adults.[10] Exercise protects memory and alleviates symptoms of depression. A 2022 review of 21 randomized controlled trials found that exercise is as effective as antidepressants in reducing depressive symptoms in people with mild to moderate depression.[11] Physical activity can also ease anxiety and panic attacks.

Many healthy, enjoyable sports will not compromise your child's brain health and their future. Tennis, Ping-Pong (Dr. Amen's personal favorite), pickleball, swimming, basketball, volleyball, ballet, and other forms of dance are wonderful, safe ways to exercise a growing body. Encourage your child to have fun doing what's good for them. Get your kids to move and play and run around. Their brains and minds will be stronger, more flexible, and faster.

BRAIN WORKOUTS FOR MENTAL STRENGTH

While physical activity benefits the brain and body, you also want to exercise the brain with mental activities. One of the best brain workouts is to learn something new every day, which is easiest in childhood.

Einstein is attributed as saying that if a person spent 15 minutes a day learning something new (within one subject), it would only take one year to become an expert. So encourage your kids to find life applications from the topics they are learning in school. By learning something new, the brain establishes new connections and maintains and improves the function of less-used brain areas.[12]

Just like you would never go to the gym and only do left leg lunges for strength training, make sure your children get a variety of brain training. Encourage the following activities on a regular basis:

- Sign them up for a class outside their interests.
- Nudge them to learn to play a musical instrument.
- Encourage them to go deeper in their interests.
- Play a new game together (e.g., word games, card and board games, memory and math games).

- Cook a new recipe.
- Make up a game to look at similarities and differences in similar items, such as how different baseball pitchers throw a curveball, the colors and images in paintings, or the flavors of different spices.
- Cultivate different friends for your kids, so they are exposed to different points of view.
- Laugh a lot.
- Improve coordination with activities such as juggling, table tennis, dance, or yoga.
- Cross-train (try another sport position or someone else's chore).
- Kill the ANTs (see chapter 7).

Don't Encourage Multitasking

Multitasking is not good for the brain—surprise! Instead of making your kids more productive, it actually leads to more distractions. Multitasking is actually an inefficient use of time and decreases their performance (this is true for adults, too). Gray matter in the brain (brain cells where a lot of the brain work is happening) actually shrinks with too much multitasking. So encourage your kids to focus on one task at a time. They will be much more effective in whatever they are doing, and success builds more confidence and even greater success.

When your child is learning a new skill or activity, encourage them to practice perfectly; have them take their time to do it correctly over and over. Practice does not make perfect—unless they practice perfectly.

As you are encouraging them to work hard, praise the desired behavior, not the end result. If you praise your kids for being smart, they become more performance oriented and assume that intelligence cannot be improved. This can actually be demotivating and may contribute to a fear of failure that holds them back in life. But if you praise kids for working hard, the effect on the brain is profound. They will actually enjoy working, have more persistence, and assume that they can get smarter with new strategies. These are signs of mentally strong kids.

Dr. Amen's wife, Tana, learned this lesson from her mom, Mary, early on.

Mary was a single working mother who often held three jobs to make ends meet. At that time, women couldn't work more than eight hours of overtime, and without a high school education, Mary had a hard time finding well-paying jobs. Tana was a latchkey kid and hated not having her mother home. Mary would try to comfort Tana by talking about her dreams for Tana's future. Mary explained it would require a lot of hard work to get from where they were to where they wanted to go.

One day, a friend of Mary's who lacked ambition saw Mary exhausted and run-down. With a cigarette hanging out of her mouth, the friend said, "You need to stop working so hard. You should just go on government assistance and stay home with your kid." Mary noticed 9-year-old Tana listening in the corner and correctly assumed that Tana thought this would be a great idea—anything to have her mom home more. Choosing her words carefully, Mary said, "I will never allow the government or anyone to have that much control over my life or my destiny. I know my hard work will pay off. This is temporary. Taking the easy way out will lead to long-term suffering, and we will be stuck in this hellhole forever. If I act like a victim and give up now, I will never win because victims can't win. Someone else controls them."

That conversation stayed with Tana for the rest of her life. It taught her to work hard—and see the payoff. Her mom started her own business (in her garage) that became a successful company for 30 years.

MENTALLY STRONG KIDS COPE WITH STRESS

Stress can either reinforce your child's mental strength or sap it. Positive stress motivates a child to do their homework or a teen to get a job. Positive stress enhances the immune system; everyone needs some stress so their brain and body know how to handle it. But when your child is exhibiting signs of too much stress, they need tools to help them relax. Several simple techniques help:

- Warming their hands—hold your child's hands, give them a warm drink to hold, sit by a fire, or have them think about being at the beach.

- Slow, deep breathing from their belly—teach your kids to do this any time they get stressed, angry, anxious, or panicked (all times when we stop breathing or breathe more shallowly).

- Prayer or meditation—reciting prayers silently or aloud can be comforting; many forms of meditation are simple. Teach them to meditate by telling them to close their eyes and pay attention to their breathing and thoughts.

- Visualization—help them think of places or things that make them happy, calm, or peaceful, such as a pet, a vacation, or a certain person.

- Start each day with intention, gratitude, and appreciation (this should already be part of daily goal setting). At Dr. Amen's house, they start each day by saying, "Today is going to be a great day" at breakfast, and at dinner or bedtime they discuss "What went well today."[13] This helps to direct the mind to what they love about their lives rather than focusing on the trouble.

Remember: No matter what changes you create in your family to promote healthy brains and bodies, they'll only be effective if you've created a loving, engaging home environment full of attention, eye contact, touch, and play. Everything your family does helps or harms the brain, body, and mental strength. With a better brain and body always comes better mental strength and a better life because kids will make better decisions. And the more you talk about brain and body health around your kids and model that behavior, the more it will become a natural part of their life.

Action Steps

- Feed kids foods they love that love them back.
- Only keep healthy foods in the house.
- Let children decide how much they eat.
- Make it a habit to exercise or play sports with your kids.
- Make sleep a priority for everyone in your home.
- Encourage your child's curiosity and inspire them to learn new things.
- Teach your child simple stress-reduction techniques.

CHAPTER 10

WHEN PARENTS HAVE DIFFERENT STYLES: CREATING A UNITED TEAM

*When parents can't agree about parenting, the result
is anxiety and confusion for their kids.*

Rose and Antonelli were good-hearted people and basically good parents. They sought some help from a Love and Logic coach to help them manage their four wonderful children, ages 11 months, 2 years, 7 years, and almost 16. Chris, their 7-year-old, was the main reason they needed help. He had been suspended from school twice in one year and had a general attitude of entitlement and disrespect.

During their second coaching session, Rose lamented, "Antonelli is the fun one. He won't stand up to them. He's always so worried about whether they like him or not."

Obviously, Dad was not impressed with his wife's depiction of his parenting style. "That's not true. Rose, you are so critical. Not just with the kids but with me. How about last week when you said, 'You need to get a backbone! You're not man enough to raise these kids'?"

By their third week, while their oldest daughter remained an honor student, Chris continued to act out, their 2-year-old wouldn't poop in the potty, and their youngest spit food. Nothing had changed except that it had become clear that the kids were anxious spectators in an epic battle between two good people who wanted the best for them but couldn't agree on how to make it happen.

Dr. Fay has seen this scenario unfold countless times. Parents come to him about their "problem child." After a session or two, he discovers the difficulty with their perceptions: Each believes the other parent is the real misbehaving child. When parents choose to point fingers at each other, the built-up tension generally vents through the behavior of their kids. Like steam from a boiling teakettle, this conflict often manifests in a sad way: At least one of the kids acts out, another often tries to keep things on an even keel by being perfect, and the others develop variants of those roles.

When parents begin to realize that the change they want lies within their own skin, they often see big improvements in their children, as well as in their relationship with the other parent. The relief children experience when the parental tug-of-war ends is immense. "During one of our sessions, it hit both of us at about the same time," Antonelli and Rose commented. "We realized that our blaming and arguing over our different parenting styles was doing far more damage than our different parenting styles."

Let that sink in for a moment.

Conflict over different parenting styles does far more damage than different parenting styles.

HOW CARING COUPLES FALL INTO CONFLICT

The following descriptions depict this fundamental concept playing out between another couple with different personalities. As we see, the roles are often the same, but the people playing them, the intensity of the conflict, and many particulars depend on the unique family.

Before Kids

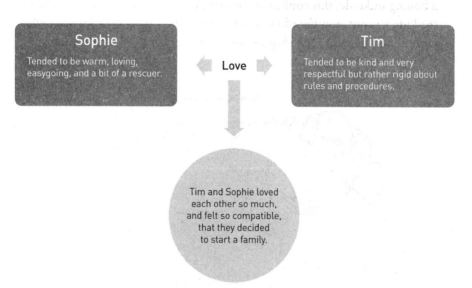

Before the kids arrived, love and respect primarily characterize the interactions between Sophie and Tim. Notice the arrow in the middle of the page. This points to the impact of their interactions, not the impact of their individual styles, per se. Both played a role in their happiness, and both will play a role in the conflict and unhappiness lurking on the horizon.

The Kids Arrive

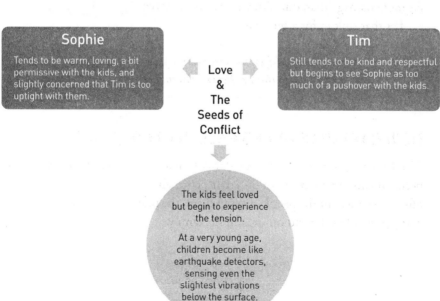

Sophie and Tim are still madly in love, but they are also mad at each other more frequently than before. Trying to rescue the kids from each other's style, they create conflict. This battle has begun to leave their kids feeling progressively more anxious.

In elementary school, did you ever do the basic science experiment with a bottle of vinegar, a box of baking soda, an empty glass bottle, and a cork? Like different personalities and different parenting styles, nothing happened until a teacher combined the ingredients in the bottle and corked it. The combo fizzed, bubbled, and eventually blew the cork sky high.

The baking soda didn't cause the bottle to blow. Neither did the vinegar. The combination of the two, which led to the pressure inside the bottle, did the trick. So remember this concept: Family problems aren't always caused by problem people; instead, problems often happen when good people blame each other, experience the pressure to change each other, and fail to learn new ways of thinking and reacting.

The Kids Age and Begin to Present Some Challenges

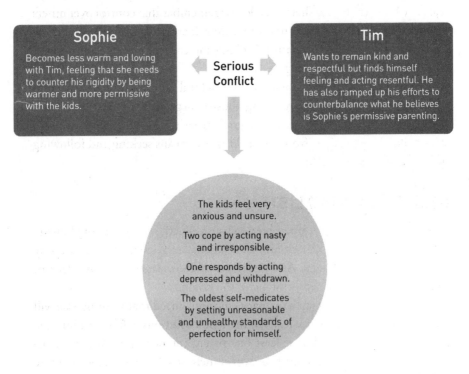

Sophie

Becomes less warm and loving with Tim, feeling that she needs to counter his rigidity by being warmer and more permissive with the kids.

Serious Conflict

Tim

Wants to remain kind and respectful but finds himself feeling and acting resentful. He has also ramped up his efforts to counterbalance what he believes is Sophie's permissive parenting.

The kids feel very anxious and unsure.

Two cope by acting nasty and irresponsible.

One responds by acting depressed and withdrawn.

The oldest self-medicates by setting unreasonable and unhealthy standards of perfection for himself.

Tim and Sophie now wonder why they have drifted apart. They have little to no intimacy between them, and they are constantly battling over how to parent the kids. Sophie believes that Tim is a major Drill Sergeant, and Tim sees her as a high-powered Helicopter. The kids are doing their best to keep things together, while their parents remain distracted by the power struggle between them.

In truth, Tim and Sophie are still good-hearted people, and there is great hope for their relationship and their kids. At the heart of their challenges is their habit of seeing each other as the problem, rather than seeing their interactions as the problem. As a result, they've also fallen into the trap of trying to control each other rather than allowing each other to learn and grow. Their fear that the other's style will harm the kids creates a self-fulfilling prophecy: Their children are suffering.

Control battles typically grow from the seeds of fear.
Fear is often our most terrifying adversary.

We'll share a plan for preventing or resolving the fear, conflict, and damaging differences that haunt so many intelligent and caring parents. Well-meaning parents who chronically disagree over parenting are letting their fears and worries control their lives. Please remember that control over others is an illusion. Real change comes from exterminating your own ANTs, those thoughts that perpetuate negative thinking and conflict rather than cooperation, and taking the following steps.

Note: There are times when fear is a helpful emotion. It's necessary to fear and control a situation involving abusive, neglectful, or other otherwise dangerous behavior. This means doing whatever it takes to protect yourself, your children, and others from harm. This also means seeking and following qualified professional help.

STEP 1: LEARN TO LISTEN

Most people have never learned how to listen effectively. Instead of allowing others to fully express their emotions, opinions, and desires, they constantly interrupt by sharing theirs. As a result, frustration, anger, hurt, and lack of unity become the prevailing climate of the home.

Being listened to is such a primary emotional need that nothing else will work until others experience it. Even the wisest solutions will be cast into the furnace, forever lost, unless at least one parent interacting makes an intentional effort to close their mouth and open their ears. Listening requires more than good intentions:

- Nobody cares how much you know until they know how much you care. While it is an old cliché, this statement is tested and true. First allow the other parent to express their hopes, dreams, fears, and frustrations without interrupting (even when you feel triggered).

- Demonstrate that you are listening. Sitting like a bump on a log does little to show that you hear and care about what the other person is saying. Good listeners provide little doses of empathy, reflect the feeling being expressed, and communicate their understanding by occasionally repeating what the other has said.

- Watch your body language. Eliminate frowning, eye-rolling, checking your phone, and other immature, passive-aggressive behavior. Sit where you can maintain closeness, loving touch, and healthy eye contact. This may mean you need to schedule some time alone. Turn off your phone, and ready your heart to give rather than receive.

- Remind yourself throughout the conversation that the loving act of listening will have a bigger impact on your success as a family than all the nifty psychological tools you apply. It's really that important.

Let's take a look at how this might play out. An exchange starts like this:

MOTHER: I'm so sick of the kids leaving things all over the house. They never pick up.

FATHER: That's because you aren't consistent about making them do it. If you would just take the things that they leave around, then . . .

Stop!

We included that quick example to demonstrate how it *shouldn't* be done. Here's a better example:

MOTHER: I'm sick and tired of the kids leaving things all over the house. They never pick up anything. I'm worn out.

FATHER: (*resisting the urge to give his opinion on how to fix things*) It's exhausting.

MOTHER: Every day, exhausting! And you don't help at all.

FATHER: (*This is the real test of his listening skills! He passes by using empathy.*) This is really hard, and you wish that I would help.

MOTHER: Yes! You need to tell them that this is not okay.

FATHER: I will do that. Do you have any other ideas about what should be done?

MOTHER: My parents just give them too much crap. They have so much stuff that they don't even know what to do with it.

FATHER: So part of this has to do with the sheer volume of stuff they have?

MOTHER: Yes! It's crazy too much!

FATHER: Let me get this correct: This whole thing is exhausting and super frustrating to you. Something I can do is set more limits with the kids about putting things away. It seems like you feel that your parents giving them too much stuff that they don't need is also part of the problem. Do you feel like I am listening?

For most of us, learning good active listening skills is a long and challenging process. This is especially the case if your parents didn't use them while you were growing up. Practice listening skills in all kinds of conversations, especially ones without high emotions. This will help you get into the habit. You could also practice with a professional counselor, read books on the subject, rehearse the skills with your spouse and kids, or take a relationship class.

STEP 2: UNDERSTAND HOW POWER STRUGGLES MAKE DIFFERENCES WORSE

Many books, articles, blogs, podcasts, and seminars have focused on the concept of "getting on the same page" as parents. The implication is that you should consistently parent in the same way so that your kids will blossom like roses in a well-tended garden. This is surely a noble goal, but many people have put their heart and soul into improving their skills *and unfortunately* trying to perfect the skills and attitudes of the other parent.

As you know, it's always enjoyable to be around someone who is dedicated to remediating your faults. There's nothing more uplifting than frequently hearing that you ought to behave in more psychologically, socially, or morally beneficial ways. It's even better when someone provides you with a book or web link that will help you eliminate your defective actions and attitudes. . . . Do you detect our sarcasm?

How many relationships have been destroyed through one or both parents' efforts to improve or control the other? The concept of ANTs discussed in chapters 5 and 7 is central to this dynamic. A common ANT goes something like this: *If I can just get _____to_____, then the kids will _____.* Perhaps the challenge with this thought is that it's frequently true. Often the other parent does need to change. Maybe they are too permissive, lack consistency, make critical comments, use language that would make a pirate blush, micromanage the kids, or have other cringeworthy habits.

The problem with this ANT has less to do with its potential validity and more to do with its lack of practicality. When you allow it to dominate your mind, you become more fearful, frustrated, and likely to engage in controlling behaviors that often backfire. Subconsciously, the other parent begins to entertain options for regaining control, such as developing severe hearing loss, displaying other passive-resistant behaviors, harboring resentment, and becoming even more devoted to their existing parenting approach.

Liana, while attending one of our trainings, shared her tremendous frustration with her husband Eddie's lack of limit setting with the kids. "We've been to multiple trainings, read your books, and even saw a counselor," she shared. "He always says that he is going to be firmer, but it never lasts long. I hate having to be on his case, but he's like a child."

After doing his best to listen and validate her feelings, Dr. Fay inquired, "Would it be okay if I asked a rather personal question?"

"No problem. I need any help you can give," she answered.

Dr. Fay took a calculated risk based on his sense that Eddie was a good and kind man, "So are you telling me that Eddie doesn't care about you and the kids and that he's just plain irresponsible? I mean, he sounds really nasty."

Suddenly, she came to his defense. "No! He's very kind and responsible. It's not like that. He just lets them play too many video games, lets them complain about the food I serve, and isn't consistent about bedtime. It's things like that."

"So . . . he's a really good guy who loves you and the kids?" Dr. Fay clarified.

Liana nodded. "Yes. Definitely. He's a great guy."

"How often does he hear that from you?" Dr. Fay asked.

She answered with a sheepish smile. "I think I know what you're getting at."

As they continued their conversation, Liana admitted that she was focusing way too much on what she perceived as Eddie's faults, and way too little on what would really motivate him to become a stronger father: experiencing the appreciation and respect of his wife. She also began to realize that her attempts to control her husband were causing him to tighten his grip on less-than-optimal parenting practices.

Truth be told, all of us fall short of the ideal, and all of us need to grow. Are we motivated to change by being controlled, or are we inspired to do so by being around others who love us, respect us, and model healthy behavior? Again, nothing works without positive relationships.

Changing Our Perspective on Change

Change is hard, but here are some ways that we can make it easier.

- **Follow the 10-to-1 rule:** Share 10 positive things about the other parent for every one negative thing. Even if the other parent doesn't change, you'll tend to see them in a more positive way.
- **Make it safe to make mistakes:** If it's not safe to make mistakes, people won't take the risks required to grow. You'll also remain frustrated with your own shortcomings.
- **Demonstrate empathy, forgiveness, and unconditional love:** People will do almost anything for someone who gives these gifts. Even if they don't respond the way you want, your heart is free from the poison of unforgiveness.
- **Confront your fears:** When you refuse to let fear determine how you relate to others, you begin to see that situations often work out better when you don't try so hard to control them.

STEP 3: END YOUR ROLE IN THE POWER STRUGGLE

When asked about his former wife, Joel moaned, "We've been arguing about parenting since the day we brought our child home from the hospital. I tried to tell her that going over to Evans Street was the fastest and safest route. Can you believe she took Hampton down to University Boulevard instead?"

His therapist replied, "So you've been arguing with her all of this time?"

Joel nodded. "And she always does the opposite of what I think is best."

"So, every time you try to get her to do something, it starts a battle?" the therapist continued.

Joel pursed his lips and nodded silently.

"If you know this always starts a battle," the therapist proceeded, "why do you keep doing it?"

What's the only thing that you can control? The obvious answer is yourself. Although doing so doesn't necessarily lead to the rapid change you dream of for someone else, committing to this course of action—100 percent of the time—results in a more favorable long-term result.

Liana, whom we mentioned earlier, found a quiet time to have an uninterrupted talk with her husband, Eddie. Realizing that she needed to take the lead in ending the power struggle, she started by holding his hand, looking into his eyes, and apologizing. "Eddie, I am so sorry. I love you dearly and have been spending way too little time recognizing what a great man you are."

Eddie was speechless.

Liana continued, "I've been trying to get you to parent the kids differently and have ignored how much you care about them and about me."

Unsure how much to trust his wife's admission, Eddie mumbled, "It's okay. I love you too."

"It's not okay, Eddie," she replied. "I need to stop trying to control what you do and focus on how I handle things. You are a great man, and you love our kids. I know that you would never intentionally do anything to hurt them, and I know that our arguing about how we are raising them is doing more harm to them than us just being different. I need to focus on improving what I do rather than trying to control you."

Is it possible that Eddie's heart might have softened a bit? Regardless of whether he changes, Liana put an end to the power struggle and focused on herself.

The difficulty associated with ending our role in power struggles is generally commensurate with the amount of fear, worry, and associated anger that's shackling us to conflict.

Fear and Worry: Enemies of Problem-Solving and Freedom

The problem: Research clearly shows us that unhealthy fear and worry negatively affect the brain and problem-solving,[1] including:

- Distractibility
- Impulsivity
- Ineffective attempts to control a situation or others, leading to poor interactions
- Poor short-term memory and other cognitive processes
- Failure to identify effective solutions
- Less confidence when solutions are implemented

Since kids take their emotional cues from the adults around them, witnessing unhealthy fear and worry also rubs off on them.

The solution: The negative effects of unhealthy fear and worry dramatically decrease when we:
- Identify and focus on our goals
- Place our mental focus on the solutions not the problem
- Replace worry ANTs with more accurate thoughts, such as "Problems are part of life. We can solve this."
- Intentionally breathe deeply and slowly.
- Take action through experimenting with solutions rather than ruminating on which one will solve the problem.

Psychology researchers Sandra Llera and Michelle Newman recently demonstrated that the steps above help people develop more effective solutions and feel far more confident and satisfied with these solutions.[2]

The challenge: If you recognize fears and worries controlling you, give yourself and your kids a great gift: Find a qualified mental health professional who can help you become free from the corrosive impact those ANTs are having on your life.

Since the beginning of time, imperfect parents have raised responsible, good-hearted adults. Keep that in mind. Letting go of control is generally the best way to regain it. Only when we hold on to anger and resentment do we destroy the physical, emotional, social, and spiritual health (four circles of mental strength) we desire. Forgiveness is the only solution. It might help to ask yourself this difficult question: "Do I need to hold on to anger and hurt even though I know that it's hurting my kids?"

STEP 4: DEMONSTRATE LOVING LEADERSHIP BY STRETCHING AND EXERCISING

Most people are aware that stretching before exercise goes a long way toward preventing injury. Stretching is also one of the most helpful things we can do to enhance our relationships, love our kids, and strengthen our brains. It involves intentionally yet gently moving away from any comfort zone that prevents us from relating to others in healthy, loving ways. Here's an example of what we mean.

Sean grew up in a home full of rather rough humor, much of which involved teasing and being sarcastic. "You knew you were loved," he'd often reminisce, "when dad messed up your hair, bear-hugged you, and said something like, 'Ah, there's a face only a mother could love.' Believe it or not, we never got bent out of shape when we heard little put-downs. It was just a family tradition."

Using sarcasm represented one of Sean's comfort zones. For his wife and kids, this was not the case, and it was contributing to hurt feelings and conflict. Perplexed and frustrated by that, he vented to an old friend, "They just can't take a joke. Why are they so thin-skinned?"

"Maybe it's because you're being a jerk," his friend replied.

While used to tough talk, Sean was a bit hurt by the comment. "What kind of crap is this?" he retorted.

"Real friends get straight with each other," his friend shared firmly. "Even though it worked for you when you were a kid, Nina and the kids are different. If they don't think you're being funny, you aren't being funny. I know you love them, but you are messing this up. I love you, man, so don't be a jerk and mess this up."

The conflict between Sean and Nina, his wife, was not simply because of his sarcasm. Her overindulgence of the kids also stoked the flames. The more she coddled and spoiled them, the more he tried to toughen them up with his brand of humor. The more their kids felt hurt, the more Nina overprotected and overprovided.

Sean reluctantly decided to stretch, and he shared his goal with Nina. "I didn't realize that I was being a jerk by teasing you and the kids and being sarcastic. I'm sorry. I don't want to hurt you guys."

The changes you decide to make are not focused on trying to manipulate others into behaving how you want. Instead, they fall under the category of doing the right thing by doing your part. When change in others happens as a result, it is merely a welcome side effect, not an expected payoff for your efforts.

Stretching is helpful, but we also need consistent exercise. Exercise for Sean involved replacing the ANT *They need to learn how to toughen up and take a joke* with a far more productive thought, *A joke is only funny when both people are enjoying it.*

Doing the right thing is always the right thing to do,
regardless of whether it improves the behavior of others.
Doing the right thing is what we do for our own integrity
and health, not something we do to control others.

STEP 5: REVIEW YOUR GOALS

It's easy to fall into the trap of thinking that there is only one effective way to accomplish a set of goals. That's how cults form. Cults have rules and procedures that everyone must rigidly follow in the same way. As such, cults create people who cannot think. Instead of celebrating healthy relationships, creativity, and differing gifts, they punish them.

In parenting, we sometimes battle so much over how things get done that nothing good gets done. Before reading further, take a moment to review your goals (chapter 2). Goals aren't cult doctrine. One of the reasons healthy families remain healthy is because they remember that their goals can be met in a variety of ways. For example, one parent may handle a child's lying by calmly yet firmly informing the child that they take kids to soccer practice when they feel that the kids are being honest and respectful. The other parent in the same family may handle lying by firmly yet calmly expecting the child to make restitution through extra chores.

Together, you establish goals that you adhere to so tightly that you will constructively confront one another if you behave counter to them. At the same time, relax when it comes to *how* you achieve those goals. In fact, actively embrace the fact that each of you may very well handle situations differently based on personality, skill set, and context. Free each other to have a unique and positive influence on your children. Many helpful leadership books have incorporated this concept of "tight and loose" leadership. For those interested in learning more we recommend the book *Learning by Doing*.

The wonderful question, "Does it fit?" embodies the essence of this form of leadership. It provides direction while allowing the flexibility to handle challenging situations with creativity. It also protects you from stepping into the snare of fighting unnecessary and unwinnable control battles with the other parent.

STEP 6: DEVELOP A PLAN FOR HANDLING THE MOST COMMON CONFLICTS

The most frequent conflicts come up when one or more of the following happens:

- The kids say things like, "Well, Dad lets me" or "Mom said it was okay" or "Why is Dad always so mean?"
- One or more of the kids is acting out, and each parent feels different about how to handle it.

Tina and Jim's marriage was on the rocks, largely because their toddler and their teenager had realized that pitting their parents against each other allowed the kids to run the home. While Mom and Dad argued over various points, they were distracted from the real task at hand: teaching their kids that manipulation doesn't pay. Because the drama had exhausted these parents, they also didn't have the energy to set and enforce other essential limits.

From a brief article Dr. Fay posted online, Tina and Jim realized that they were spending way too much time being upset with each other and way too little time expecting their kids to adapt to their parents' differences. When their teen would say, "Well, Dad lets me," Tina would respond with two bad habits: believing her daughter instead of her husband and trying way too hard to be "fair" in her daughter's eyes. When their toddler grumbled, "Mommy is being mean," Jim would feel sorry for her and give in. He realized that he had allowed his daughter to get way too much sympathy by pretending to be a victim.

Tina and Jim changed their conflict when they discovered a nasty habit that people often fall into: When person A has a problem with person B, they complain to person C.

Instead of continuing that pattern, Tina and Jim committed to following this rule:

- When person A has a problem with person B, person A works it out with person B.
- Person C stays out of it except for providing occasional consultation services.

They discussed how they would handle it when their kids used their differences to divide them. Listed below are some examples of how they decided to respond:

Example

CHILD: Mom is being mean.

PARENT: It sounds like you are having a problem with Mom. She loves you, and I'm sure that she would be willing to listen to how you feel.

Example

CHILD: Well, Dad lets me.

PARENT: What did I say?

CHILD: You said no but . . .

PARENT: What did I say? No is my answer.

Example

CHILD: Mom just told me no.

DAD: Sometimes we will have different answers because we are different or the situation is different. She is a wise mom, and I trust her. This is something between the two of you.

Example

CHILD: Can I have some money? Dad is so stingy.

PARENT: One of the reasons I married him is because he has such great judgment about things. I might have some extra jobs around here that I'd be willing to pay you to do.

CHILD: But I need it now!

PARENT: That's a tough spot to be in. My offer still stands.

Now what about potential conflicts when kids have fallen into a pattern of misbehavior that needs to be addressed in a united way? You will face situations like that. How do you handle them when you have different DNA and experiences? The goals you developed while reading chapter 2 are the key to success.

For example, let's imagine that your child has developed a habit of displaying disrespect and even occasional defiance. First, the two of you need to discuss your goals, not your child's disrespect or defiance. Too frequently decision makers get bogged down in differences of opinion over strategies because they haven't first refreshed their agreement over goals. Focusing on the problem feels overwhelming and contributes to the type of fear and worry that interferes with problem-solving. Focusing on solutions helps our brains go from survival mode to problem-solving mode.

Next, brainstorm possible responses:

- Maybe we could lecture and threaten to take away his phone.
- Maybe we could yell and let him know that he's the kid and we are the parents.
- Maybe we could calmly repeat, "I love you too much to argue" when he tries to pull us into debates.
- Maybe we could get him involved in more service activities so that he learns the value of putting others over self.
- Maybe we could lovingly say, "We provide privileges in this home when we feel respected and see you doing what we ask."

Remember to breathe. Don't rush this or try to come up with perfect solutions. At this point, don't evaluate the quality of ideas. Just perform a mind dump. Taking the pressure off the process actually results in producing a larger list of potentially effective experiments. Creativity requires a calm brain.

The last step requires asking each other, "Which of these fit our goals?" and experimenting.

"Which of these fit?" is not the same as "Which ones will surely work?" Again, the goal is to remain calm and objective, instead of becoming wracked with fear and worry. The greatest problem-solvers *experiment* with reasonable solutions rather than getting locked into analysis paralysis or interpersonal conflict trying to agree on the perfect strategy. Experiment is a powerful word, capable of freeing us from unnecessary anxiety and control battles with others.

Dr. Fay worked with a director of special education at a large school district. She was known and loved statewide for fostering cooperation among a large and diverse population of teachers, school administrators, and parents. Intrigued by her success in getting so many people to cooperate, I asked her, "What's your secret, Dr. Barber?" The gist of her response went as follows:

We look at our shared goals and then run experiments. Just about anything is okay to experiment with as long as it is legal, moral, and doesn't violate any of our core values and goals. When someone suggests something that I think isn't great but doesn't do any harm, I usually suggest that we run an experiment. Then I sit back, provide the support they need, and allow us all to learn from the results. When things go well with the student, we learn. When things go poorly, we learn. Regardless of the outcome of the initial experiments, we move closer to finding strategies that people can agree on and that work with the unique child in question. The biggest challenge for me is to remember the importance of using patience and empathy as people navigate this challenging process. The rewarding part is that we often bond with each other during the journey.

What might happen if you applied this wisdom to making decisions about parenting your kids? This "goof and grow" approach might help you bond and learn from each other rather than fighting so many battles.

Action Steps

- Remember that conflict over different parenting styles does far more damage than different parenting styles.
- Practice active listening skills with your spouse (and your kids).
- Recognize any ANTs about the other parent and challenge any beliefs that are contributing to conflict.
- Take responsibility for your part in the parental power struggle.
- Stretch out of your comfort zone and be a leader in reconnecting with your partner.
- Review your shared goals for your children and let that drive your behavior.
- Commit to following this rule in your household: When person A has a problem with person B, person A works it out with person B. Person C stays out of it except for providing occasional consultation.

CHAPTER 11

REACHING THE UNDERACHIEVING CHILD

If your child lacks motivation, be curious, not furious.

Underachievement is one of the most complex challenges facing children, parents, and schools, and it can have devastating effects on a young person's sense of self-worth and mental strength. Too often, parents start with the assumption that the child is simply being lazy. Then these well-meaning adults often resort to practices that make the problem worse. These include:

- Threats, lectures, and reminders
- Punishment
- An excessive focus on remediating weaknesses at the expense of nurturing strengths
- Providing consequences that restrict the child from healthy social and physical activities

Those approaches look like they should work, and decades of parents and teachers have used them. In fact, those tactics may yield some positive short-term results. In the long run, though, they make underachievement worse by creating resentment, dependency, entitlement, anxiety, and hopelessness. Those practices also lower feelings of self-competence, especially with kids who are dealing with problems related to learning, family and peer relationships, mental health, and other deeper issues. As perceptions of self-competence diminish, so does motivation and social and emotional health.

Years ago, a book written by Dr. David Sousa called *How the Brain Learns*[1] heavily influenced Dr. Fay. From it, he was reminded of something he'd seen for decades in his own children and the students he taught. In essence, humans are born with a built-in drive to explore, learn, and master (curiosity), and a built-in system for rewarding curiosity and mastery when it happens. For instance, watch a toddler discover ways to play. They might find a set of blocks and start stacking them. When the blocks topple over, they will likely try again. Nobody told them to do so. The toddler just responded to their brain's desire for achievement and closure. The question, "I wonder if I can do this?" begins to dominate their minds.

We're all born with "I wonder" thinking, and it drives our natural curiosity about how the world works. When you allow youngsters to learn and explore in a safe environment, it promotes even more curiosity, experimentation, innovation, and the joy associated with success. Their brain provides a variety of feel-good chemicals, largely dopamine, that serve to reward their efforts. Curiosity becomes king, as they naturally begin to see that it leads to accomplishment and delight. In 1954, psychologist Abraham Maslow wrote about this discovery without the benefit of modern brain-imaging technology.[2] Observing thousands of people for decades, he developed a robust theory concerning the needs that must be met before we feel safe enough to experience academic achievement, creativity, and innovation (all categorized as "self-actualization"). Dr. Fay's adaptation of Maslow's pyramid keeps the original progression of needs but with descriptions that more closely reflect how these needs must be met for children and teens today. Start at the bottom of the pyramid where the most basic needs are. When the first level of needs are met, then the brain moves onto the next level of need. Fulfillment at each level is required for progression to the next.

From the day your child is born, you start meeting their most basic physical and safety needs, as well as bonding through love and acceptance. This sets up your child for curiosity and learning. As they grow, sadly, intrinsic motivation can get derailed in the lives of too many children. Anxiety, insecurity, and fear—associated with family challenges, dangerous neighborhoods, physical illness, permissive parenting, harsh educational methods, trauma, and other hardships—are the enemies that can strip away the joy of learning. When challenges related to physical, mental, or emotional survival confront the brain, the inborn drive for learning takes a back seat to meeting the more pressing survival needs. That's when children may go into a mode of self-preservation, interrupting the natural process of the curiosity-learning-reward cycle. This may sound scary; that's why understanding the progression of needs your child has will help you. Your efforts at home affect whether your child succumbs to anxiety, insecurity, and fear or faces them with confidence and competence.

Self-Actualization
Morality, creativity, spontaneity,
problem-solving, lack of prejudice,
spiritual focus & growth

Esteem
Healthy beliefs about the connection
between effort & achievement, confidence,
motivation to achieve, respect for self & others

Love & Belonging
Parental affection, encouragement, opportunites
to contribute to the family, opportunities to make decisions &
to experience freedom, loving discipline

Safety
Physical protection; emotional protection through supervision, limits &
appropriate boundaries; protection from the harmful effects of social media

Physiological Needs
Clean water; healthy food; shelter; protection from
disease, toxins, excessive exposure to screens; clothing; and more

Anxiety and the Brain

Deep within the brain are important structures called the amygdala and basal ganglia, which play a role in setting the body's anxiety level among other functions. Our brain-imaging work at Amen Clinics shows that when there is too much activity in these areas, people tend to be more anxious, tense, nervous, and fearful. They are also more likely to freeze in stressful situations, avoid conflict, and be excessively fearful of criticism or judgment from others. Lack of sleep, a high-glycemic diet (e.g., sugary breakfast cereals, candy, and chips), caffeine, alcohol, marijuana, skipping meals, and believing negative thoughts without challenging them can exacerbate anxiousness. See chapter 13 for natural ways to calm your brain or your anxious child's brain.

NINE TIPS FOR RAISING AN ACADEMICALLY SECURE AND MOTIVATED CHILD

Tip #1: End the control battle.

As soon as a control battle begins, anxiety increases and academic motivation decreases. As soon as power struggles start, the bond we have with our kids weakens. Glancing back at the pyramid of needs, it's easy to see how control battles could damage many aspects of our children's development. Let's consider how a parent might end a war that's been going on between them and their child over learning. Keep in mind that the following conversation is effective with kids as young as early elementary school all the way to adulthood. Of course, you may decide to change the wording based on your child's age and ability. This is also not a "one and done" conversation; it's simply the start of an overall program to end hurtful power struggles.

PARENT: I need to apologize to you, son.

CHILD: For what?

PARENT: I love you so much that I've forgotten that you are the only one who can decide what type of life you will lead.

CHILD: What do you mean?

PARENT: Can anyone make you take advantage of school so that you have the knowledge and skills required to have an easier life as an adult?

CHILD: No.

PARENT: That's right. You call the shots. I've been making the mistake of thinking that I can make you decide to choose an easier life. This has gotten us into a lot of arguments, and I'm truly sorry about that.

CHILD: You're always nagging me about school.

PARENT: Yes. I've done way too much of that in the past. Now I'm realizing that my job is to offer help, not to try to force you to get good grades. I will love you regardless of whether you take advantage of school and learn things that make your life easier—or you don't and end up having a more challenging life. I will love you the same either way. Just let me know how I can help.

Take a moment and consider the basic needs met by the parent in that exchange (love and esteem). What would happen to the overall tone of the home? Is there far less anxiety in the air?

It may seem that this parent is giving away a large amount of control. In truth, they are giving away the power they never had.

Tip #2: Transition responsibility for learning to your child.

Whose learning are we talking about? Is it yours or your child's? Obviously, you can't do school for your kids. While true, this doesn't stop many parents from taking way more ownership in their kids' learning than their kids do. Do you fall into this large category of well-meaning parents who are consistently working harder on their child's education than their child is? What are the underlying, yet powerful messages sent when you make this mistake? It communicates to your child that they aren't capable and that they don't need to take responsibility for the challenges they encounter because someone else will do it for them. Stop this harmful pattern as early in elementary school as possible. The longer it goes on, the harder it becomes for you and your child. Below is a parent-child dialogue that many parents have used as a guide. Like so many examples in this book, change the wording based on your child's age and ability:

CHILD: You need to email my teacher and let her know that there is no way that I can get all of this work done by the end of the week.

PARENT: It sounds like you are feeling really overwhelmed.

CHILD: Yeah! Isn't that obvious?

PARENT: What do you think you are going to do? Would you like some ideas?

CHILD: You need to talk to her.

PARENT: Honey, whose schoolwork are we talking about here? Is it mine or yours?

CHILD: Well . . . it's just too much for me to handle.

PARENT: I'm happy to share some ideas about how you might talk with your teacher about this. I'm even happy to go with you as you talk to her.

CHILD: What am I supposed to do?

PARENT: Being a kid is hard. I feel for you. I will always be willing to help you as long as I never feel like I am working harder on your learning and grades than you are. Let me know what you decide to do. If you would like to hear what some people decide to do, please ask.

When you take this smart but often scary leap, what should you expect? Mistakes. It's that simple. The child will make more mistakes because they have been handed a new and significant responsibility. Don't panic. This is part of the learning process and offering shared thinking. When you hand your kids the responsibility of taking primary responsibility for their learning, they will make plenty of affordable mistakes, but they will also be free to make many wonderfully great decisions. This meets many of the esteem and self-actualization needs and gives your child a sense of freedom (shared control). Do they also experience feelings of competence when they see that they can learn from their mistakes? Do they feel love and belonging when we can remember to respond to their errors with empathy rather than anger?

Tip #3: *Respond with empathy and reasonable, logical consequences.*
Anger shuts the door on learning. Empathy opens the door to learning. Anger implies that the problem is ours. Empathy allows it to remain our child's. Empathy, in and of itself, assists in meeting most of the needs for love and belonging. It calms anxiety, and it helps us communicate that we understand our child's feelings. Let's see how this works:

> PARENT: Thanks for showing me your report card. I can't imagine how disappointing this must be for you.
> CHILD: You're just mad at me!
> PARENT: I sure hope that you can see that I'm not. I just feel bad for you.
> CHILD: It's not fair. All of my teachers have attitudes . . . like they don't even care.
> PARENT: Please let me know how I can help. Remember. I will always love you . . . good grades or not.

Sincere empathy is essential. So is reasonable, logical accountability. You have two choices when it comes to creating accountability: Will you be motivated by the desire to use consequences as a way of punishing your child into being a better student? Or will you be motivated by the desire to simply help them develop an accurate view of life's struggles and how they can overcome them? The first motivation will lead to disappointment on your part, as well as damage your relationship. The second maintains your relationship while giving your child a chance to see that they can solve the problems they create. Below are two brief parent-child interactions illustrating the flavor of each.

> PARENT: These grades are completely unacceptable. What's it going to take to get you to start taking school seriously? There will be no more video games until I see your grades improving.

While this parent's basic approach may seem reasonable, their tone is all about their own anger and their own need to control the situation. Let's consider how this might unfold in a way that depicts the parent as an ally rather than an enemy.

PARENT: How are you feeling about these grades?

CHILD: I don't know. It's no big deal.

PARENT: I can imagine that it's hard to admit how discouraging this can be. I'd like to help.

CHILD: What can you do?

PARENT: I've been learning a lot about technology use lately and how kids who spend a lot of time on screens, playing video games and doing social media, have a harder time doing well in school.

CHILD: Oh great! Here we go. I guess you're just going to take everything away.

PARENT: I'd like to experiment with seeing if it helps to shorten the amount of time you spend on these things. Would you like me to decide how much less time you have, or do you have some ideas about that? If so, I'd like to hear them.

CHILD: You're just punishing me!

PARENT: I can see how it might feel that way. I hope for your sake that you can see that my desire is to help . . . not make your life horrible. I love you.

The parent is being kind while holding their child accountable. By being a participant in problem-solving, their child is far more likely to develop a sense of competence than a kid who is held accountable through punishment. Experiments can lead to discoveries that build self-competence and wisdom. Feelings of competence will leave them feeling more hopeful and motivated to tackle the other challenges they face.

Tip #4: Follow some guidelines for helping with homework.

Successful parents care about their children's homework, and they follow some basic guidelines for helping in productive ways:

Guideline #1: Help as long as your child wants it from you. Too often we force help on our kids without offering them the option of declining it. A sense of control is an important emotional need. If you ask, "Would you like me to help you with that?" and they respond no, honor their request, yet keep the door open by saying, "If you change your mind, please let me know."

Guideline #2: Help only when your child can prove that they listen to their teacher. Quite frequently, children will tune out in class and then get one-on-one help from a parent at home. Before automatically helping, ask, "What did your teacher tell you about this? How did she describe this?" If your child responds by acting clueless, reply with, "I will help you when you can share some things about how your teacher described doing this. Maybe you can ask her about it tomorrow."

The child may answer, "But it is due tomorrow."

You can reply, "That's sad. If any kid can get through this, you can."

The price of a child doing poorly on a homework assignment here and there is worth the benefit of them learning to listen more carefully to their teachers. If you sense that the teacher is not explaining things clearly, the first step is to coach your child on how to talk to the teacher about the problem. The last resort is getting involved and communicating directly to the teacher. When you enable your kids to solve most of the challenges they face, they become mentally strong and resilient people.

Guideline #3. Help only as long as there is no anger or frustration. The goal is to develop and maintain positive feelings around learning. As soon as a pattern of frustration or anger rears its ugly head, it's time to say, "I help as long as we are getting along and enjoying each other. It seems like this is something you might visit with your teacher about." Even if this means that your child gets a poor grade on the assignment, it's worth it to avoid an ongoing pattern of negative schoolwork-related interactions.

Guideline #4: Help in brief segments, so that they can see themselves succeeding. Something interesting begins to happen when a parent or teacher consistently sits with a student as they guide them through the learning process. Each time the child is guided to success, they begin to reason, *I experienced these good feelings because some adult helped me.* It takes relatively few repetitions for them to believe that they can only achieve success when an adult is nearby.

A better approach involves guiding your child a bit, moving away to do some other task, guiding them a little more, moving away again, and hoping that they will discover the solution when you are not nearby. When this happens, they have an opportunity to see that they can learn without constant help, which builds their internal motivation. While a true art form, great parents gradually develop the intuitive sense of when a child is about to have a "learning moment" and put some distance between themselves and the child.

Tip #5: Let school be school and home be home.

As parents of a child with learning disabilities, Dr. Fay's parents were inundated with notes and calls from his elementary school about his behavior and

lack of work production. Along with notes and calls came makeup assignments, possible consequences he should experience, and plenty of extra activities to remediate Charles's learning problems.

Being the concerned and compliant parents they were, they did their
best to follow the recommendations. Charles was home from school around
3:00 p.m. By 3:10 he was busy completing worksheets and complaining to
his mother that he couldn't do most of them. Trying to help, she started with
calmly explaining, progressed to swallowing her frustration, and eventually
she lost it around 5:00 p.m. in a flood of lectures and tears. Dad was home
by 5:45, and he began drilling Charles on multiplication facts, mathematical
orders of operation, and the basics of grammar, which were his weaknesses
and part of the school's remediation plan. Still on the agenda was the fact
that Charles had thrown his math book on the floor during class and yelled,
"Long division sucks!" Completely drained, the only thing his parents had
the energy to do was yell, "You threw your book at school. That earns you
early bedtime!" The only good that came out of all of that was his father was
motivated to research more effective strategies and to eventually develop the
Love and Logic approach.

Let's imagine how Dr. Fay's parents' old strategy might work for Tammy.
She's an adult struggling with her new job and quite stressed. "Tammy, I love
you," her husband, Jon, says as she walks through the door after a hard day.
He continues with concern. "I talked to your boss today, and he mentioned
that many of your computer skills are lacking."

Tammy is astounded. "He talked to you? Why did he do that? That's crazy.
Besides, he is never clear about what he wants me to do, and I wasn't aware
that I would need to learn a program for computing multilinear equations!"

Jon continues, "You don't have to get so defensive. We are just trying
to help. Your boss sent me some links to tutorials that will really help you
improve on your missing skills. I'll be happy to sit down with you and see if I
can help. He also mentioned that you failed to get one of your reports done,
so it looks like we won't be going to the beach this weekend."

Without a doubt, this approach would fail with spouses. It works no
better with kids. Home needs to be a sanctuary, where children can enjoy
their family, recharge their batteries by doing things they are good at, and rest.
Homework and academic remediation should take up relatively little of their
home life. We agree with many other experts who recommend this general
guideline: 10 minutes of homework per grade level per evening. Of course,
this may differ slightly, depending upon the subject matter and the child's
ability. Most important, remember that kids grow when they are challenged

but not stressed. They also develop in healthy ways when they have time to participate in other beneficial activities, including exercise, play, fun discussions with family members, meals with family, and age-appropriate chores. Besides, research conducted on the benefits of homework has clearly revealed that it has very small positive effects on academic achievement until students reach high school where they are studying more complex subjects, such as chemistry, physics, and advanced mathematics.[3]

Maintaining a distinction between what happens at school and what happens at home is also important for parents who homeschool. Parents need predictable times when they can take respite from the role of teacher, and kids need these times to take a break from the role of student. Work these times into your schedule each day, and stick with them—even when school time hasn't gone well and your child has struggled to complete their work. Dr. Fay and his wife, Monica, chose to homeschool their youngest son, Cody, who was born quite a few years after his two older brothers, who attended public schools. Monica learned early on that it was important to maintain a consistent schedule that was similar to what Cody would experience if he attended school outside the family home. School was over at the same time each day. Now that their son is in college, Dr. Fay often recalls those homeschooling days and feels extremely grateful for her wisdom in this regard. He says she has taught him many wonderful things over the years.

While it's wise to establish healthy boundaries between what happens at school and what takes place at home, it's unrealistic to suggest that kids will never have homework or need help on assignments. It's also unrealistic to think that your kids will never encounter a teacher who assigns too much homework. When this happens, refrain from saying or doing anything that contributes to your kids having less respect for the teacher in question. Instead, first help your child learn to advocate for themselves by offering suggestions and practicing with them how to talk to the teacher. Doing so provides your child with an opportunity to learn that they can respectfully advocate for themselves. If your child is younger, say elementary school age, it's smart to schedule a meeting with the teacher and accompany your child in a supportive way. This means allowing your child to do most of the talking while filling in the gaps when needed.

Teaching is an incredibly challenging profession, and most teachers admit that they occasionally err by assigning homework that takes too much time. When kids and parents approach them in grateful, graceful, and goodhearted ways, teachers are usually willing to make adjustments.

Tip #6: Celebrate their strengths often.

As Dr. Fay often mentions, nothing is more demotivating than a constant diet of constructive feedback. When we say, "constructive feedback," we're referring to criticism. Feedback becomes truly constructive only when it comes from someone we trust, someone who believes in us, and someone who understands we are far more likely to work on new habits when we are loved and appreciated for our strengths. The basic principle goes as follows:

Build them up in their areas of strength so that they are willing to take risks in their areas of weakness.

People don't take risks for people they don't trust or respect, but they're often willing to walk through fire for those special people who've constantly communicated, "You are the apple of my eye. I believe in you!"

As you know by now, Dr. Fay struggled in school as a kid. He struggled a lot. In fact, most of his early life was spent reviewing flashcards, practicing grammar, reviewing the multiplication table, and memorizing spelling lists. It didn't work. He was still a below-average student, becoming less motivated by the day. About that time, his father attended a motivational speech that changed his mind. The speaker said, "Help your kids discover their God-given talents. Put most of your focus on these talents. Train them up in such a way that they focus on these gifts, rather than their weaknesses. Teach them to live in this way, to gift others with their gifts, and they will find joy in the work."

His entire perspective on motivation, education, and parenting was turned upside down by this revelation. So much so that he hugged Charles tightly one day and encouraged him to spend most of his energy pursuing his gifts and much less energy fighting with his weaknesses. Charles's greatest gift was the ability to fix just about anything that broke. Pursuing that, he became a mechanic and spent a couple of years after high school repairing Oldsmobile cars. (Their quality control was horrible at that time, so he found great satisfaction in helping customers who'd had the misfortune of buying them.)

From this, Charles realized that he could learn and be productive. He also discovered that helping others was immensely rewarding. As time passed, he attended college and graduate school, graduating with top honors. Somehow the mechanical gifts God had given Charles unlocked other gifts that were not yet expressed, such as the ability to explain higher level statistics to young graduate students on the verge of nervous breakdowns. On one occasion one of those students slid his book off a table in a fit of frustration. Dr. Fay was able to whisper, "This is tough stuff, but you have what it takes to do it." He'll never forget the student's surprised and sheepishly thankful look.

When you begin to adopt a gift-focused approach, chances are that your children will experience a profound level of relief and growth when they are allowed to build their lives around their gifts. Their anxiety will lift, and they'll be free to discover and pursue their dreams.

Tip #7: Set effective limits.

Children with permissive parents are far less likely to succeed in school.[4] That's a scientific fact. This makes sense when we consider the pyramid of needs and remember that limits mean safety and limits mean love. Although we covered limits in chapter 5, the limits we are talking about are not just limits over schoolwork, homework, or grades. Instead, they are also limits over respect, chores, keeping us aware of their location, acceptable behavior while playing sports or engaging in other extracurricular activities, food, bedtime, and other daily issues. These daily limits, most of which look like they have nothing to do with academic motivation, have a lot to do with meeting your child's need for safety and structure.

One of the most important sets of limits involves the use of digital devices, particularly with kids who are struggling in school. We implore parents to provide a nearly screen-free home when they have children suffering from these problems. In fact, Dr. Fay suggests that parents request homework and other assignments that do not require the use of the internet or digital devices. Handwritten essays are a good example. Math largely done with a small calculator yet no computer is good for kids. Those types of activities reduce the overstimulation and anxiety that so often hinders the academic success of fragile learners. Once these youngsters experience some success and their brains begin to heal, gradually reintroduce them to learning with the help of digital technology.

Tip #8: Teach them to think like high achievers.

Early in his career Bernard Weiner, one of America's leading social psychologists, became fascinated with the thinking patterns of high- versus low-achieving research subjects, observing that high achievers often attributed both their success and lack of success to factors within their control.[5] These factors included amount of practice or preparation, amount of effort, degree of perseverance, and so on. Conversely, he noticed that low-achieving subjects attributed performance to factors beyond their control, such as luck, quality of instruction, inborn ability levels, or task difficulty. Those who attribute their performance to factors beyond their control will lack motivation to improve or stick with difficult tasks. Conversely, those who attribute their performance to changeable qualities will be far more motivated to improve their skills and persevere.

More recently Stanford University scientist Dr. Carol Dweck identified a similar pattern, as well as data supporting the notion that these attribution styles can be learned.[6] From her research, she discovered that subjects receiving consistent nonspecific feedback, such as "You are so smart" or "You are so bright" were more likely to give up or avoid difficult tasks. In essence these children were trained to attribute their success to high ability, a factor often viewed as genetic and fixed. Consequently, when they found themselves facing tasks requiring more skill, they gave up, assuming that they could do nothing more. In contrast, subjects who received specific feedback related to their effort, such as "You worked hard" or "You kept trying" were more likely to persevere and to attempt more difficult tasks in the future. In her wonderful book, *Mindset: The New Psychology of Success*, Dweck articulates this helpful distinction between the "Fixed Mindset" and "Growth Mindset."

Concurrent with Dr. Dweck's research, we've identified similar patterns in the underachieving students we've seen. Based on these observations of achievers and underachievers, we created the following process for teaching kids to think like high achievers:

- *Step 1: Catch the child doing something well and describe it in very specific terms.*
  Example: "You completed math problem number nine correctly."

- *Step 2: Ask the child, "How did you do that?"*
  Important: Resist the urge to praise the child with something like, "You are so bright" or "That's great!"

- *Step 3: Provide a menu of three possible reasons for success.*
  1. "Did you work hard?"
  2. "Did you keep trying?"
  3. "Have you been practicing?

  Note: all of these represent attributions to effort, so it doesn't matter which one the child chooses.

- *Step 4: Ask them to tell you what they believe is responsible for their success.*

We believe that children are far more likely to internalize a belief when they speak it. This is why I recommend doing whatever you can to get your child to choose and to say aloud one of these three reasons for success. Similar to the way the mind takes what it sees and makes it happen, which we described in chapter 2, the brain also uses what it hears to turn it into reality. Dr. Fay has even been known to smile at a child who is not sure and ask, "Well, if you did know which one it was, which would it be?" One bright little girl responded to his request to share why she was successful on her spelling test. Giggling, she replied, "You are silly! All three of those reasons are the same." Then she continued, "I guess if I had to pick one it's because I've been practicing."

Kids are far happier when we use this approach than when we provide praise focused on their brightness, smartness, or giftedness. Perhaps it's because such praise carries along pressure to perform, which many children find overwhelming. Remember: Anxiety is the enemy of motivation. When children begin to feel that they cannot measure up to our perceptions of them, it doesn't take long for them to shut down. In contrast, when they know that we simply love them for who they are, they are free to explore, make mistakes, and turn those mistakes into the type of learning that shapes their lives in positive ways.

Tip #9: Look for underlying causes of underachievement.

If you've tried the strategies in this chapter but still aren't seeing increased motivation or achievement in your child, don't beat yourself up and don't get angry with them. Be curious, not furious. Investigate what might be causing the problem. A biological condition or brain health issue may be at play. That's what happened to Dr. Fay. As mentioned in the introduction, when he was just starting school, he got Rocky Mountain spotted fever, a bacterial illness from infected tick bites. The most common symptoms include a fever, headaches, and a rash. He had them all, but he also felt like the sickness was making it harder for him to think clearly and tougher to learn in school. He was right. What his parents and he didn't know at the time is that tick-borne diseases, including Lyme disease and others, can lead to cognitive and psychological issues. For example, Lyme disease has been associated with impaired attention and focus, slower mental processing speed, poor problem-solving, depression, and other issues.[7] That's likely why all the coaching and helpful strategies didn't help Charles. He was still falling flat in terms of achievement because of the effects of the disease. When he got healthier, he was able to tap into his motivation and become highly productive and more successful.

Tick-borne diseases are just one form of health issue that might be contributing to underachievement. Other such issues include:

- ADHD
- Dyslexia
- Irlen syndrome (a visual processing problem often seen in kids and adults with low motivation)
- Mold exposure
- Long COVID
- Undergoing anesthesia
- Eating a poor diet

Diagnosing and addressing these issues can be the key to overcoming stubborn underachievement. See chapter 13 for more help for brain health issues when nothing is working.

IT'S ALL ABOUT CHARACTER

The proportion of chronic academic difficulties that stem from legitimate disabilities interfering with the learning and development of academic skills pales in comparison to the percentage caused by basic character problems, such as lack of self-control, difficulty managing emotions, lack of experience with struggle and perseverance, lack of connection and contribution to the family, problems accepting limits, etc. When Dr. Fay's first son was struggling with learning math in second grade, his teacher was an older, wise woman with over 35 years of experience. Dr. Fay will never forget her words: "Teach Marc to be a good man. That's even more important than reading, writing, and arithmetic. If you do this, he will always find a way to be successful."

Dr. Fay took the teacher's advice and placed most of his focus on teaching his son how to work hard on his chores, treat people nicely, wait for what he wanted, and experience thankfulness. As the years passed, Dr. Fay noticed that his son still struggled in school, but he was becoming a kind and responsible man. As an adult, his son has discovered that treating his wife, his coworkers, his customers, and everyone else with dignity is what it means to be successful. When we raise kids who know how to treat others well, do what they say they will do, and take responsibility for their mistakes, the odds are high that success will take care of itself.

Action Steps

- Give up trying to control what is out of your control.
- Transition the responsibility for learning to your child.
- When your child underachieves, respond with empathy.
- When kids, especially younger ones, are at home, let them focus on "homework" such as helping with cooking, learning about how to fix things around the house, and other fun and interactive activities.
- Before diving in to help your child with school homework, ask them if they want your help.
- Focus on your child's strengths rather than harping on their shortcomings.
- If kids are struggling in school, set limits on screen time.
- When your child does have success, ask them what helped them do well, such as working hard, trying multiple times, or practicing.
- If nothing is working, look for underlying biological conditions or brain health issues.

CHAPTER 12

TECHNOLOGY MISUSE AND ADDICTION

No screen-locking device or parental control function
is as effective as parental supervision.

Technology is wonderful when used for good. "I love the fact that I can use my phone to conference with coworkers and clients from almost anywhere on the planet," Dr. Fay says. "I'm crazy about the fact that I can use it to keep an eye on my 16-year-old's whereabouts as he's driving. I'm extremely thankful for the woman who resides in my phone, always willing to guide me turn by turn to where I need to go. Without her, I'd be lost. Technology is awesome, and we are fans of it."

Most people agree that technology can be terrible when misused. Like a chainsaw, it can make life far easier when used with extreme care yet cause great injury when misused. A growing body of research suggests that heavy tech usage—phones, internet, social media, video games—is associated with increased risk for anxiety, depression, impulsivity, substance abuse, and more.[1]

TECHNOLOGY CANNOT ENTIRELY SOLVE OUR PROBLEMS WITH TECHNOLOGY

Some parents think the solution to technology problems involves more technology, such as parental controls, monitors, and such. These can be helpful, and we recommend that you do everything within your power to monitor and control your children's devices. Dr. Fay has worked with many parents who think they've got the phone, social media, and gaming situations under control only to discover that their child bought a secret "burner" phone or some other device.

One of the biggest challenges we face is that our children have more time and energy than we do. They're not working full-time jobs, trying to complete tax returns, driving multiple kids to activities, and doing all of the other things required to keep a family going. Our kids also have an army of bright consultants willing to share their expertise on simple workarounds for monitoring and blocking programs: their friends and the mind-numbing quantity of blogs and web posts sharing strategies for sabotaging the safeguards we work so hard to provide.

Tech safeguards can provide a false sense of security for many busy parents. Something similar happened in the early 2000s when aircraft flight management systems became so advanced that pilots began to rely on them over their hands-on aviation skills. By 2013, this issue had become a major safety risk, brought home by the crash of Asiana Airlines flight 214. Approaching San Francisco International Airport too low, it hit the seawall. Three passengers were killed in the crash, and hundreds more were injured. The National Transportation Safety Board concluded that the pilots "over-relied on automated systems that they did not fully understand."[2] The incident sparked a major change in pilot training.

What's the moral to that story? Technological safeguards can be good, but there is absolutely no substitute for solid supervision and parenting skills. Listed below are six tips that can help you and your kids navigate these turbulent issues without creating unwinnable power struggles and rebellion.

Tech Tip #1: Strengthen the prefrontal cortex. A strong PFC is essential for impulse control, so make sure your child is developing habits that enhance PFC function. We have covered this in other chapters, but here's a quick recap of PFC boosters:

- Setting goals with the One Page Miracle
- Adequate sleep
- High-intensity exercise
- Prayer or meditation (yes, even small children can learn to meditate)
- A healthy diet with protein at every meal
- Finding meaning and purpose

Tech Tip #2. Focus on building relationships. The stronger your bonds with your kids, the more influence you will have to keep them from falling into a digital black hole. A key contributor to this connection also has to do with the extent to which you've discussed the principles of addiction (coming up on pages 232–238). When we have the courage to broach challenging topics with our tweens and teens, it communicates that we love them and trust them enough to handle deep and important issues (a sign of shared control). Our primary job is to listen to their opinions, knowing that they will often say things that they don't really mean. Why so? One of their prerogatives as teens is to test the trust level of our relationship with them. When we listen without judgment, we pass the test. When we start to issue edicts or argue, we make it more likely that they will find a need to do something stupid.

PARENT: It seems like a lot of teens get pulled into giving away too much information about themselves online. What do you think?

TEEN: I don't know what you're talking about.

PARENT: Well, they tell strangers where they live, they take pictures of themselves and their stuff, and they even talk about where they like to hang out.

TEEN: It's no big deal. Everybody does it.

PARENT: (*calmly and sincerely*) So everybody does it. It's no big deal.

TEEN: That's what I said.

PARENT: I wonder if some of the teens online are actually adults posing as teens, trying to find out where kids live?

TEEN: You worry about everything way too much.

PARENT: (*still calm and sincere*) So you think that I worry too much.

TEEN: Well, you're always talking about this stuff.

PARENT: Why do you think I do that? Is it because I love you, or because I don't love you?

TEEN: (*smiling*) You're so annoying.

PARENT: (*smiling and hugging his kid*) Thanks. I take that job very seriously. See you after school.

This interaction between father and son could have turned into an argument and a power struggle. Dad did the right thing by resisting the urge to debate and choosing to listen. Interestingly, when you do that, teens tend to come around to your point of view, even when they can't admit it to you (or even themselves).

Tech Tip #3. Model the behavior you want your kids to adopt. Be a good role model in terms of limiting the use of tech devices. Rather than sitting on the couch next to your child while you scroll through your social media feed, say something like, "Let's go do something together that doesn't involve technology." Initially you may hear a lot of moaning and see a lot of eye-rolling. Don't let this stop you. Get on those bikes (be sure to wear your helmets to protect your brains) and ride, play catch, do some maintenance on the car together, or go for a walk. As you do, express your love for your child while ignoring any nasty attitudes. If you make this a consistent habit and find activities that your child truly likes to do, they will eventually stop acting as if the sky has fallen.

Tech Tip #4. Set firm and loving limits. Effective limits build and maintain positive relationships while also providing boundaries to keep your kids safe and healthy. Both sides of this coin are essential. It's the bond you have with them that will largely determine whether they learn to accept your limits or rebel. Kids who view their parents as allies are far less likely to be the ones who openly defy them or lie and become sneaky.

Clearly, maintaining the balance between remaining firm and staying loving is no easy task. First, remember that all healthy parent-child relationships require boundaries that the adult provides. Especially with technology issues, kids need the very same limits they often protest the most. Being loving doesn't mean allowing them to do what they *want*; it means giving them what they *need*. Second, keep in mind the supreme importance that many of us, especially young people, place on technology.

Dr. Fay once asked a young girl, "How important do you think smartphones are to most people your age?"

She responded with a gasp, "It's like they are more important than air!"

With that context in mind, communicate tech limits in loving, sincere, and dignified ways. Most of what we communicate comes through our tone of voice and body language. While a loving attitude does not mean that your child will respond with enthusiasm, it will model the behavior you desire and increase the chances that they will gradually mature toward seeing you as an ally rather than an enemy.

TECHNOLOGY MISUSE AND ADDICTION • 231

Listed below are some examples of important technology-related limits. Notice the message of love, concern, or empathy woven into each:

- "I love you. You may enjoy your devices as long as you are pleasant with me when I ask you to shut them off."

- "I love talking with you and seeing your expressive eyes. Thanks for waiting until after dinner meals to use your phone."

- "We all need someone who cares enough about us to watch over us. That's why I will allow you to keep your devices as long as I have access to them with the passwords."

- "It seems like you are like a lot of us who struggle with feeling anxious, edgy, or even angry when we have too much screen time. That's why I'm asking you to take a break so that we can enjoy each other's company."

- "I understand that this is frustrating to you, but I believe in allowing kids to have phones when they are at least 13 and appear to be ready for the responsibility."

- "I find myself being very concerned about kids who are allowed to have their devices with them in their rooms all night. That's why I expect that you place yours in the basket on my nightstand by 8:00 p.m. each evening."

Again, the fact that these limits are tempered with love does not mean that your child will not try to argue with you about them. Respond consistently by calmly repeating, "I love you too much to argue about this. What did I say?"

Tech Tip #5. Provide good supervision. Some parents make the mistake of thinking that once their kids reach their tween or teen years, they've got the tech situation figured out. Wrong! Kids at these ages need even more supervision than toddlers, particularly when it comes to digital devices. Kids need us to search their rooms from time to time or do surprise checks on their phone. They will protest it. Nonetheless, they desperately want us to love them enough to protect them from others—and themselves. One of their deep needs is to see that we are strong enough to set and enforce limits.

Teens are testers. They test our intentions, they test to see if we are sincere or hypocritical, and they test to see if we are willing to remain firm to our commitment to supervision. Track their cell phone. Track their car (newer cars come with the ability to be tracked, but you can also equip older cars with a tracking device). These tools can play an incredibly helpful role in our supervision, as long as we make it clear that they are always enabled and functioning.

A parent recently shared how her teenage son's phone would suddenly stop showing his location about the time he happened to be within a five-mile range of his girlfriend's house. Apparently this is a "glitch" affecting almost every teen's electronics. As soon as they enter any form of temptation zone, they flip off location services or the entire phone. This parent, being savvy with teens but not so much with tech, shared this with her son: "It looks like your phone, tablet, and even your car is unsafe. It would be best if these stayed at home in my room and the garage. That is, until I can figure out why they keep failing."

Of course, the mom eventually "discovered" that nothing was wrong with her son's devices and that "PFC Error" was the main culprit.

Tech Tip #6. Provide loving accountability. If you see your child getting overly obsessed with their tech gadgets, their PFC making bad choices, or they are being victimized, step in. It might go like this:

FATHER: Son, I'm really concerned. It seems like you're getting addicted to that phone, and the only way we're going to know for sure is if you don't have it for some time.

SON: You can't do that! That's not fair! I need it for school.

FATHER: What did I say, son?

SON: When do I get it back?

FATHER: I'm not sure. It will depend on how well you follow the rules of our home, your general level of respect toward us, and how well you use your time in general.

The natural response for many teens is to become angry, attempt to deflect blame, and argue. Remember these two goals: Be firm, and be kind.

BASIC PRINCIPLES OF TECH ADDICTION

Technology firms are big businesses, highly motivated to build profits, and have invested tremendous resources into studying and applying the science of addiction. Habitual use of their products supports their financial bottom line. When you understand the basic principles of addiction, you can better help your children learn its dangers and how to avoid it. You can also spot addiction in yourself and take the steps to remain the role model you want to be.

Tech addiction is brain-based. At Amen Clinics, we have treated many teens with video game addictions. One teenager became violent whenever his parents limited his play. We scanned his brain while he played video games and then later after he had been away from them for a month. It was as if we were looking at the brains of two different people. The video games caused abnormal firing in his left temporal lobe, an area of the brain often associated with violence. When he was off video games, he was one of the sweetest, most polite young men we had met.[3]

In simple terms, a network of brain systems drives us to seek out experiences that bring us pleasure—whether that's scrolling through social media, eating a hot fudge sundae, or petting the dog. The PFC helps keep unhealthy urges in check by putting on the brakes when we are about to engage in risky actions or behaviors that don't serve us. A strong PFC provides impulse control and good judgment to fight cravings. The problem, as you may recall, is that the PFC is not fully matured until the mid- to late twenties, while the drive systems have already developed. This gives the drive systems the advantage, and they can overpower the PFC. This means tweens, teens, and young adults are more vulnerable to developing unhealthy habits and falling into addictive behavior—and brain-imaging research proves it.[4]

Thrill seeking and avoidance. Addictions develop under some identifiable conditions: First, the substance or activity is highly stimulating or allows the user to escape from some aspect of their life that feels dull or painful. How many children, teens, and adults are extremely susceptible to this because of anxiety, depression, or the lack of connection they are experiencing? In our clinical practices, we see many who use gaming, social media, and other digital distractions to escape from social or family pain. This is one of the many reasons why it is so important to stay close to your teens, doing your best to keep a finger on the pulse of their emotions. If you are feeling stressed or unhappy about conflict in your family, it's a sure bet that your kids are too. Don't ignore your feelings. Your children's will likely be the same. Get guidance now so you can restore your family to a place of health and peace—a place where your kids get their needs met far more effectively than through interaction with their devices.

Unpredictability. Another principle is the unpredictability of the desired thrill or escape. Slot machines operate according to this principle, delivering payouts on an unpredictable basis. That's why some people will sit for hours, believing that the next coin they deposit will yield the jackpot. Believing this, often referred to as the "gambler's fallacy," leaves them emotionally chained to a machine, devouring their time and their hard-earned money. Will the next

YouTube video or Instagram post make you laugh or learn something new? It can keep you—and your fully mature adult brain—hostage for hours, wading through a lot of nonsense. So imagine the impact this can have on your child's developing brain. The gambler's fallacy can interfere with brain health, development, and decision-making. The famous behavioral psychologist B. F. Skinner discovered this basic principle of conditioning. Observing that lab animals were far more likely to develop very strong learning when they received rewards on an unpredictable basis, he coined the term "intermittent reinforcement schedule."[5]

FOMO (fear of missing out). This shackles many digital device users to their keyboards and screens.[6] Social media isn't the only contributor to FOMO. Even a simple online search leaves the user mostly encountering uninteresting content. After a random number of clicks, however, they eventually find something exciting or interesting. Video games are designed in the same manner, keeping the user wondering how many moves or how much time will be required to advance to the next level? Checking and responding to phone calls and texts is another example. FOMO plays a role in the destruction and death we see happening on our roads and highways, as both teens and adults feel compelled to immediately check texts, listen to voice messages, and answer calls while driving.

Teach your children about why people do some of the things they do and how they can be controlled or manipulated. This provides your kids with the awareness of who's trying to make choices for them. One bright high school student responded to a discussion about this with anger: "I don't like being controlled by anyone—even my parents. I guess they are supposed to do it, but my phone? That's another thing. It sucks that they treat us like lab rats just to make more money."

Interestingly, abusive relationships also operate this way. While unknown to most abusers, their peaceful *and* painful actions operate in an unpredictable fashion. Victims walk on eggshells, never knowing what will come but often believing that if they can crack the code to the abuser's behavior, the abuser will start treating them nicely: "Maybe today will be the day when I find a way to measure up and gain his approval." This misguided hope is often why someone stays in a toxic, hurtful relationship. Below, we will discuss how to help kids understand online relationships that operate in this way.

The need for attention. People who feel important and valued only when they are noticed easily fall prey to obsessive, unhealthy social media use. They post pictures of themselves constantly, comment incessantly, and often contribute to unpleasant drama through a need to stir the pot so attention comes back to them.

Where do you and your kids find your satisfaction? A bit of being seen and sharing the exciting details of your life is healthy and relational. Too much creates an insatiable quest to be the center of attention. Since this unhealthy behavior can elicit just enough online accolades to trigger a dopamine rush, it's easy to see why so many people become addicted to it. Before long those who idolize them unwittingly lead to their despair. Celebrity comes at a cost. Some can keep it in perspective. Others become chronically anxious and depressed.

That's why it's so important to help your children develop a purpose beyond their own needs rather than seeking to make themselves the center of attention. Only a healthier source of satisfaction will last a lifetime. The other will only last as long as they are young, attractive, or extremely socially relevant.

Guide your children also toward developing perspective. It can help them understand that being bored or experiencing disappointment with the performance of their tablet does not qualify as a crisis. It can help them see that they have the power to find meaning in other ways and that personal peace comes not from the things they heap up, but the people they help up. This perspective also helps them develop a sense of gratitude. When they get in the habit of looking at the bigger picture and attending to the needs of others, the positive aspects of their lives will come into sharper focus. This perceptual habit does not come naturally for many people. Instead, it requires practice and help from those who love us enough to gently yet assertively guide us toward focusing on the positive.

Desire based on social comparison. The dangerous desire to always want more was born far prior to digital technology. Since people covet with their eyes, all that's required is an enticing image. Enhanced images of beauty, shiny new gadgets, toys, Pokémon characters, and "new and improved" features draw in kids of all ages—making them want more stuff, more beauty, more money. Both girls and boys see images and ads and compare themselves with what others have. Unfortunately, many become addicted to pursuing impossible, impractical, and unhealthy goals. Every family needs to discuss this issue and ask these important questions: Are we content with what we have? Are we basing any of our worth and self-esteem on having certain possessions or comparisons with standards that aren't real?

Evil. This a big, bad four-letter word. To some it connotes battles in the spiritual realm. Some find it so distasteful that they don't believe it exists. Without a doubt, though, there are people whose behavior is sadistic and opportunistic. These individuals prey particularly on teens but sometimes on adults and seniors. And the nature of the online world makes it so much easier to be exposed to predators. They use manipulation to leave teens feeling excited and hopeful—then shamed and fearful. Once this happens, the victim often becomes addicted to the fantasy that they can please the manipulator and once again become adored and special in their eyes. The sadistic opportunist keeps the teen on the hook, giving just enough affection and praise to keep them involved.

These evil people are masters of disguise and often seem like the best thing since the invention of the refrigerator to tweens and teens. So we must help our children spot the cycle of manipulation and be cautious about who they interact with online.

Do not allow children of elementary school age or younger to access the internet without your supervision or the supervision of an adult you trust. As they become young teens and have earned a bit more freedom, be sure to teach them to recognize signs of manipulation or predatory behavior. The most common tip-off is that the manipulator begins to make the victim feel excessively special in some way. Perhaps they praise the music they've posted, or their ideas about a certain subject, or their fashion, their attractiveness, or the car they drive. This meets a need for love, belonging, and esteem. With more accolades from the perpetrator comes more interest and intrigue from the victim, even as the perpetrator becomes progressively hurtful and opportunistic. This is when a manipulator begins to pull young and old alike into schemes, stripping them of their dignity, their money, their hope, and sometimes their lives.

You've probably read news on children and teens who've been manipulated into posting inappropriate photos of themselves. Then the perpetrator demanded money to keep things quiet. Tragically, the young person is so overwhelmed with guilt and shame that they become depressed and afraid.

Just this week Dr. Fay had a discussion with his 16-year-old son about a tragic case of a teen who fell prey to this form of extortion. Tragically, the situation ended in his suicide. The child could have been yours. Every parent needs to discuss this danger with their children. Our kids need to know that such things happen, and even more important, that nothing in heaven or earth would cause us to love them less if they got caught in an online problem and came to us admitting they needed help. One useful preventative strategy: search for "scams targeting teens" online. Many reputable sites can open everyone's eyes to what's out there. One of our favorites is komando.com. Sit at the dinner table and read some of this information with your kids and talk about what they can do to protect themselves (shared thinking). The best prevention is knowing that such things can happen to anyone.

Uncharacteristic behavior. Addiction may cause someone to do things we didn't believe they would ever do. For example, surely our kids would not get so obsessed with an online group that they would divulge their personal information, take life-threatening challenges, or arrange to meet someone they don't know. Surely our kids would not share compromising pictures of themselves or their friends. This could never happen.

Denial lurks in the shadows of every heart.
It's hiding in ours, and it's hiding in yours.

Surely our teen would not allow themselves to be ridiculed, abused, and bullied by others. They would stand up for themselves. They would never become so depressed that they would attempt to end their lives. They would have the strength to simply stop going online to be abused.

That's also denial.

Mom and Dad would never "update" their banking information by filling out an online financial form, requiring them to provide their account numbers, dates of birth, social security numbers, and other highly sensitive information. They are too smart for that.

Another case of denial.

When someone becomes clinically addicted to a substance, their reaction can be much more extreme, even violent. In one case, an 11-year-old Indiana boy shot and injured his father when he discovered that his collection of video games was confiscated.[7] In another incident, a 16-year-old shot his father and killed his mother when they refused to let him play a violent video game.[8] Unfortunately, these tragic cases are just a sample of serious incidents taking place when kids (and adults) become addicted to technology use. This is why we must prepare ourselves for any reaction, particularly if our child has a significant history of serious behavior problems and brain health issues. It may be essential to seek professional consultation. A skilled counselor can provide invaluable assistance in planning and implementing an accountability session, as well as following up with the needed inpatient and at-home treatment. Yes, sometimes kids need to enter a behavioral health program to receive the assistance needed to conquer their unhealthy dependence on digital technology. A good program can also help them heal any brain health and psychological issues that have contributed to the problem. The reSTART program is one of our favorites, run by a staff very familiar with the Love and Logic approach. Learn more about this very helpful resource by visiting restartlife.com or calling 800-682-0670.

You now possess an extreme advantage in raising kids who are able to navigate a world of technology without being consumed by it. One parent admitted, "With the advice of a trusted psychologist, we felt it necessary to remove access to all of my son's video games and online gaming. He was furious. When we removed the door to his bedroom, this made him even angrier. We felt it necessary because he kept closing and locking it, keeping us unaware of what he was doing in there. As the months passed, he slowly became the boy we remembered. He started to go outside, and he started to have real friends. He began to laugh at the dumb jokes shared by his grand-father, and he even went fishing with his dad. They had a good time. The first 'good time' they'd had together in years. The other day he thanked me. We were riding in the car, and he said, 'Mom, I was so mad at you guys for taking all of my games away. Now, I'm so thankful. Now I know that I was out of control. I love you.'"

Action Steps

- Strengthen your child's prefrontal cortex by encouraging physical exercise.
- Work on bonding with your child by listening to them without judgment.
- Be a good role model—put down your phone when you are with your kids.
- Create a general rule regarding limits on tech devices for everyone in the household.
- Don't forget to supervise your kids. Do spot checks on their phone.
- Be prepared to take your child's phone away or seek professional help if they're becoming addicted to it.

CHAPTER 13

WHEN NOTHING SEEMS TO BE WORKING: HELP FOR BRAIN HEALTH ISSUES

Mental health is really brain health.

Whenever Dr. Amen gives lectures, people from the audience approach him afterward to share personal stories. One woman, Sarah, was crying when she came up to him. Through her tears, she told Dr. Amen that she was having trouble with her teenage son, William. He had been diagnosed with ADHD years earlier and had done better on medication, but as he got older, he refused to take it. He said he didn't want to have to take pills and that he just wanted to be normal like the other kids his age. Without the medication, William was on the verge of flunking out of high school, his room looked like a cyclone had just passed through, he impulsively said rude things to Sarah to get a rise out of her, and he wouldn't follow through on anything his mom asked him to do. Sarah was at her wit's end and thought she was a terrible parent.

Sarah told Dr. Amen she was surprised to hear him say on a public television show that most people will have a mental health—or rather, a brain health—problem at some point in their lifetime. In fact, it's more normal than not having a problem. He'd often tell his patients, "Normal is a myth." Sarah recorded the show and later showed it to her son. When William realized how common it is to have an issue with mental health and that mental health issues are really brain health issues that steal your mind, he agreed to start taking his medicine again. He did much better, and Sarah's parenting strategies were much more effective. Her life was less stressful, she didn't feel like a failure, and she and William developed a closer relationship.

If you have been working diligently to put the parenting concepts in this book into practice, but your child is still misbehaving, creating conflict,

239

lacking motivation, procrastinating, underperforming at school, having trouble making friends, or having other problems, a brain health issue may be the culprit. Psychiatric issues and learning disorders—all of which are actually brain health problems—are rising among the more than 73 million kids ages 0 to 17 in the US.[1] Just look at these statistics:

- 75 percent of all brain/mental health issues begin before age 25.[2]
- Nearly 50 percent of children who struggle with brain/mental health issues are unidentified and receive no treatment.[3]
- 46 percent of students with a brain/mental health issue drop out of school.[4]
- 65–75 percent of jailed teens have a brain/mental illness, including brain injuries.[5]
- 57 percent of teen girls in 2021 report feeling persistently sad and hopeless (a nearly 60 percent increase since 2011); 29 percent of teen boys report the same persistent sadness and hopelessness.[6]
- Suicide is the second leading cause of death, behind accidents, among teens ages 15 to 19.[7]
- 30 percent of high school girls in 2021 report seriously considering suicide in the year prior.[8]
- 24 percent of high school girls in 2021 made a suicide plan.[9]
- 13 percent of high school girls in 2021 say they actually attempted suicide.[10]
- The three percentages cited above for teen girls are roughly double what teen boys reported.[11]
- 86 percent of teens know someone with a brain/mental health issue.[12]
- Over 86 percent of teens say mental health is an important topic.[13]
- Over 84 percent say there is a stigma surrounding mental health.[14]

Although approximately half of all brain/mental health issues show up by the mid-teens,[15] most children aren't diagnosed and don't receive treatment until several years after symptoms first appear. This is not surprising because most parents aren't experts in the differences between "normal" and "abnormal" behaviors, emotional health, or brain and mental wellness. Parents are usually only exposed to their own children, their nieces and nephews, and their kids' friends. So, when a youngster seems consistently down in the dumps, constantly worries, or acts aggressively, it's natural to assume it's just your child's nature or that they have an attitude problem. If you misread an underlying brain/mental health issue as an attitude issue, your knee-jerk reaction may be to increase discipline and consequences, which may be harmful. Many kids who have brain/mental health problems are actually trying hard to do what Mom and Dad ask, but they just aren't able to do it because of the way their brain is wired.

If your child is consistently struggling at school, routinely having trouble getting along with others, or frequently losing their temper, take a moment and ask yourself, "Could this be a sign of something else?" If you have a feeling that your youngster or adolescent may have a behavioral, emotional, or learning issue, don't wait. Bring up any concerns with your child's pediatrician or other healthcare provider. Small issues that remain untreated can morph into big problems. On the flip side, early intervention can put a halt to unwanted issues and can improve your child's future. In some cases, simple lifestyle changes or nutritional supplements may be all they need. If you're noticing problematic behaviors or emotional issues, it's important to get your child on a brain-healthy program sooner rather than later.

When these issues remain untreated, they can have lifelong consequences that make parenting exponentially more difficult. In the short term, these issues are associated with increased family discord, academic underachievement, and more. Over time and into adulthood, they are linked with increased risks of school dropouts, traffic accidents, substance abuse, job failure and unemployment, financial problems, obesity, divorce, and suicidal thoughts and behaviors. It's critical to be aware of the signs and symptoms of common brain/mental health problems and to seek professional help when necessary. After working with thousands of children, we can assure you that seeking treatment for brain/mental health and learning problems is not a sign of weakness; it is a sign of strength and love for your child.

THE FOUR CIRCLES APPLY TO MENTAL HEALTH TOO

In chapter 1, we introduced you to the concept of the Four Circles of Mental Strength, which include biological, psychological, social, and spiritual factors. These same four circles also play an important role in your child's—and in your own—brain/mental health. When the four circles are balanced and strong, it enhances kids' brain/mental well-being and their ability to make good decisions, follow the family rules, finish what they start, and get along with others. However, problems in any of the four circles can contribute to psychiatric illnesses, behavioral issues, and learning disorders. Check out this quick overview of issues that can fuel problems.

Biological factors

When there is too much activity or too little activity in the brain, or there is damage to regions in the brain, it is associated with increased risk for problems. Anything that hurts the brain (such as the BRIGHT MINDS risk factors mentioned in chapter 1) can negatively influence mental health. As a quick example, let's look at blood sugar levels, which have a strong impact on brain function.[16] Dr. Amen once treated a child actor who was constantly getting into trouble for fighting. Testing his blood sugar level revealed that it was very low on a routine basis. Low blood sugar levels are associated with a loss of self-control and can also produce feelings of anger, as well as anxiety or depression.[17] An important element of his treatment plan was to eat small meals that included protein four times a day to help keep his blood sugar more balanced. The result? He no longer picked fights and stopped getting in trouble.

Psychological factors

The way we think, talk to ourselves, and view ourselves has a major influence on our well-being. Additional psychological factors that play an important role include a child's upbringing, development, successes or failures, sense of self-worth, and sense of control over their own life. Trauma is one of the biggest negative influences on your child's mind. (See Adverse Childhood Experiences on the next page.)

When a child is chronically exposed to traumatic experiences—such as the death of a loved one, parents going through a nasty divorce, or living through a pandemic—it can cause changes in the brain that can lead to challenges with self-control, emotional regulation, social skills, learning, and more. The COVID-19 pandemic has had a significant effect on an entire generation of kids and adolescents. Alarming research shows that brain/mental health-related emergency room visits for children ages 5 to 11 jumped 24 percent, and 31 percent for those between the ages of 12 and 17.[18] Surprisingly, a family history of trauma can also fuel problems in children. Adverse experiences alter a person's genes, which can then be passed down to the next generation. This is referred to as generational or ancestral trauma. For example, a child whose grandparents survived a major trauma, were alcoholics, or survived a major loss is at greater risk for mental health issues.

Adverse Childhood Experiences (ACE) Questionnaire

From 1995 to 1997, the CDC and Kaiser Permanente conducted a large-scale study involving over 17,000 adults to investigate the prevalence of adverse childhood experiences (ACEs) and any long-term consequences.[19] This groundbreaking research found that approximately one in five of the study participants had been exposed to three or more of the eight ACEs included in the original study. The ACE questionnaire has since undergone some minor modifications and currently includes 10 questions covering adverse and traumatic childhood experiences.

Scores range from zero to 10, with zero indicating no exposure and 10 meaning a person was exposed to significant levels of trauma prior to 18 years of age. The higher the score, the higher the risk for long-term physical and mental health consequences. Please answer Yes (Y) or No (N) to each question for yourself and for your child to get an idea of how trauma may be impacting you.

1. Before your 18th birthday, did a parent or other adult in the household often or very often swear at you, insult you, put you down, or humiliate you? Or act in a way that made you afraid that you might be physically hurt? _____

2. Before your 18th birthday, did a parent or other adult in the household often or very often push, grab, slap, or throw something at you? Or ever hit you so hard that you had marks or were injured? _____

3. Before your 18th birthday, did an adult or person at least five years older than you ever touch or fondle you or have you touch their body in a sexual way? Or attempt to or have oral, anal, or vaginal intercourse with you? _____

4. Before your 18th birthday, did you often or very often feel that no one in your family loved you or thought you were important

or special? Or your family didn't look out for each other, feel close to each other, or support each other? _____

5. Before your 18th birthday, did you often or very often feel that you didn't have enough to eat, had to wear dirty clothes, and had no one to protect you? Or your parents were too drunk or high to take care of you or take you to the doctor if you needed it? _____

6. Before your 18th birthday, was a biological parent ever lost to you through divorce, abandonment, or other reason?

_____

7. Before your 18th birthday, was your mother or stepmother often or very often pushed, grabbed, slapped, or had something thrown at her? Or sometimes, often, or very often kicked, bitten, hit with a fist, or hit with something hard? Or ever repeatedly hit for at least a few minutes or threatened with a gun or knife? _____

8. Before your 18th birthday, did you live with anyone who was a problem drinker or alcoholic, or who used street drugs?

_____

9. Before your 18th birthday, was a household member depressed or mentally ill, or did a household member attempt suicide? _____

10. Before your 18th birthday, did a household member go to prison? _____

SCORING

Add up the number of yes responses you have and enter it here: _____. This is your ACE score.

Social factors

Does your child have strong bonds with family and friends, or do they lack deep connections to others? Are they happy at school, or is it a source of pressure or problems? Are their stress levels too high? When a child's everyday life or relationships are filled with stress, it affects their needs for love and belonging and raises the risk of brain/mental health problems. Loving relationships boost the brain by triggering the release of a neurochemical called oxytocin, which enhances bonding and trust. Higher levels of oxytocin are associated with less anxiety, stress, and fear, while low levels of the neurochemical may play a role in depression, autism, and other psychiatric issues.[20]

Spiritual factors

The concept of spirituality goes beyond a belief in God to include your child's sense of meaning and purpose, values, and morality. Whether your child feels connected to the past (such as with grandparents), to future generations, to the planet, and to the world as a whole influences their spiritual health. Without any form of spiritual connection, people are more likely to feel as though their life has no meaning, which increases the likelihood of issues such as depression, addictions, and in some cases, suicidal thoughts.

SIGNS AND SYMPTOMS OF COMMON BRAIN/MENTAL HEALTH ISSUES IN KIDS

This section will introduce you to some of the more common mental health issues seen in children along with the signs and symptoms that can help you recognize them. You will also discover some natural strategies to help support the brain and improve symptoms.

Attention Deficit Hyperactivity Disorder (ADHD)

ADHD is characterized by a short attention span, distractibility, procrastination, disorganization, and poor internal supervision (such as problems with judgment and impulse control). Notice that hyperactivity is *not* one of the five hallmark symptoms. Children can have ADHD without hyperactivity, which can make it harder for parents to notice. Our brain-imaging work at Amen Clinics has helped us identify seven types of ADHD, and each type requires its own treatment plan. For example, stimulant medication, the standard treatment for ADHD, may help some types but will make other types worse. It's important to know your child's ADHD type to find the most effective treatments. (Take the free assessment at ADDtypetest.com for more information on the ADHD types.)

ADHD Symptoms in Kids
- Inattention
- Being disruptive in class
- Picking fights with siblings or schoolmates
- Easily distracted
- Waits until the last minute to start chores or homework
- Misses deadlines
- Chronic lateness
- Messy room and desk
- Doesn't learn from mistakes
- Impulsivity
- In constant motion—fidgeting, jumping, roughhousing

Natural Strategies That Help All Types of ADHD
- Eliminate artificial dyes, preservatives, and sweeteners from the family's diet.
- Minimize or eliminate processed foods (anything in a box).
- Try an elimination diet for three weeks, eliminating sugary foods, gluten, dairy, corn, soy, and other categories of potentially allergenic foods. Then add these back one at a time and watch for reactions to them, which would indicate that your child should permanently avoid that food.
- Boost exercise to 45 minutes four times a week.
- Increase sleep and good sleep habits.
- Decrease screen time.
- Work closely with an integrative physician to check ferritin, vitamin D, magnesium, zinc, and thyroid levels, as well as all the other lab chemistry tests, and balance any that are not optimal.

- Neurofeedback: This noninvasive, interactive therapy helps children strengthen and retrain their brain to achieve a more focused state.
- Individualized Education Plan (IEP): If needed, consider seeking an IEP to provide appropriate accommodations at school.
- Start kids a bit later in school (the youngest kids in class are more likely to be diagnosed with ADHD).
- Provide nutritional supplements, such as:
  - EPA-rich fish oil 1,000 mg/day of EPA+DHA per 40 pounds of body weight, to maximum 3,000 mg/day EPA+DHA
  - Phosphatidylserine (PS) 100–300 mg/day
  - Zinc as citrate or glycinate 30 mg (34 mg/day for adolescents, less for younger kids)
  - Magnesium as glycinate, citrate, or malate 100–400 mg/day

If a child truly has ADHD, they will still have it in a few months, so taking some time to get their brain health/mental health optimized is worth the investment before starting a medication that they may be on for years or even decades. After that, then consider nutraceuticals or medications targeted to their specific type of ADHD. (see *Healing ADD: The Breakthrough Program That Allows You to See and Heal the 7 Types of ADD* by Daniel G. Amen, MD.)

In the case of ADHD, which has been one of Dr. Amen's primary areas of expertise, there is a great deal of negative bias against medication. He's heard countless parents say:

"I'm not going to drug my kid."

"If you take this drug, you won't be creative."

"You won't be yourself."

The problem is that most physicians assume ADHD is one thing, so they start everyone on the same class of medications—stimulants, such as Ritalin or Adderall. These medications help many who have ADHD, but they also make many others much worse. Both miracle and horror stories about stimulants abound. One of Dr. Amen's own children went from being a mediocre student to getting straight As for 10 years while using a stimulant medication to optimize the low activity in her prefrontal cortex, and she was accepted to one of the world's best veterinary schools. The medication stimulated her frontal lobes (the area of the PFC), giving her greater access to her own abilities, which also enhanced her self-esteem. On the other hand, Dr. Amen had another patient who was referred to him because he became suicidal on Ritalin. His brain was already overactive to start, so stimulating it only made him more anxious and upset. The problem is that physicians assume everyone with the same symptoms has the same brain patterns, which is just not true and invites failure and frustration. When medication is needed, it is more effective when it is targeted to the type of ADHD.

Anxiety Disorders

All kids feel anxious from time to time. It's completely normal to get the jitters before a test, giving a speech at school, or on the first day of class. As we mentioned in chapter 11, making sure your child's basic needs are met can alleviate a lot of anxiety. When anxiety becomes nearly constant, however, or it is so overwhelming that it prevents your child from performing up to their potential or keeps them from participating in activities, it may be an anxiety disorder. Many parents misinterpret anxiousness or physical symptoms as complaining or whining and react in a negative way to their child, which can exacerbate the problem. Anxiety is the most common mental health condition in the US, affecting more than 9 percent of all children, and that number jumped 29 percent from 2016 to 2020, according to a 2022 study in *JAMA Pediatrics.*[21] Rates of anxiety have soared even higher due to the pandemic, so it's a good idea to be aware of any signs of this condition. Brain imaging shows us that there are seven types of anxiety (and depression), and it's important to know which type your child has.

Anxiety Symptoms in Kids
- Frequently feeling anxious or nervous
- Excessive worrying
- Being easily startled
- Avoids conflict
- Heightened muscle tension
- Headaches and stomachaches
- Being excessively shy or timid
- Easily embarrassed

Natural Strategies That Help All Types of Anxiety

- Eat small meals and healthy snacks: Hypoglycemia (low blood sugar), which can occur when skipping meals or eating too many refined carbohydrates (think candy or baked goods) is a common cause of anxiousness, so give small meals and healthy snacks to your kids throughout the day to maintain balanced blood sugar levels.
- Deep belly breathing: Teach your child to inhale for four seconds, hold it for one second, exhale for eight seconds, and repeat 10 times to help them learn to self-soothe quickly.
- Hand warming: Teach children to visualize holding a cup of hot cocoa, which can warm their hands, counteract stress, and help with relaxation.
- Get rid of ANTs: Teach your child to challenge their anxious and worrisome thoughts (see chapter 7).
- Calming exercise: Doing yoga or taking a walk in nature can have a relaxing effect.
- Hypnosis: Powerfully soothing, hypnosis can help shift a child's state of mind from anxious to calm.
- Neurofeedback: This non-invasive technique uses EEG (electroencephalogram) biofeedback to measure brainwaves in real time to help retrain the brain to achieve a healthier, more balanced state of mind. If you're interested in exploring this treatment, look for a licensed mental health professional who is trained in neurofeedback.
- Nutritional supplements, such as:
  - L-theanine 100–300 mg
  - GABA 125–500 mg
  - Ashwagandha 125–600 mg
  - Magnesium as glycinate, citrate or malate 100–400 mg

Mood problems and depression

All kids feel sad or hopeless at times. When a beloved family pet dies, when a school friend moves away, or when a child doesn't get selected to be on a sports team or in the school play, it's common to experience sadness, despair, or worthlessness. But when low mood persists for weeks or months, it could be a sign of depression, which increased by 27 percent in kids from 2016 to 2020, according to the *JAMA Pediatrics* study mentioned earlier.[22] This means nearly 3 million children are affected by depression, but the number has increased since the pandemic. Here are some of the signs that a child may be experiencing depression.

Depression Symptoms in Kids
- Feeling sad, hopeless, or helpless
- Lack of interest in hobbies or activities they used to enjoy
- Feeling fatigued
- Changes in appetite—eating substantially more or less food than usual
- Sleeping a lot more or less than usual
- Difficulty concentrating
- Appearing to lack motivation
- Having body aches and pains
- Irritability
- Engaging in self-destructive or self-injurious behavior (including suicidal thoughts and behaviors)

Natural Strategies That Help All Types of Depression
- Encouraging children to question their ANTs (see Dr. Amen's book *Captain Snout and the Super Power Questions*)
- Being in nature—walking or playing outside
- Adequate sunshine—or using a bright light therapy lamp during winter or on dark days
- A diet high in fruits and vegetables
- Working with an integrative or functional medicine physician to optimize your child's thyroid, folate, vitamin D, and other levels
- Eliminating processed foods, artificial dyes, preservatives, and sweeteners
- Trying an elimination diet for three weeks (See the ADHD section for more detail.)
- Exercise
- Nutritional supplements, such as:
  - Saffron 10–30 mg

- Curcumin 100–400 mg
- Zinc as citrate or glycinate 30 mg (34 mg/day for adolescents, less for younger kids)
- Omega 3 fatty acids EPA+DHA 1,000–3,000 mg. (Dr. Amen is convinced that without these nutritional fixes, children are unlikely to respond to medications.)

Depression can be devastating, but too often people are put on SSRIs (selective serotonin reuptake inhibitors) in a quick office visit before attacking the underlying cause. SSRIs are often hard medications to stop and have been shown to make some children worse. If the above interventions are ineffective, then it's time to try other nutraceuticals or medications targeted to their specific type of depression (see Dr. Amen's book *Healing Anxiety and Depression*).

Obsessive-compulsive disorder (OCD)

OCD is characterized by unwanted, unpleasant recurrent thoughts that cause worry, shame, guilt, and/or compulsions that interfere with daily life. The most common repetitive behaviors involve counting, handwashing, checking, and touching. Children with OCD, which affects 1 to 4 percent of the population,[23] feel the need to perform these behaviors in a strict or rigid manner according to certain self-imposed rules. A child with a counting compulsion, for example, might feel compelled to count every crack on the pavement on the way to school. What would be a five-minute walk for most people could turn into a one-hour trip for the kid with OCD. These kids have an urgent sense of "I have to do it" inside.

Dr. Amen has treated many people with OCD, the youngest of whom was 5 years old. This young boy had a checking compulsion, and he had to check the house locks at night as many as 20 to 30 times before he could fall asleep.

OCD Symptoms in Kids
- Obsessive thoughts
- Compulsions—counting, excessive handwashing, etc.
- Excessive or senseless worrying
- Overfocused tendencies
- Oppositional—their favorite word is *no*
- Argumentative
- Holding grudges
- Getting upset when things don't go their way

- Unhealthy perfectionism
- Being upset when things are out of place

Natural Strategies to Help All Kinds of OCD
- Make sure to check for underlying infections, such as strep, post-COVID, or Lyme disease. Pediatric autoimmune neuropsychiatric disorders associated with strep (PANDAS) and pediatric acute-onset neuropsychiatric syndrome (PANS) associated with other infections can cause new-onset OCD symptoms. See the next section.
- Eat a diet higher in complex carbohydrates: Foods like sweet potatoes and garbanzo beans can help increase levels of serotonin.
- Avoid high-protein diets: These diets increase focus and can exacerbate OCD symptoms.
- Behavior therapy: This helps strengthen the prefrontal cortex so it can calm overactivity in the anterior cingulate gyrus.
- Distraction: When you notice your child getting stuck on worries or behaviors, distract them by singing a song with them, taking them for a quick walk, or playing a game.
- Nutritional supplements may help, such as:
  - 5-HTP 50–300 mg
  - Saffron 10–30 mg
  - St. John's wort 300–900 mg

PANS and PANDAS

Eric was a good-natured kid until he turned 5. Suddenly, he developed intense rages and a strange tic, shrugging his shoulders and jerking his head to one side. His parents took him to a psychiatrist, which eventually led to other doctors and several diagnoses, including ADHD, OCD, oppositional defiant disorder, and others. When Eric's parents brought him to Amen Clinics, he was taking numerous medications, which weren't working. Following a complete evaluation, including SPECT scans and lab work, Eric got a different diagnosis: PANDAS.

Pediatric autoimmune neuropsychiatric disorders associated with streptococcal infections (PANDAS), which are considered a subset of pediatric acute-onset neuropsychiatric syndrome (PANS), are mental and behavioral issues that occur suddenly following an infection. Considered controversial in traditional psychiatry, PANS/PANDAS are very real conditions, and they affect an estimated 10 percent of children diagnosed with OCD or Tourette's syndrome. The primary characteristic of PANS/PANDAS is sudden acute and debilitating onset of neuropsychiatric symptoms. Bacterial and viral infections that are associated with PANS/PANDAS include:

- Strep
- Mononucleosis
- Lyme disease
- Epstein-Barr virus
- Mycoplasma pneumoniae (walking pneumonia)

Researchers are currently investigating if there is a relationship between infection with COVID and PANS/PANDAS. Treating the underlying infection is critical for the healing process.

PANS/PANDAS Symptoms in Kids
- OCD
- Restrictive eating
- Intense anxiety panic attacks or new phobias
- Inattention and/or hyperactivity
- Vocal or motor tics
- Depression and/or suicidal thoughts and behaviors
- Anger or aggression
- Oppositional behavior
- Sensory sensitivities
- Behavioral regression
- Decline in math and handwriting abilities
- Trouble sleeping
- Bedwetting
- Symptoms associated with autism
- Psychosis
- Decrease in school performance

Natural Strategies to Help PANS/PANDAS
- Eating a brain-healthy diet: Fueling the brain with nutritious foods can be beneficial.
- Reducing exposure to toxins: Avoiding toxins that further harm the brain is important.
- Stress management: Helping kids learn to self-soothe can be helpful.
- Work with a PANS/PANDAS expert clinician for more strategies.

Brain and mental health issues are treatable, including those described here as well as oppositional defiance disorder, autism, bipolar disorder, post-traumatic stress disorder (PTSD), schizophrenia, eating disorders, and more. Early intervention can make a major difference in the trajectory of your child's life, so don't wait for symptoms to go away. Seek help when you need it.

WHEN TO SEEK PROFESSIONAL HELP

So how do you know when it's time to get help? If your child's attitudes, behaviors, feelings, or thoughts interfere with their ability to be successful at home or at school, and when brain-healthy habits and Love and Logic principles have not helped alleviate the problem, seek professional help. In addition, if symptoms impede your child's ability to function, be productive, or feel joy, then they need help. If you understand some of the signs to look for, then you'll also know when something is off with your child.

Finding a competent professional

Even those with the best parenting skills and brain-healthy habits struggle when they're up against the day-to-day stress of a child with a brain/mental health issue. Siblings are often embarrassed by the child's behavior, and parents often feel guilty. Getting professional help is crucial to a healthy outcome for the child and the rest of the family. Finding the right healthcare provider is even more important.

Eight Steps to Find the Best Mental Health Professional

1. *Get the best person you can find.* Don't rely on a therapist solely because he or she is on your managed care plan or has an affordable rate. That person may not be a good fit for you or your child. Saving money up front may cost you a lot in the long run. The right help is not only cost-effective long-term, but also saves unnecessary pain and suffering.

2. *Use a specialist.* Brain science is expanding at a rapid pace. Specialists keep up with the latest developments in

their fields, while generalists (family physicians) have to try to keep up with everything. If you had a heart arrhythmia, wouldn't you rather see a cardiologist than a general internist?

3. *Get referrals from people who are highly knowledgeable about your problem.* Sometimes well-meaning people give bad information. Dr. Amen has known many physicians and teachers who make light of brain system problems, such as ADHD, learning disabilities, or depression, and discourage people from getting help. One family physician told one of Dr. Amen's patients: "Oh, ADHD is a fad. You don't need help. Just try harder." Contact specialists in the field, people at major research centers, and people in support groups for your specific problem. Check out online medical support groups in your area. Support groups often have members who have visited the local professionals, and they can give you important information about doctors and providers, such as bedside manner, competence, responsiveness, and organization.

4. *Check credentials.* Physicians should have board certification. To become board-certified, physicians have to pass certain written and verbal tests. They have had to discipline themselves to gain specialized skill and knowledge. Don't give excessive credibility to the medical school or graduate school the professional attended. Dr. Amen has worked with some doctors who went to Yale and Harvard who did not have a clue about how to treat patients appropriately, while other doctors from less prestigious schools were outstanding, forward-thinking, and caring.

5. *Set up an interview to see whether you want to work with a certain professional.* Generally, you have to pay for their time, but it is worth the time to get to know the people you will rely on for help. If you sense the fit isn't good, keep looking.

6. *Many professionals write articles or books, or speak at meetings or local groups.* If possible, read some of their writing or

go hear them speak to get a feel for who they are and their ability to help you.

7. *Look for a provider who is open-minded, up-to-date, and willing to try new approaches.*

8. *Look for a provider who treats you with respect, who listens to your questions, and who responds to your needs.* You want a collaborative and trusting relationship.

It can be hard to find a professional who meets all of these criteria and who has the right training in brain physiology, but it is possible. Be persistent. The right caregiver is essential to helping your child heal.

Action Steps

- Accept that brain/mental health problems are common.
- Understand how the Four Circles of Mental Strength can have a negative or positive impact on your child's brain/mental health.
- Be aware that untreated brain/mental health issues can have significant long-term consequences on your child's life.
- Know the signs and symptoms of common brain/mental health issues in kids.
- Recognize that pediatric brain/mental health problems are really brain health problems.
- Try natural strategies as soon as you notice problems.
- If you suspect a problem, start by talking to your child's pediatrician.
- For treatment, seek a brain/mental health specialist who is well-versed in brain health.

PART 2

TIPS AND TOOLS FOR TURNING COMMON CHALLENGES INTO STRENGTH OF CHARACTER

The road to wisdom, strength of character, and faith is paved with potholes.
The drive is hard, but the destination is delightful.

Now that you have proven tools and techniques for raising respectful, responsible, and brain-healthy kids, we'll provide to-the-point tips for responding to common challenges. These include potty training, sibling rivalry, bullying, participation in sports, friendships/peer pressure, dating, divorce, and step-parenting. With the right strategies, you can overcome everyday challenges and turn them into learning opportunities that promote mental strength. When you approach common issues using brain-based techniques and love and logic, you can help your child become a better problem-solver, develop greater self-esteem, and shore up a can-do attitude. If your efforts aren't effective or you suspect that something more serious is causing issues, it's a good idea to check in with a mental health professional (as described in chapter 7).

CHAPTER 14

COMMON CHALLENGES: MAKING POTTY TRAINING A POSITIVE EXPERIENCE

Who knew teaching kids to use the potty could be so much fun?

Potty training can be frustrating for both parents and their little ones, but much of this turmoil is unnecessary when parents understand three things:

- The unhealthy messages we often get about the age when all kids should be trained
- The timing and trajectory of normal development
- How to apply the Love and Logic MAP to help kids enjoy the process

Inaccurate and unhealthy messages about potty training come from a variety of sources, including other parents, social media, blogs, and some so-called parenting "experts" who don't have the credentials or experience to back up their claims. Here are some of the most damaging messages.

- **Unhealthy message #1: All kids are the same.** The truth is that each child's biology and development is unique. Don't expect your second child to be on the same timetable as your firstborn. And don't assume your little one will develop at the same pace as your best friend's child.

- **Unhealthy message #2: It's a competition.** Think of those moms who put a sticker on their child's shirt saying, "I'm potty trained" as if it's some sort of status symbol. Most childcare providers can figure out pretty quickly whether a child has mastered this skill even without the child having a sticker.

- **Unhealthy message #3: It's a matter of the correct consequences.** Some parents think if you just punish the toddler enough, their bladder will cooperate.

- **Unhealthy message #4: It's just a matter of the correct rewards.** Occasionally using tangible rewards can be a fine way of shaping desired behaviors; however, they don't always work as planned. Keep in mind two things: (1) rewards will not speed up developmental readiness; and (2) rewards are rarely effective if they aren't accompanied by positive relationship messages. The greatest motivator is your love, encouragement, and enthusiasm.

These untruths lead to frustration for parents and kids.

In reality, there is a wide range of "normal" when it comes to the timing and trajectory of development. The average age for potty training in the US is 2 to 3 years old,[1] but some children begin to achieve success earlier or later than that. For example, research shows that girls typically achieve potty training two to three months earlier than boys.[2] Something to remember is that a staggering number of complex physical and neurological growth processes must happen before a child is ready. When we interfere with healthy development, often trying to rush the process, we introduce undue stress which often backfires by slowing development.

The development of potty skills is like the development of many others. Its progression is not smooth or linear. Your child may make rapid advances then reach a plateau or even regress a bit. This is normal. When you understand that, you are far less likely to panic, experience frustration, or get short with your child when lulls and backslides happen.

Learn to apply the Love and Logic MAP:

- Model healthy behavior
- Allow safe mistakes
- Provide empathy

Look at how one single mom turned things around with her daughter who was becoming resistant to using the potty. When Jessica came to Dr. Fay, she said that she had tried everything, including getting a bit stern with her daughter. Dr. Fay asked if being scolded made Jessica want to do something, or if watching other people have fun doing it would be more helpful. Dr. Fay suggested that Jessica model using the toilet and making it fun.

About a month later, Dr. Fay asked how it was going. Jessica said the new strategy was working. She was even having fun by making silly faces and adding sound effects. When she backed up to the toilet, she'd go, "Beep, beep, beep," just like a big truck in reverse. This made her daughter giggle and want to try it too.

"But there's a problem," she said. "Lack of privacy. Every time I go in there now, she's staring at me. But we're making some progress. The other day, she said, 'Mommy, do you need some privacy?' And I said, 'That's so sweet of you to ask, and yes, a little privacy would be nice.' So, she shut the bathroom door and kept staring at me."

The moral of this story is that this busy single mom kept things simple and fun by remembering that optimal development is fostered when children's physical and emotional needs are consistently met. She didn't let the unhealthy messages in the air around her lead her into practices that introduce cortisol (the stress response hormone) into the mix. Instead, she modeled the behavior for her daughter in a way that continued to build a bond of trust and affection that will last a lifetime. Here are potty-training tips to help you get started:

- Wait until toddlers are 2 to 3 years old to start potty training.
- Model the behavior, and make it fun. Sing songs, make funny sounds, clap your hands, or do something else that shows how much fun it is to use the potty.
- Use a doll to demonstrate how to use the potty.
- When your child successfully goes in the potty, celebrate!
- Set a schedule to help kids understand when it's time to use the potty.
- Avoid punishment. No amount of scolding will make a child's bladder cooperate.

- Teach your child to say "pee-pee" or "poo-poo" when they have to go.
- Don't make setbacks a big deal.
- Gradually transition from diapers to training pants to underwear.

What about bedwetting? Although enuresis, the medical term for nighttime bedwetting, is not a serious condition, it can be frustrating for parents. One study shows that roughly 30 percent of youngsters still wet the bed at age 4 ½, and nearly 10 percent of kids who are 9 ½ years old experience bed-wetting.[3] This can cause guilt and embarrassment in children that leads to issues with low self-esteem. Dr. Amen used to wet the bed as a child, and it filled him with shame. Every morning, he woke up in a panic wondering if the sheets would be soaked through. Stress and anxiousness are common triggers for bedwetting, and research shows that kids with ADHD are more likely to experience it.[4] For parents, the trick is to be patient and let your child's nighttime bladder control develop on its own time.

Do not get angry with your child or make them feel like it's their fault or that they're doing something wrong. This can be damaging in many ways. As an extreme example, look at Louis Peoples, who was convicted of murdering four people in 1997.[5] At Amen Clinics we scanned his brain, which showed abnormal activity in the prefrontal cortex consistent with drug abuse or head trauma. We also learned that he had a history of bedwetting that lasted into his teens. If he wet the bed, his parents would take the wet sheets and use them to tie him to a tree outside. Although this horrific punishment doesn't excuse his murder spree, it was extremely harmful to his brain health.

Several strategies help reduce the chances of bedwetting. For example, have your child stop drinking liquids in the evening and avoid any caffeine, which is a diuretic. Make sure your child urinates right before bedtime and once again if some time has passed before going to sleep. Moisture alarms may also be helpful. If bedwetting continues beyond age 7, consult your child's healthcare provider to rule out any underlying health issues such as sleep apnea or constipation. In some cases, medications may be helpful.

Action Steps

- Use the training tips that are most effective for you and your child.
- Keep it fun, and don't make it stressful for your child.
- Don't expect progress to be linear. Setbacks are common.

CHAPTER 15

COMMON CHALLENGES: SIBLING RIVALRY

As parents, we can't make brothers and sisters love each other,
but we can teach them how to respect each other.

Siblings can be best friends or seem like the worst enemies, and this important relationship either fuels the development of important social and emotional skills and self-confidence or breeds fear, resentment, anxiousness, and depression.[1] Good outcomes depend on understanding that sibling relationships can provide a safe and effective training ground for children.

When you view sibling rivalry as an opportunity for learning, you'll tend to be less panicked about making certain that your kids treat each other with kindness. In fact, sibling spats can build skills only when parents understand the steps required for children to learn:

1. Encounter a problem or conflict.
2. Struggle to solve the problem or conflict.
3. Limits and guidance provided by an adult.
4. More struggle with the challenge.
5. Eventual success due to the struggle invested.

The struggle, limits, and direction provide a framework for kids to develop solutions, which builds mental strength and healthy relationships. When you allow children to work through their conflicts, they tend to have far greater respect for each other in the end. (The same goes for adults.) Remember: It's not your job to make them love each other. It's your job to help them learn to cope with conflict and how to deal with people who are different.

Perhaps the biggest factor in the health of sibling relationships is how you model respect, forgiveness, and grace toward others. Let's remember, kids do eventually become more like us than we can imagine. That's why it's so important to model healthy self-care, calmness, and good boundaries as you respond to sibling eruptions. Here's how to help resolve sibling rivalry while promoting shared control and thinking:

1. **Celebrate each child's unique strengths.** Don't compare your kids with each other. They're individuals, and they need to see you respecting and loving them for their uniqueness. This also models what you hope they will do with their siblings. As we've emphasized frequently, the quality of your kids' relationship with you will influence every other relationship they encounter. If they love and respect you, they are far more likely to eventually learn to love and respect each other.

2. **Teach them that rivalry with you will not work.** Many instances of sibling rivalry are really instances of kids not respecting their parents enough to stop fighting when the parent asks them to. If your kids have not learned to comply with other simple requests, such as taking out the trash, cleaning their rooms, or washing and putting away the dishes they use, what are the chances that they will comply when you ask them to stop hitting or yelling at each other? If your kids have not been trained to listen, review chapter 6 on discipline.

3. **Take good care of yourself and let their interpersonal problems remain theirs.** You may be tempted to jump into the fray when your kids are bickering or fighting. This teaches that someone will always come to the rescue when they have, or create, a problem with someone else. A better tactic involves keeping the problem theirs to solve. Let's say that you're in the car and the kids are yelling, roughhousing in the back seat, and kicking the back of your seat. The dialogue may go something like the following:

PARENT: This is really sad. You guys have a problem you need to solve. You need to solve it because it is becoming a problem for me. What are you going to do?

KIDS: Yeah, but he called me . . . / But he's on my side! / She pinched me.

PARENT: What are you going to do to solve this problem? If you want some ideas, I'll be happy to share them with you. If this behavior continues, I'm going to have to do something about it when we get home.

KIDS: What are you going to do?

PARENT: I'll need to think about it, but it seems that you guys could use some bonding time to help your relationship.

ONE CHILD TO THE OTHER: Bonding time means us doing chores together.

PARENT: Chores really help people bond, don't they?

KIDS: (*suddenly hugging each other*) We love each other. We don't think we need any.

PARENT: (*smiling*) Well, that's great. I'm so glad to see that your relationship has improved.

As you might imagine, this was not the first experience these kids had with Love and Logic. Their first went something like:

PARENT (*calmly with empathy*): Oh, this is sad. Each of you is getting close to having to do a lot of chores to replace my energy and learn how to bond with each other.

ONE CHILD: That's dumb. I don't care.

THE OTHER CHILD: I don't want to bond with her.

PARENT (*still calmly*): I'm going to have to do something about this, but not now. I need to focus on driving. We'll talk later.

KIDS: What are you going to do?

PARENT: I'm not sure. We'll talk later.

KIDS: You have to tell us!

PARENT (*calmly yet firmly*): We will talk later.

At home a couple of hours later:

PARENT (*with empathy*): The way you were fighting with each other really drained my energy in the car. What might you do to replace it?

ONE CHILD: He's such a pain! It wasn't my fault.

THE OTHER CHILD: No way! You started it.

PARENT (*sure that both kids were involved in the problem, replies firmly but with empathy*): Oh, this is very sad. I love both of you so much that it really does drain me when you refuse to try and get along. I suppose that you can replace my energy by staying home instead of having me drive you to activities this week, or you might do some bonding time by finishing some of my chores like vacuuming, dusting the furniture, cleaning the bathrooms, and anything else you can think of. I've learned that doing chores together really helps people bond so that they get along better, but it's your choice. If you decide on doing the chores, I will show you what needs to be done by Monday at six in the evening.

Notice how this parent took good care of herself instead of getting pulled into the battle with her kids. Notice also how she applied the energy drain technique from chapter 6. It's important to remember here that the "energy drain" technique is not designed to be used with sarcasm or anger. Further, it's not intended to be done in a way that intentionally lays a guilt trip on your kids. It's designed to provide an opportunity to make restitution for the effects of their misbehavior. An added benefit is that they often feel very proud of themselves after doing so.

4. **Don't try to figure out who started it.** If we could bottle the wasted energy expended by parents attempting to determine "who started it?" we'd be capable of fueling a large metropolitan area for months, maybe years. Typically speaking, everyone "started it" in some way, shape, or form. Often, the child who appears to be the victim initiated the grudge match by casting a nasty look or whispering a jab. Unless you know beyond a reasonable doubt, don't become a detective. Doing so can end up reinforcing some covert but unhealthy behavior performed by the child who looks like they are just minding their own business. No parent wants to perpetuate this pattern into adulthood.

Action Steps

- Find a way to celebrate each child's unique strengths today.
- Don't jump into the fray when your kids are bickering.
- Ask your kids how they are going to solve their problem.
- Don't waste time trying to figure out who started it.

CHAPTER 16

COMMON CHALLENGES: WHEN YOUR CHILD IS TEASED OR BULLIED

*Teaching your child how to deal with teasing is
a skill that can be beneficial at all ages.*

Few things are more upsetting and angering than discovering that your kid has become the target of teasing or bullying. While it's tempting to step in and rescue your child, this is not always the wisest approach—unless the bullying has transitioned into abuse or assault. Recently, Dr. Fay watched a video of a smaller boy being strangled, punched, and slapped on a school bus. The aggressor looked to be older and much larger than he was. The news commentators kept calling this bullying. No, that was abuse. That was assault. Both abuse and assault are against the law, and parents must become extremely involved to the point of filing legal charges.

With that said, too often children who are being teased or bullied come to believe that someone will rescue them any time they encounter a conflict or mistreatment from someone else. This happens when the drama triangle, which Stephen Karpman, MD, extensively discusses, persists on a chronic basis.[1] This dynamic, depicted on the following page, creates a situation where the person being mistreated begins to perpetually take on the role of "victim" because they receive more attention and sympathy when they are having a crisis than when they are actively working on preventing or solving the crisis. Strangely, as depicted by the double-pointed arrows, it's common for the roles to reverse, leaving the victim criticizing the rescuer for failing to provide the desired form of rescue. The victim displays entitlement behavior and feels justified in lashing out at the original bully. It's the messy type of drama that nobody in their right mind wants happening in their family or school.

With children, Dr. Fay has observed that the quickest way to help them avoid or exit the damaging pattern of the drama triangle is by empowering the victim to prevent or minimize taking on the emotional role of victim. This means helping them learn how to handle situations with assertiveness, humor, calmness, or any other demeanor that proves to the bully that the would-be victim is *not* a fun and exciting target.

Let's not steal from kids by too frequently playing the rescuer. When we do, this automatically places them in the victim role. When your child is not in clear emotional or physical danger, it's often wise to allow them to struggle a bit while they learn wonderful skills that will come in handy for the rest of their lives. When they see themselves being successful, the joy and improved self-esteem is priceless. As we're all aware, bullying doesn't stop after elementary, middle, or high school. Most of us have witnessed or encountered it as adults. Listed below are some keys to educating and empowering kids of all ages:

1. **Help them understand the difference between bullying and disagreement.** Take a look at these examples of minor disagreements mistaken as bullying:

   - A second grader went to the school administration office in tears, saying she was being bullied. When asked what happened, she said, "Emma said she didn't like my shoes."

   - A junior high school student told his parents he had been bullied when a classmate told him that his favorite NFL quarterback, Tom Brady, sucks.

Disagreements don't automatically qualify as bullying. A good way to explain this is to say that everybody has an invisible internal device that controls their reaction to others disagreeing with them. We call it an "Offend-O-Meter." Some people's Offend-O-Meters are set very high, meaning they get upset about the tiniest disagreements. For instance, if someone says that they don't like the color of another person's shirt—zing!—that other person's Offend-O-Meter goes off, and their whole day is ruined. Isn't it sad for people like that? Other people have a medium setting on their Offend-O-Meter or a low setting. The people with a low setting are usually the happiest because somebody can say something that they disagree with, and they don't care very much. They just brush it off and continue to have a great day.

2. **Teach them the "power of cool."** An effective approach is to help your children understand that one way to decrease the odds of repeatedly being targeted by a bully is to show, or at least pretend, that they are not upset or flustered by the bully's words. Ask your child to describe what happens when their Offend-O-Meter gets triggered and they start to do or say things that show that they are upset or angered. Then ask, "Does this make it more likely or less likely that you will get bullied?"

Many children are quick to reply that bullies seem to like picking on kids who get emotional. In other words, many kids intuitively understand that bullies feel powerful when they are able to create emotional distress in others. If your child has difficulty understanding this concept, gently explain that an emotional response is like a reward to a bully.

Mr. Menendez understood this concept, so he taught the kids in his second-grade class how to act cool when somebody said something nasty. In class they would practice pretending to be calm, cool, and collected when they started to feel their "Offend-O-Meters" triggered. Mr. Menendez helped his class get plenty of practice pretending that they didn't care about their Offend-O-Meters or what other kids said or did. He described this as "Having the power of cool."

Manny, a boy in Mr. Menendez's class, was being teased by some older students in the hall. Just about every day, they would chide, "Yo mama does . . ." "Yo mama is . . ." "I saw yo mama at . . ." After learning about the "power of cool," Manny stopped getting angry and frustrated. Instead, he smiled and replied, "Yeah, I've been telling her to stop doing that stuff, but she just won't listen." The bullies soon realized they couldn't get a rise out of Manny and began to look for someone without the "power of cool."

3. **Remind them to challenge their ANTs about being bullied.** All of us need to remember that ANTs always make things worse, regardless of the situation. Being teased or bullied is no different. In fact, this is the time when we need to have the healthiest thoughts possible. Some common teasing and bullying-related ANTs include:

- *I'm a victim.*
- *I'm a loser.*
- *It's my fault they're being mean to me.*
- *I hate those kids. I'm gonna get them.*
- *There's nothing I can do. It's hopeless.*

Dr. Fay was conducting a school assembly about bullying in Houston, Texas. "We were visiting about how to confront ANTs when a little girl raised her hand. She said, 'My daddy says to use magic sentences. You've got to have magic sentences you say to yourself when somebody's picking on you or something's going wrong.' I asked her for an example, and she said, 'When I get picked on or somebody's mean to me, I just say to myself, *Do not be overcome by evil but overcome evil with good.* I say that all the time to myself. My dad told me not to say it out loud, just to say it to myself.' This little girl is fortunate to have such a wise father!"

Challenging the accuracy of ANTs and replacing them with an appropriate accurate thought, or "magic sentence," can help any child learn to see bullies as people *in* pain rather than people who *are* a pain. They can help teens understand that they don't have to believe everything someone says, and they don't even have to believe what they say about themselves, unless it's accurate. One teen shared his favorite magic sentence: "The day I'm having depends on me." This simple phrase reminded the teen that how he responded to things was entirely within his control. A woman Dr. Fay coached gave him the one she used when her extremely critical mother-in-law bullied her: "I'm so thankful that her son has a different personality." For more great ideas on this subject, read Sally Ogden's incredibly helpful book, *Words Will Never Hurt Me.*[2] Most kids can read it themselves and successfully apply her suggestions.

4. **Teach them to avoid starting or maintaining it.** Preeminent expert on bullying Dan Olweus spent over 40 years investigating why it's such a problem and what to do about it. In his helpful book, *Bullying at School: What We Know and What We Can Do*, he describes what he called the "provocative victim."[3] This is the child who plays a role in their mistreatment by instigating conflict and maintaining it by subtly transitioning back and forth from playing the roles of helpless victim and snide instigator. These are children who often do things like quietly calling others names, casting nasty looks, engaging in gossip, using sarcastic barbs, needlessly arguing with other kids, teasing, or playing way too roughly. Children who have ADHD are more likely to be bullied and may be "provocative victims" because of their impulsivity, hyperactivity, and being easily emotionally aroused.[4] Kids who have overactivity in the brain's anterior cingulate gyrus (ACG) may be overly persistent and doggedly continue in a dispute even when they are losing the fight.

Mr. Menendez, the teacher who taught his students the "power of cool," used an effective strategy to help his students see that they were expected to do whatever they could to avoid being part of the teasing or bullying problem. Of course, he would help them when they needed rescue, but otherwise, he would pull them aside and whisper, "Are you using the skills we learned for handling teasing and bullying?" These skills involved using the power of cool and avoiding behaviors that provoke others.

He noticed that it was usually clear which students were using the "power of cool" and doing whatever they could to be peacemakers. In those instances, he'd take a more active role in solving the problem and ensuring that bullying stopped. In other cases, however, it was obvious that the student was safe but was trying to extract as much drama and attention as possible by maintaining the conflict. In these cases, he would say, "This sounds like a good time to use your skills. Let me know how it goes."

Sometimes this strategy prompts the child to use their skills and the situation is resolved. What a boost for their self-esteem. Other times, you may need to take action to stop the problem.

5. **Teach kids to develop a support system and how to use it.** Dan Olweus discovered three groups, each of which played a role in the bullying problem: (1) the bully, (2) the victim, and (3) the bystander.

Bystanders are those who see the bullying happening and fear getting involved. Schools can make great strides in reducing bullying behavior by helping students see it for what it is and intervene in numbers. Let your child know that if they are being teased or bullied, they should slowly move toward their friends or an adult, without saying anything about the problem at that time. When a child moves toward the safety of their support system, but they point at the bully and say something like, "He's calling me names!" or "He's picking on me!" they invite retribution by the bully.

Our kids also need to report the event to their teacher and to describe the things they are doing to prevent the problem. When our kids can do so calmly, and describe mature strategies for handling it, this helps the adult better understand that the situation is very serious.

6. **Take action when bullying continues or escalates.** While it's difficult to provide hard-and-fast answers for when we need to intervene, two principles are generally true: (1) if abuse or assault is taking place, we do whatever we can to stop it; and (2) when teasing and bullying are happening, we try our best to help kids see that they can successfully solve the problem without our help. If they aren't able, we step in. When rescue is warranted, parents must play a role in addressing school personnel in ways that continue to empower their child. Describing the incidents in writing and carefully detailing how you have empowered your child to solve the problem is an important follow-up to an in-person meeting or phone call.

Action Steps

- Help your child learn the difference between bullying and disagreement.
- Teach your kids how to use the "power of cool."
- Encourage your kids to challenge their ANTs regarding bullying and teasing.
- Make sure your kids know how to avoid encouraging bullying.
- Let kids know how their friends and adults can act as a support system when bullying occurs.
- If your child's efforts don't resolve the bullying, or it becomes abusive, step in.

CHAPTER 17

COMMON CHALLENGES: KEEPING SPORTS HEALTHY AND FUN

Don't expect sports to build character.
Expect character to enhance the sports experience.

Starting around elementary school, sports can be good for kids, helping them learn teamwork, the value of effort, and goal setting. Other benefits include improved academic performance, enhanced self-regulation, better physical health, and more.[1] In some cases, however, involvement in sports can test the emotional stamina, self-control, and maturity of everyone involved. To keep sports fun, as well as physically and emotionally healthy, be sure to follow these next tips.

1. **Protect their brains.** Soccer, tackle football, and some other sports are associated with injuries that can derail your child's future. As many as 3.8 million traumatic brain injuries occur annually in the US, with an estimated 10 percent of them due to sports- and recreation-related head trauma.[2] Head trauma can be devastating to mental strength, considering it is associated with increased risk of mental health issues later in life such as anxiety, depression, ADHD, drug and alcohol abuse, learning problems, aggression, and more.

   Although wearing helmets offers some level of protection, impacts—even mild ones—can still cause injury to the brain. When a child gets hit in the head, the brain can slosh back and forth within the skull, hitting sharp areas in the skull and causing damage. One of the many problems with such closed-head injuries is that they often *appear* to cause no harm in the short term. A single injury or repetitive blows—think heading soccer balls repeatedly—can add up over time. We often see children, teens, and adults with serious problems with self-control, focus, anxiousness, low moods, anger, impulsive decision-making, and other issues that may be related to brain trauma.

2. **Protect their bodies.** Protocols for rest and proper mechanics in school and recreational sports have progressed light years in the last decade. Many coaches are careful about the type and number of reps they allow kids to practice, protecting their growing bodies. Some aren't because they lack the knowledge or simply don't care. Don't leave your child's physical health up to the coach. Learn everything you can about this subject and speak up if there is a problem. Dr. Fay pulled his 10-year-old son from a baseball team because the coach would not abide by the recommended limitations on pitch counts and rest.

3. **Expect your kids to display responsibility and good character at all times.** Competition can bring out the best and the worst in all of us. Set strong limits with your children over who is responsible for making sure that their equipment is organized and brought to practices and games. When your child forgets a baseball glove, tennis racquet, or golf shoes, think of it as an opportunity for them to learn from affordable consequences. Set limits also over how your kids conduct themselves while playing and practicing: no phones; no snide

comments directed toward others; no arguing or nasty looks directed at officials or coaches; no profanity; no acting lazy or disinterested. In fact, expect them to behave better than many professional athletes do.

In Dr. Fay's home, he and his wife made it clear that they would allow participation only when none of those things was a problem. Yes, they were prepared to pull the plug on any sport if attitude became an issue. When kids know that you are willing to do so, you are less likely to be forced to do it.

4. **Expect *yourself* to display responsibility and good character at all times.** As a parent of a high school varsity level pitcher, Dr. Fay found it tough to keep quiet and behave while sitting on the sidelines. "Fortunately, I have two prefrontal cortices—one inside my skull and the other inside my wife's. Together we've managed to keep things sane." Yelling at coaches, yelling at kids, having adult temper tantrums, and other nasty behavior embarrasses your children, is demotivating, and sets a terrible example. They don't witness this behavior and think, *Gee, I'm so glad I have parents who are willing to fight for me.* One player confided in Dr. Fay, "Sometimes I wish that my bat was a shovel so that I could dig a hole in the ground and hide. My mom is so out of control."

5. **Be your child's parent—not their coach.** Why ruin your and your child's enjoyment of the game by trying to coach your kid? It's fine to have fun playing at home, but refrain from trying to refine or change their skills. Besides, their coach or trainer has likely taught them certain drills or fine mechanics for them to focus on. When you try to provide instruction, it too often becomes confusing to your child. We also prefer parents not to coach their child's team. We've seen some do it well, but it becomes more complicated and conflict prone as the child becomes older and enters competitive play. Sadly, some parents choose a coaching role to groom their child for the major leagues, completely oblivious to the fact that this is not fair to their own child or the other kids on the team.

6. **Err on the side of allowing your child to directly communicate and solve problems with their coach.** Most youth coaches are fine men and women who care deeply about the health and welfare of

their young athletes. They understand that young people are more motivated to work hard for those they view as firm and caring. They have high standards but help their athletes meet these standards in positive ways. Our hats go off to these coaches! Kids benefit greatly from parents staying out of most matters, allowing kids to discuss issues directly with the coach.

Unfortunately, some coaches act like jerks. "Jerk" is a clinical term for someone who is selfish and cares more about their own desires for control and glory than the health of their athletes. Occasionally, it's not horrible for kids to have a low-level jerk (LLJ) for a coach. LLJs can help kids become stronger and more capable of handling a world full of LLJs. Such LLJs may occasionally yell a bit too much, make sarcastic comments, play favorites, or get cross with officials. Even with LLJs, it's wise to place responsibility on your child for communicating directly with their coach. Stay out of most issues so that your kids have the skills to face other LLJs in the future.

MLJs (maximum level jerks) are toxic narcissistic bullies who model everything that goes against your family values. They physically push kids around, direct frequent profanity toward officials, scream at people, kick and throw things, and usually play favorites. They are masters of deception, saying and doing all the right things in front of their superiors. They often make their players feel like they must keep secrets from their parents or other adults. Many parents are afraid of MLJs, so don't expect things to change. Too many parents are willing to let their kids, and others, suffer just so they can get to play or get that coveted college offer. Sadly, many school district leaders are also afraid of, or deceived by, these manipulative coaches. Stirring up a hornet's nest by taking on a bully coach is often more than they can handle.

So, what do you do if your child is experiencing harm from an MLJ type coach? Don't expect your child to rehabilitate an MLJ, and don't feel badly if you have to intervene. Typically, the best approach is to change teams. While a painful tactic, your child's mental and physical health is worth it. It's also helpful to remember that the percentage of high school athletes that compete in college is about 7 percent.[3] The percentage of athletes who go from there to the pros is about 2 percent. Less than one percent of Little League baseball players end up reaching the Major League.[4] By keeping sports in perspective, you can make participation in sports a healthy opportunity for your kids.

Action Steps

- Encourage your kids to play sports that don't increase the risk for head injuries.
- Don't let your kids head soccer balls or play tackle football, and make sure they wear a helmet when needed.
- Be aware of the physical demands being placed on your child.
- Expect good behavior from your child and model good behavior at all sports events.
- Spend time playing sports with your child, but refrain from providing instruction.
- Unless you have reason to believe that a coach is abusive or a maximum level jerk, don't step in to talk to your child's coach whenever there is an issue. Encourage your child to speak directly to the coach.

CHAPTER 18

COMMON CHALLENGES: FRIENDS AND PEER PRESSURE

*When you have developed a strong bond with your child,
they will likely choose friends who share the same values.
When that bond is lacking, they are more likely to seek out friends
who won't meet with your approval.*

Friends are essential for the social circle of mental strength. Kids who have at least one or two faithful friends are far less likely to experience mental health problems, behavioral issues, and substance abuse.[1] While some introverted youngsters want just one or two close pals, the extroverted ones want the entire school. Both personalities are healthy, both are part of the child's prenatal wiring, and both are unlikely to change as a child ages.

Friendships can provide some of the greatest joys in children's lives, but in some cases, they can also present some anxieties for you. For example, when children choose friends that you don't think are good for them, it creates friction. Dr. Fay sees this in families where Drill Sergeant and Helicopter parents are too controlling, causing the child to rebel by becoming friends with kids their parents don't like. This situation requires finesse because you don't have any practical control over the issue. You can move to another city, change your child's school, live in an isolated community, or enter some form of witness protection program. All are drastic measures that wouldn't work anyway. Your kids would still find people that you are slow to like.

In desperation, you could forbid your children from befriending anyone who didn't meet your preestablished criteria. While drastic, too many parents try it:

PARENT: We forbid you to see Zack ever again!

KID: You can't make me stop seeing him.

PARENT: He's a bad influence on you.

KID: He's really cool. You just don't understand him.

PARENT: If we find out you're hanging out with him, you're going to be in big trouble.

KID: My friends are none of your business.

That type of conversation isn't practical or effective and likely sparks more rebellion. It can make your child even more determined to keep seeing that friend *because* you disapprove. Ultimately, when you try to control your kid's friendships, you send an unhealthy message: "You're not capable of thinking on your own." This fuels more friction and can damage your relationship.

When faced with a situation where your child is hanging around with what you think are questionable friends, try a different approach. Give your child a vote of confidence, while pointing out any potential challenges they may face, by choosing to spend time with the person. Here's how it might go:

PARENT: I see that you really like to hang out with Zack.

KID: Yeah. What's wrong with that?

PARENT: Oh, nothing. This is great. I think it's nice for him to have you as a friend.

KID: Well, you seem like you don't like him.

PARENT: It's not that. I think I worry about some of the things he does because they seem to be a little risky or maybe not healthy. Fortunately, I worry less about him now that he has you as a friend. If anyone can show him how to make better decisions about tough things like drinking, drugs, and other risky things, you can.

KID: Are you for real?

PARENT: Yes. Who needs to be the one to decide how you live your life? Is it me or you? Is it Zack or is it you? I think your mom and I have done a pretty good job teaching you how to make decisions for yourself. That's why I think you have what it takes to handle these sorts of things.

That is a more positive and practical approach because it sends a high-expectation message. Research shows that expectations are incredibly powerful. Our kids will either live up or down to them.[2] This strategy also tends to minimize rebellion and supports your relationship. Dr. Fay has worked with many parents who have tried this tactic, and it works. These parents often find that their child's interest in the friend begins to wane. Many report their kids discovering on their own that the friend is not so fun to be with because they create too much trouble.

Another strategy is to get to know and build relationships with such friends. This gives you an opportunity to have a positive influence on them. Invite the friend over for dinner or a family outing. By doing so, you provide a safe environment for the child or teen and provide an example of how a caring family operates.

Even if you're not a person of faith, you might want to check out the Bible for a beautiful example of how Jesus loved people and used this love to reach those traditionally seen as bad or sinful. Too often, parents will say something like, "You shouldn't hang out with that kid; she's bad news." In response, a child or teen who has attended church may even retort, "Well, Jesus ate with sinners, so why can't I?"

When you open your home to your kid's friends—kids who may be broken or hurting—it allows you to build healthy relationships with them. Perhaps you'll have a positive impact on them. Perhaps they'll be less likely to lead your own children astray. Perhaps it's wiser for them to relate to your children within your home rather than somewhere beyond your watch. Certainly, you can model the type of compassion your kids need to see. As a result, they will be more likely to respect you and less likely to see you as a hypocrite worthy of rebellion.

Action Steps

- Don't try to control your child's friendships.
- Point out potential challenges your child might face with certain friends.
- Invite your child's friend over for dinner or to go on a family outing to build a relationship with them.

CHAPTER 19

COMMON CHALLENGES: WHEN YOUR KID WANTS TO BEGIN DATING

When young love makes kids do crazy things,
it's better for parents to empathize, not criticize.

As preteens and teens begin to see other kids their age "date," they want to do it too. Although don't be too quick to call it "dating" these days or you're likely to hear your kids protest that that's not what's happening. They may be "talking to" or "seeing" someone or just "hanging out"—the terminology can get confusing during a time in a teen's life that can already be confusing. And if they ever get to that "serious" stage where you might think they are dating someone, the problem is that many of them have no idea what dating really means. In fact, we could argue that our society in general has an incomplete or inaccurate view of what dating or romantic involvement is. This lack of understanding can also lead parents down one of two conflict-laden, bumpy roads.

1. **The "free for all" road:** This is the street without a speed limit, and with no center lines, no passing zones, and no guardrails. It's the one that too many parents took themselves and, as a result, ended up making mistakes that followed them for the remainder of their lives. The problem with this approach is that it sends our children into situations requiring skills, information, and prefrontal cortex maturity they don't have. It also sends a damaging message: "I don't care enough about you to say no, and I don't care enough about you to give you the guidance you need."

2. **The "not until you're 40" road:** Although 40 might be an exaggeration, many parents make it clear that their children will not "date" (aka hang out with someone they're romantically interested in) until they are older teens—say, 17 or 18—or even adults. This is the street with the cement barrier and a "Road Closed" sign. It's the one that many parents believe will prevent their kids from making mistakes that will plague them for a lifetime. Ironically, this approach is equally dangerous as the "free for all" road, because it deprives kids of skills that will prove absolutely essential for healthy dating when the barrier is removed and the "Road Closed" sign is taken down. This approach also sends a damaging underlying message: "I don't believe that you are bright enough to make good decisions or to take healthy control over your life." This covert yet loud message often leads to severe rebellion, where kids jump the barrier and race ahead on what could be a path that leads to much physical and emotional fallout. Imagine if you've never driven a car and then suddenly you find yourself behind the wheel on a highway full of hairpin curves, steep drop-offs without guardrails, and speeding traffic veering your way.

So, what exactly is dating? We define dating simply as a deep friendship. That's it. While saving physical intimacy for marriage seems like an archaic view, can you imagine how the divorce rate would plummet if this perspective were adopted on a grand scale? We imagine that many adults wish they could turn back the clock and spend more time on friendship and less time on physical passion. It's likely that they would still have chosen the same person. They just would have developed more skills before they made a long-term commitment to each other.

During dating, or deep friendship, teens have an opportunity to learn how to establish healthy boundaries. This is the basis of all good relationships. Most of this they will have learned earlier through your modeling, where they experienced you saying no and setting limits. How will your children learn how to say no to others if they never hear it from you? How will your kids know how to set boundaries over how someone they like treats them if they haven't seen you doing it at home? If you haven't taught your adolescent about boundaries, it's not too late to catch up as they approach the age when they want to date.

Adopting a Practical Neuropsychological Approach to Parenting at Any Age

It's never too late to change your approach to parenting. Whether your kids are toddlers, tweens, or teens, you can successfully shift to a more effective game plan that involves enhancing brain health, identifying goals, developing relationships, and setting limits. When you're ready to incorporate these new strategies into your daily life, show some accountability with your children. Let them know you've learned a better way to love and care for them. Give them a heads up that some changes may be startling at first, but that they will ultimately benefit all of you. Encourage your kids to share their perspective as you implement new techniques. This doesn't mean allowing them to tell you how to parent. It means demonstrating an openness to change when you believe their feedback is helpful. This will help you make greater progress toward raising a mentally strong child.

To avoid teen romance drama, it's also essential to have brief discussions about topics such as:

The causes and consequences of premarital sex: Physical intimacy can stunt the friendship learning process. It puts the focus on sex rather than learning healthy relationship skills. This can be a painful time for tweens or teens who must endure the hills and valleys of young love. Dating is even harder in our sex-saturated culture, leaving many young people feeling like they are so in love that they just can't—or shouldn't have to—wait. When your child starts dating, be a good listener, show empathy, set limits, and do your best to supervise their every move.

How love impacts decision-making: Intense feelings can affect decision-making. Brain-imaging research shows that people who are madly in love experience changes in the brain that ramp up dopamine production and can cause us to fixate on our new love and think of little else.[1] Ask your child or teen if they think they make the best decisions when they are obsessed with a person they think is perfect. Ask them if they think they make the best choices when they are feeling insecure about whether someone still likes them. Inquire whether they make their best decisions when they are feeling jealous or angry. This line of inquiry is not designed to break your child down or leave them feeling interrogated. It's meant to be a gentle way of planting seeds about the importance of waiting until your mind is working more actively than your feelings.

Who is responsible for the happiness of another: This is so important for young people to understand. If your child is constantly trying to appease their special friend to make them feel happy, or if their own happiness becomes dependent on the other person, it's a problem. Let your kids know that healthy people find joy within themselves and don't need to get it from somebody else. They also don't need to control others to feel okay. Encourage them to remain assertive about their convictions and to pay close attention to how others react. Share with your teen that the way others behave when your teen says no to unhealthy activities or experiments is very telling. People who display anger, put them down, get pushy, try to make them feel guilty, isolate them from family and friends, or do other unhealthy things are not the people they should want to be around. A good friend is one who readily values and accepts your wishes even when theirs are different.

When someone treats them poorly: This topic goes back to knowing how to set healthy boundaries. Let your child know that it's okay to say to their friend, "I really like you a lot, but you're being so mean right now that I'm going to choose to spend time away from you. I'm happy to spend time with you when you're being nicer."

It's important for children to know that they should never feel put down or constantly criticized. They should never feel like they are walking on eggshells, constantly afraid that their "friend" will become angry or physically hurtful or reject them. Your child should never have to witness their friend controlling and hurting others and wonder whether they will be next. Even knowing how someone treats animals is often a good indicator of how they will eventually treat people. Your child needs to know that charm is fleeting. How people treat them when they are upset or stressed shows the most about their character. Help your kids learn to recognize these red flags that signal trouble on the horizon.

When someone makes them feel unsafe: Make sure to let your child know that it is never okay for someone to make them feel unsafe. Reassure them that you will come to get them at any time of day or night if they feel threatened or scared.

When your child likes someone but realizes they have different goals: Explain to your kids that they may like someone, but if their values and plans don't match up, it's okay to just be friends.

By having these discussions, you can help your adolescent or teen develop better skills and make better decisions regarding special friendships.

Action Steps

- Talk to your child about dating and explain the concept of deep friendship.
- Talk to your child about premarital sex and its consequences.
- Talk to your child about how romantic love impacts the brain and decision-making.
- Talk to your child about how they are responsible for their own happiness but not for anybody else's.
- Talk to your child about how to set healthy boundaries when someone doesn't treat them well.
- Talk to your child about what to do if they ever feel unsafe in a relationship.
- Talk to your child about how it's okay to let someone go if they don't share the same values.

CHAPTER 20

COMMON CHALLENGES: KEEPING YOUR PARENTING HEALTHY WHEN YOU DIVORCE

When it comes to your ex, always be a class act.

Most people who've gone through a divorce admit that it was one of the most painful experiences they've ever encountered. Often fraught with feelings of loss, anger, fear, guilt, doubt, and uncertainty, parents can find it difficult to muster the emotional resources to help their children cope with those very same emotions. Making matters more difficult, many former spouses act out their anger and hurt through the kids. As this happens, differences in parenting style become accentuated. The parent who was once a mild rescuer now becomes a Helicopter with sidewinder missiles. The one who struggled a bit with anger or micromanagement often becomes a full-fledged Drill Sergeant. Some even begin a campaign of alienation, effectively brainwashing the kids into believing that the other parent is untrustworthy and essentially evil. How might you keep your parenting healthy, regardless of how crushed you feel or how badly your former spouse may behave?

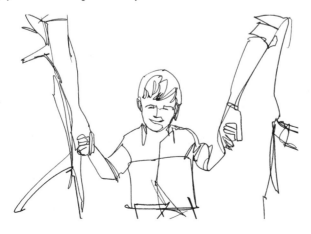

Stay focused on what you can control. When marriages end, former spouses can get caught up in trying to control their ex's behavior as it pertains to the children. Most of the time, this is a losing battle and contributes to even more conflict. Dr. Fay often asks parents in this situation, "If you couldn't control their behavior when you were married, is it more likely or less likely that you can do it now?" This question is not meant to leave anyone feeling worse. Instead, it's intended to free the person from the pain of banging their head against a wall. If we try to control someone who is unwilling to budge, more feelings of anger, frustration, and hopelessness are sure to result.

If you are navigating these turbulent waters, view your own physical and emotional resources as limited and very precious. These resources must go toward staying healthy and showing your children what it looks like to remain rational and calm under difficult circumstances. Dr. Fay has taught many parents to remind themselves, "Be healthy and be a class act." Doing so helps them focus on how to help themselves and their kids the most. Doing so also assists in reminding them that great satisfaction comes from controlling their own behavior—even when someone else is not.

Consistently maintain healthy routines and standards in your home. When kids transition from the other parent's house to yours, they'll likely experience different rules and routines in each. One mom's kids, ages 3 and 6, often came back from their dad's house acting completely out of control. They'd also say things like, "Dad lets us do that. That's not fair. Why don't you let us?"

From Love and Logic, she learned a helpful skill for resetting the tone when they arrived home acting this way. She'd smile and excitedly say, "Hey, let's go outside!"

Her kids would reply, "Why? What's going on?"

She'd answer by gesturing toward the door, taking each by a hand, and saying, "C'mon, we're going outside."

Once outside, she would ask in a rather whimsical manner, "I'm confused. Can you help me? Whose house is this?"

They would reply, "Your house. Mommy, you are being too silly."

In response, she'd ask, "And how do we do things here?"

The kids would think for a moment, then say, "We come in quietly and take our shoes off."

Then Mom would say, "That's right. So, let's try it again." Sometimes, she had to repeat this a few times to get them to settle down, and for a while she had them do this "reset" each morning as needed. With love, humor, firmness, and consistency, she helped her young children understand how to make the transition in a calmer and happier way.

Helping older children and teens isn't much different. A dad from Denver helped his teens understand that he and their mom had different expectations.

"Why do you think that I handle things differently from mom?" he asked.

The strong-willed one of the pair replied, "Because you want to make our lives miserable."

Choosing to ignore that comment, he continued, "It's because we're different. That's all. She has her ways, and I have mine. They aren't better ways or worse ways. They are just different."

Dad understood how important it was to never demean the kids' mom and how it was equally important for him to retain his expectations consistently. If you budge just a bit, your kids quickly learn that they can manipulate you by acting sullen, nasty, or noncompliant. Consistency is king. Although maintaining it is a huge challenge in the short term, it will pay off big-time in the long term. Kids come to love and respect the parent who provides and enforces limits in firm and loving ways.

If necessary, educate yourself about parental alienation syndrome. Sadly, sometimes divorced parents can do everything well yet experience alienation. This painful and extremely damaging issue is quite common. It occurs when one, or sometimes both, parents either consciously or unconsciously attempt to brainwash the children into believing that the other parent is completely evil. One of the hallmarks of true parental alienation syndrome is that the child's view of the alienated parent is completely negative. The child sees no good in the parent who is truly doing their best to be firm and loving. No matter how much pleasure the child and parent experience together during visitation, the child relays the event as completely horrible, awful, or even torturous. This skews a child's perspective and introduces them to a mindset in which they tend to see things as all good or all bad (one of the ANTs discussed in chapter 7). This type of thinking can be harmful throughout their lifetime. A great resource on this topic is Dr. Richard Warshak's *Divorce Poison: How to Protect Your Family from Bad-mouthing and Brainwashing*.[1] In some cases, this type of situation may require help from both an attorney and a mental health professional who specializes in the subject.

Action Steps

- Realize that you can't control your ex's behavior, so stay focused on what you can control.
- Let your kids know that you and your ex do things differently because you are different, and that's okay.

- Consistently maintain healthy routines and standards in your home.
- Don't use your kids to get back at your ex.
- If necessary, educate yourself about parental alienation syndrome.

CHAPTER 21

COMMON CHALLENGES: YOUR ROLE AS A STEPPARENT

Creating healthy boundaries is the first step as a stepparent.

By far the most common question we receive about stepparenting is: "What's my role? Should I start by being the disciplinarian so that the kids know they must obey me, or should I start with only building a relationship and allowing their parents to handle the discipline?"

Another common concern is this: "They treat me with so much disrespect. Sometimes they even play games and act like I don't exist. I find it incredibly hurtful. I know that I'm not their 'real parent,' which they remind me of almost daily, but it doesn't seem healthy for them to believe that it's okay to treat me so badly." These two questions are intimately related. Let's start with defining the role played by a successful stepparent.

THE ROLE OF THE STEPPARENT

Ultimately, the role of a stepparent is to demonstrate healthy boundaries so that they can remain a biologically, psychologically, socially, and spiritually healthy adult. Healthy boundaries must come first. When we have them, most things in life go well. In fact, healthy boundaries are what allow us to set the most important limits we set—those we set with ourselves. Healthy adults set these self-limits so they can maintain the habits required to take care of their brains, bodies, mental hygiene, social relationships, and sense of purpose. When you fail to consistently do that, it becomes impossible to be the type of person kids eventually grow to respect and love. As a review, take another peek at chapter 5 on limits and rules. I also recommend reading the book *Boundaries: When to Say Yes, How to Say No to Take Control of Your Life* by Henry Cloud and John Townsend.[1] When your boundaries are weak, the wheels wobble off of your life, simply because your decisions are based on emotions rather than logic. Your prefrontal cortex sits on the couch, passively watching a painful reality TV drama depicting your life. Look at these common scenarios:

- **Friendly Fixer Frank:** This is the type of stepparent who thinks, *Hey, if I just come in and be friendly and easygoing, peace will prevail. Then I'll be the hero.* This is the stepparent who operates like a Helicopter.

- **No-Nonsense Ned:** This is the stepparent who acts like a Drill Sergeant, barking orders and demanding respect.

- **Vacillating Vinny:** Vinny doesn't really know what to do, but he wants to do it well. So he often finds himself trapped in the Guilt Cycle, alternating between being the disciplinarian and the hero.

Of course, all three of these roles are doomed to failure. Fortunately, there's another role, one that tends to bring the best out of everyone involved:

- **Healthy Henry:** Henry isn't an expert on child psychology, marital dynamics, or any similar field. He's simply a healthy adult with a good heart, healthy boundaries, and some common sense.

The preferred style for stepparenting involves being like Henry, who doesn't spend much time or energy thinking about how to be friendly, how to rescue the kids, or how to get them to respect him. Instead, he demonstrates these qualities:

1. He shows love and respect to his new wife.
2. He shows love and respect to the kids.
3. He takes good care of himself by setting boundaries over how he allows others to treat him.
4. He also takes care of himself by allowing others to own and solve their problems.
5. He may decide to provide some advice, but only when others pry it out of him.

QUALITIES OF A SUCCESSFUL STEPPARENT

The first two qualities are self-explanatory. So let's skip to quality three: setting boundaries over how you are treated. Great boundaries are like great limits. They aren't about how others should act. They are about how you will act. Let's imagine that one of Henry's stepkids is hassling him with incessant arguing. Without lecturing or threatening, he might smile and say, "It seems like you are passionate about a lot of things. I will listen to you when your voice is calm like mine."

The last time Henry allowed the kids to use his tennis racket, it came back dirty and a bit scratched. When asked to lend it again, he replies with empathy, "This is sad, but I lend my stuff to people who take care of it. My tennis racket was a mess the last time you used it."

One of the kids has developed a habit of making snide comments directed toward Henry. He takes some time to think about it and decides to say, "When I hear comments like I've been hearing, I don't feel respected. I'm always more willing to do extra things for people who treat me nicely."

Quality number four is all about who should own and solve the problems encountered in the family. In healthy households, the person who created the problem is allowed to take primary responsibility for solving it. Too frequently, however, you may want to barge in and try too hard to give advice or to rescue. Healthy adults spend more time listening than talking. Let's see what this might look like when Henry discovers that his stepdaughter is getting a D in English.

> STEPDAUGHTER: Mom's going to kill me when she finds out that I'm getting a D in English.
> HENRY: It sounds like you're really worried about how she's going to react.
> STEPDAUGHTER: Well, I don't know. It's just that she's going to be disappointed in me.
> HENRY: Her being disappointed is hard for you?

STEPDAUGHTER: Yeah. Sometimes I wish she would just yell.

HENRY: I'm feeling for you. I can see that you're really dreading having to tell her.

STEPDAUGHTER: What would you do?

HENRY: I could share that with you, but I think you might already have some ideas.

STEPDAUGHTER: I guess that I could wait for her to be in a really good mood before I tell her.

HENRY: That's an option. How do you think that will work for you?

STEPDAUGHTER: I guess I should just tell her right away. She's too smart for that.

HENRY: I'm really glad you shared this with me. Like I said, I'm feeling for you. If anyone can work this thing out, you can. I believe in you.

As Henry allowed the D in English to remain his stepdaughter's responsibility, he also demonstrated the last quality of refraining from advice-giving. He artfully dodged her attempt to get him involved in the decision-making. While there are certainly times when a stepparent may offer advice, it's important that the kids or the other parent make it abundantly clear that they want such counsel.

Being a healthy stepparent means wading into the waters of swimming in a new family. In the short term, your boundaries may irritate or even anger the kids. As time goes by, the respect earned by listening and demonstrating healthy behavior often leads the stepkids to develop a tight bond of love and respect with you. In fact, many people who've had a stepparent like that come to love them and to desire their guidance. How ironic! When the respect and healthy behavior start with you, it usually rubs off on them.

Action Steps

- Don't try to be a fixer or a hero.
- Avoid barking orders at stepchildren.
- Don't waffle between acting like a Helicopter to a Drill Sergeant.
- Remember that setting healthy boundaries and listening lay the foundation for a good relationship.

CHAPTER 22

ADULT CHILDREN AND ADULTS WHO ACT LIKE CHILDREN

We teach people how to treat us by what we tolerate.

Eighteen—that magic number we see as "adulthood." Way before that age most of us hope that our kids are growing in independence, resourcefulness, responsibility, and resilience. As most seasoned parents know, however, it takes well into our children's mid-twenties, or later, for most of us to feel they no longer need our guidance. Their brains are still developing until the mid-twenties. "Guidance" doesn't mean that we need to be overly involved in their adult lives, trying to control their decisions. Nor does it mean that we are rescuing them from their poor decisions or even typical challenges. Guidance means we are showing that we care and believe in them, continuing to model what we hope they will become, and sharing our wisdom when they want it. That's why most of the parenting skills of practical neuroscience also apply to young adult children. When you face relationship challenges or hear about their struggles, don't hesitate to respond with love and firmness.

THE PRINCIPLES OF LOVE AND LOGIC REVISITED

As Rachel's senior year of high school came and went, so did her parents Mark and Robin's hopes to see her take steps into the real world. Instead of taking advantage of her academic advisor, private counselor, or either of her parents' attempts to help, she completed zero college applications. Despite her good grades, she found it more gratifying to party with her friends, obsess over social media, and build her extensive collection of traffic citations. As the days turned into weeks, and the weeks into months, she turned 18, graduated from high school, and continued to do nothing to prepare herself for responsible adulthood. Robin cried, "I just want to scream. We've given her every opportunity, but she takes advantage of none. She also shows us no respect. Sometimes I get so sick of it that I want to kick her out of the house. Then I feel horrible about myself, because I know that I've caused this problem." Although it may seem like it's too late for Rachel's parents to get through to her, the Love and Logic principles will still help.

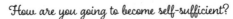

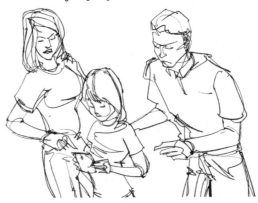

At the beginning of the book, we introduced the Five Principles of Love and Logic. Like a delicious meal, the first four principles are the ingredients. The fifth represents the wonderful results of combining them: Mutual Dignity + Shared Thinking + Shared Control + Empathy = Healthy Relationships.

Mutual dignity

The principle of mutual dignity means that both parties in a relationship treat each other with great respect and worth. Mark and Robin were good at spoiling their daughter Rachel, thinking that doing so would boost her self-dignity and give her a model of how to treat others in a dignified manner. Obviously, that didn't work. Why?

Putting someone on a pedestal and lavishing them with praise and gifts meant for royalty creates great confusion, a sense of entitlement, and anger toward the ones bearing gifts. It also plays a sad role in stunting their ability to handle adversity. Mental strength is always lacking in people who've been idolized and expected to do very little. They express more anxiety, lower academic achievement, substance abuse, and other negative outcomes.[1]

When someone tries to do everything for us and give us all that we need and want, it interferes with the hard work required to grow up and develop the hallmarks of maturity. Like wildlife consistently fed by a well-meaning yet unwise animal lover, we become dependent. This dependency leads to resentment, which often promotes aggression. Mental health professionals often call this outcome hostile dependency.[2]

Mark and Robin discovered that they could provide mutual dignity by consistently practicing three things with Rachel:

- Asking nicely
- Maintaining healthy boundaries
- Setting limits

Asking nicely

Asking nicely doesn't always get us what we want, but it always demonstrates respect and dignity. Early in his career, Dr. Fay was teaching a group of challenging eighth graders. Young and new at the job, he was completely stressed about how he might get their ringleader to stop shooting spit wads at his back every time he turned to write on the chalkboard. He peeled through his psychology and education textbooks looking for a sound psychological answer. He even thought of coming down hard on the student with threats and lectures. The teacher next door offered something so simple: "Have you tried asking nicely if he would stop?"

The next day, as this tough kid walked toward Dr. Fay's classroom door, he stopped him and asked with a smile and a whisper, "I don't want to embarrass you around your friends, so I thought I'd ask you this out here in the hall. Would you do me a favor and stop shooting spit wads at me? I would appreciate that so much."

His reaction came as a surprise. "Yeah, cool man. You got it."

Dr. Fay was shocked, but he shouldn't have been. Honey usually gets us more than vinegar. Even when it doesn't, demonstrating respect is always a good first step.

Mark and Robin experienced a rougher outcome when they used this approach with Rachel. "You are always on my case. It's so stupid that you're asking me to do all of these chores. I don't have time."

While it wasn't what they had hoped for, they achieved something important: Because of the dignity they provided, they had nothing to feel guilty about. As they began to apply additional strategies, they focused on the fact that disrespect never cures disrespect, and anger never soothes anger. One of the keys to helping their daughter become a strong and responsible woman involved their ability to remain pleasant yet firm even when she was flying off the handle. This would provide a grand model of what they hoped she'd become as a young woman: graceful under pressure.

Maintaining healthy boundaries

Scientist Kenji Kameguchi proposed that the function of human relationship boundaries is similar to cell membranes. Every life-sustaining biological process has its roots in our cells and depends on the very thin boundary of the cell membrane for survival. In a nutshell, the cell membrane has five functions:

Keeping bad things out
Letting good things in
Keeping the cell components from falling apart
Keeping individual cells distinct from one another
Allowing individual cells to interact

People with healthy boundaries recognize unhealthy situations or patterns and are good at keeping these from getting embedded in their lives.[3] Since their boundaries are permeable, like a cell membrane, they allow nourishment to enter and toxins to exit. Their boundaries also help maintain their core ethics, goals, and direction when they encounter pressures to abandon them. In essence, good boundaries allow us to help others without making their problems our own. They keep us emotionally distinct while allowing us to enjoy closeness with others. The concept of emotional boundaries is not a new one, and we didn't discover it. In 1974 Salvador Minuchin wrote a wonderful book, *Families and Family Therapy*, which quickly became the gold standard for understanding and treating families. The concept of boundaries is heavily addressed throughout this book and the approach it teaches, often referred to as family systems theory.[4] More recently, Drs. Henry Cloud and John Townsend have written extensively about boundaries in many areas of life. For a great introduction to their work, read *Boundaries: When to Say Yes, How to Say No to Take Control of Your Life.*[5]

Mark and Robin realized that their boundaries needed some shoring up. Their lives were inextricably intertwined with their daughter's. This was so much the case that it was unbearable for them to allow her to experience the trials, tribulations, and triumphs required for entry into emotional adulthood. Sitting in Dr. Fay's office, Mark and Robin discussed boundaries. Dr. Fay has a Quick Boundary Test to help people identify their boundary strengths and weaknesses in relation to specific people or situations.

QUICK BOUNDARY TEST

Boundary #1
I can't be healthy with this person if I don't take good care of myself.

```
|_____|_____|_____|_____|
1        2        3        4        5
```
I forget this often.   I never forget this.

Comments: _____

Boundary #2
I can't be healthy when I forget who the problem should belong to.

```
|_____|_____|_____|_____|
1        2        3        4        5
```
I forget often.   I never forget.

Comments: _____

Boundary #3
I'm not being healthy when I'm always working harder on the person's problems than they are.

```
|_____|_____|_____|_____|
1        2        3        4        5
```
I often work harder.   I never work harder.

Comments: _____

Boundary #4
I'm not being healthy when my self-esteem, self-competence, and happiness depend entirely on my ability to help this person be happy and overcome their problems.

```
|_____|_____|_____|_____|
1        2        3        4        5
```
They often do.   They never do.

Comments: _____

Boundary #5
I'm not being healthy when I allow excessive dependency in our relationship.

```
|_____|_____|_____|_____|
1        2        3        4        5
```
I'm not good at avoiding dependency.   I am very good at avoiding dependency.

Comments: _____

"Number 1 is a problem for us," Mark and Robin admitted. "We work ourselves to the bone in order to help her, and we are both exhausted. Looking at number 2, we realized that we have made her lack of preparation our problem by constantly nagging, complaining, and working overtime to solve it. Number 3 is obvious. Dr. Fay, we remember you saying, 'The harder you work on someone else's problem, the less concern and effort they will put into it.'" Pausing to take a deep breath, Mark went on, "It looks like number 5 is also a problem for us. She seems to be getting more and more dependent on us, rather than feeling free to jump into life with mental strength and confidence."

Setting limits

As we all know, ideas, awareness, and good intentions are unlikely to promote change unless they are accompanied by consistent action. This action largely takes the form of setting boundaries and enforcing limits. Listed below are a few examples, each designed to build healthy boundaries while maintaining the dignity of everyone involved:

- "I'm willing to help you with this as long as you are working harder on your problem than I am."
- "You may live with us as long as you are helping with daily chores, are enjoyable to be around, and are making tangible progress toward becoming independent."
- "I'm happy to provide a car for you to use, as long as you are covering the extra costs involved."
- "I will spend time with you, as long as I see that you are taking responsibility for your life rather than criticizing me for your problems."
- "We love you. What is your plan for becoming a self-sustaining adult?"
- "I will visit with you when I see that your voice is calm, and you are treating me respectfully."
- "I love you and want to help, but who needs to take the steps to overcome this addiction? Is it me, or is it the person who is using the drugs?"
- "We will love you whether you are making good choices and living someplace clean and safe, or you are making poor ones and living somewhere unhealthy and dangerous."

As you can see, setting healthy limits over tough situations is not for the faint of heart. You may have noticed something else: When we set healthy, boundary-building limits, we're mostly setting limits with ourselves. The change we hope to see in others starts with the behaviors we are willing to allow near and inside of our own cell membranes because that's all we can control.

Reflecting on the concepts of boundaries and limit setting, Mark and Robin decided there was nothing wrong with their daughter, Rachel. She was simply doing what a normal person her age would do *without* the benefit of having loving and firm limits. They also discovered that the best inheritance they could provide for her did not involve money. It involved showing her how strong men and women behave. It is true that our kids will likely have great difficulty maintaining boundaries with others if we don't establish healthy boundaries with them.

To state it mildly, Rachel was shocked when Mark and Robin acted on these concepts. "We love you, honey. What is your plan for becoming a self-sustaining adult?" That helpful limit, set in the form of a question, opened the doors to many hard yet helpful discussions about how Mark and Robin's home would begin to operate. The basic theme of those conversations? "We love you too much to continue providing the lifestyle of the rich and famous when you aren't taking any steps to grow up."

Shared thinking and shared control

Boundaries help transition responsibility and accountability to where it belongs. When you embrace them, you give up trying to control your child. You allow them to take control and learn to use their brains. That's the only way your children will grow up and you'll transition out of the parent role. When it became clear that Rachel would no longer have a free ride, she made quick strides to get a part-time job and to enroll at the local community college. An added benefit involved her use of public transportation, which immediately improved the overall safety of the community.

Mark and Robin commented, "Helping her understand that avoiding adulthood was not an option, and that we would no longer be providing a car or a place to live if she chose to be irresponsible, was one of the most gut-wrenching things we ever did. We consistently faced the fear, and it wasn't long before we began to see a far happier, dignified, and mentally strong woman, rather than an unhappy, entitled, and helpless child."

Empathy

We've written a lot about the role of empathy in parenting. It is a lifelong skill that will keep your relationship with your children healthy, even if they get off track as adults. It's essential that empathy accompanies listening, requests, and boundaries at any age.

Brenda and Tony loved their 30-year-old son, Manny, more than life itself. When he was a child, they discovered Love and Logic and applied what they learned. Manny had always been a fun kid, whom adults and kids loved. Everything seemed to be going well until he fell in with a new group of friends during high school. That's when his deep slide into drug addiction began. He had times of sobriety followed by periods of dark dependence and depression. It wasn't long before he was completely hooked on heroin and stealing anything he could to support the addiction.

While living with his parents, Manny essentially turned their home into a drug use and distribution den. Paralyzed by indecision and guilt, Brenda and Tony allowed it to happen. That is, until they also found themselves riding to the police station in handcuffs.

When Manny's life had taken a downward turn into drugs, his parents were motivated by guilt and bent over backward trying to make Manny's life perfect. *Maybe if we let him live with us*, they thought, *he won't be so anxious and need the drugs. Besides, then he'll be away from those bad kids.*

They took him to counseling, and they made sure he received treatment. Brenda and Tony learned from his counselors that relapses are part of the process, but they blamed themselves for being "bad parents" every time Manny had a setback. The more anxious they became, the more Manny devoted his time to shooting up. "It was really scary!" Tony said. "We had people banging on our doors and windows all hours of the night. Then the authorities raided our house . . . that was the breaking point."

As things got sorted out with the legal authorities, Brenda and Tony experienced even more guilt as they fantasized about not having their much-loved son and his problems affecting their lives. Both discovered that their boundaries were weak, and that they needed to set real limits with Manny. This view was reinforced by their counselor who shared a humbling truth: "Sometimes really good and conscientious parents have kids who develop addictions and other serious problems. You didn't cause this, and it's not your problem to solve. If you really care about Manny like I think you do, you need to stop trying to rescue him." They both agreed that he needed to live someplace else. Take a look at their boundaries test:

ASSESSMENT OF BRENDA AND TONY'S BOUNDARIES WITH THEIR SON, MANNY

Boundary #1

I can't be healthy with this person if I don't take good care of myself.

|①————————|————2————|————3————|————4————|————5|

I forget this often.   I never forget this.

Comments: Our guilt over this is causing us to punish ourselves and rescue Manny any time he gets himself in a jam.

Boundary #2

I can't be healthy when I forget who the problem should belong to.

|①————————|————2————|————3————|————4————|————5|

I forget often.   I never forget.

Comments: We need to make this Manny's problem.

Boundary #3

I'm not being healthy when I'm always working harder on the person's problems than they are.

|①————————|————2————|————3————|————4————|————5|

I often work harder.   I never work harder.

Comments: We think doing the healthy thing is going to make us feel horrible in the short term.

Boundary #4

I'm not being healthy when my esteem, self-competence, and happiness depend entirely on my ability to help this person be happy and overcome their problems.

|1————————|————②————|————3————|————4————|————5|

I often do this.   I never do this.

Comments: We can choose to lead healthy, joyful lives even though our son isn't. We shouldn't feel guilty for this. This will help him more than us being unhealthy and miserable.

Boundary #5

I'm not being healthy when I allow excessive dependency in our relationship.

1 2 3 4 5

I'm not good at avoiding dependency.   I am very good at avoiding dependency.

Comments: *Bad things can happen to basically good people. Manny was a strong and independent kid until he got addicted. The changes in him tricked us into being rescuers. Now we know that we need to go back to the Love and Logic skills that worked so well when he was younger.*

Brenda and Tony returned to empathy as they set a very strong limit, "Manny, we love you, and we can't imagine how hard things are for you. We want to visit you here at the corrections center as often as we can. We want you to know that we will stay for as long as we feel like you are treating us well. There's something else. We need to apologize for treating you like you can't overcome your addiction. We believe in you and promise to stop working harder on your life than you are. This means that when you are released, it will be your responsibility to find a place to live."

While heartbreaking, this discussion began to lay a large part of the foundation for Manny's recovery. Our prayers are with this family as they continued to travel this challenging road. The odds are high for a miracle as they trust God to bless their efforts to maintain healthier boundaries while still loving their son.

*   *   *

When you raise kids with a practical neuropsychological approach, you give them the foundation they need to become mentally strong adults who are confident, competent, and resilient. Other factors may come into play that make young adulthood challenging for them to navigate. In any case, remember that your grown children are the only ones responsible for their choices. Your job is to love them with firmness, kindness, and empathy. Your consistency will strengthen your relationship, emphasize that they are in control of their own lives, and assure them that they know where to turn for support.

Action Steps

- Remember the five principles of Love and Logic: Mutual Dignity + Shared Thinking + Shared Control + Empathy = Healthy Relationships.
- If your young adult child isn't behaving or making an effort to become self-sufficient, start by asking nicely.
- Take the Quick Boundary Test with a particular relationship in mind to identify your boundary strengths and weaknesses.
- Set and enforce limits on young adult children that place responsibility and accountability where it belongs.
- Be prepared for backlash when setting limits later in a child's life, and consider professional help from a psychiatrist, psychologist, or family therapist to guide you through the process.

CHAPTER 23

130 BEST THINGS YOU CAN DO TO HELP YOUR CHILD GROW UP TO BE MENTALLY STRONG

*When things seem overwhelming, start with the smallest
thing that will have the biggest impact.*

We have introduced you to many proven tips and strategies to help you raise mentally strong kids and young adults. Here we have compiled some of the most effective techniques to increase your effectiveness as a parent and build the Four Circles of Mental Strength so your kids have the foundation they need to achieve their potential. Some of them have appeared in previous chapters, but they are so important, we are including them here as reminders. We don't expect you to follow all of the suggestions listed. Choose the ones that are the most appropriate for your situation. We have gathered these "best things you can do for your child" over decades of working with both "difficult" and "not-so-difficult" children, teenagers, and young adults—and their parents.

REMEMBER WHAT IT IS LIKE TO BE A CHILD

1. Remember what it is like to be a child (the good and the bad). Remember how you felt when you were their age. This will help you relate to their worries and concerns with empathy.

2. Remember how it felt when your mom or dad were too busy for you.

3. Remember what it felt like to tell a lie and how you wish your parents would have reacted when they found out.

4. Remember how you felt when your parents fought with each other. (Do you fight in the same way with your spouse or the child's other parent?)

5. Remember how it felt when your mom or dad took you someplace special.

6. Remember mealtimes when you were a child. Were they a positive experience (and why), or were they a negative experience (and why)?

7. Remember how you felt at bedtime.

8. Remember the first time you asked someone out on a date, or were asked out, and the intense anxiety and excitement that goes along with dating.

9. Remember your sexual feelings and experiences as a child and teenager.

10. Remember the worst teachers you had, so that you can relate to your kids when they complain about school.

11. Remember the best teachers you had, so that you can tell your children how good school can be.

DEVELOP CLEAR GOALS FOR YOURSELF AS A PARENT AND FOR YOUR CHILD

12. Develop clear, written goals for raising your children and spell out the kind of person you'd like them to become. Look at your goals every day to see if your behavior is encouraging what you want. In all

of your interactions with your children, ask yourself if your actions encourage the behaviors you want.

GOALS FOR YOURSELF AS A PARENT

(The overall goal is to be a competent and positive force in your child's life.)

13. Be involved with your child. Ensure you spend enough time with them so that you can influence their direction.

14. Be open with your child. Talk with them in such a way—active listening and empathy—that will help them talk to you when they need to.

15. Be firm and set limits. Provide appropriate supervision and limits until they develop their own moral/internal controls.

16. Be a good co-parent. Whether married or divorced, it is best when parents support each other in their interactions with a child.

17. Be kind. Raise your children in such a way that they will want to come and see you after they leave home. Being a parent is also a selfish job.

18. Be fun. Joke, clown, and play with your kids. Having fun is essential to both physical and emotional health.

DEVELOP CLEAR GOALS FOR YOUR CHILD

(The overall goal is to enhance development.)

19. Be relational. We live in a relational world. It is imperative to teach your children how to get along with others.

20. Be responsible. Children need to believe and act as if they have some shared control over their own life—that when bad things happen it is not always someone else's fault. Otherwise, they will act like a victim and have no personal power.

21. Be independent. Allow your child to have some choices (shared control) over their own life. This will enable the child to be able to make good decisions on their own.

22. Be self-confident. Encourage your child to be involved with different activities where they can feel a sense of competence. Self-confidence often comes from the ability to master tasks, sports, and activities.

23. Be self-accepting. Notice more positive than negative in your child. This will enable them to accept themselves.

24. Be adaptable. Expose your child to different situations so they will be flexible enough to deal with the various stresses that will come.

25. Be emotionally healthy. Allow your child the ability to express themselves in an accepting environment. Seek help for your child if they show prolonged symptoms of emotional trouble.

26. Be fun. Teach your child how to have fun and how to laugh.

27. Be focused. Help your child develop clear goals for themselves (both short-term and long-term goals).

AUTHORITY IS ESSENTIAL

28. Authority is essential to maintaining order and structure in a family. The sixties generation lost the concept that authority is a good thing.

29. Being firm with your child is *not* the same as being mean.

30. Your child will respect you more if you believe you are supposed to be the authority in the relationship.

31. Establishing authority (in a kind way) with a child enhances creativity. They know the boundaries and do not have to test them continually, leaving energy for more productive activities.

32. Establishing authority (in a kind way) with a child will help them deal with authority as an adult.

33. Mean what you say. Don't allow guilt to cause you to back down on what you know is right.

YOUR RELATIONSHIP WITH YOUR CHILD IS THE KEY TO SUCCESS

34. Your personal relationship with your child matters to their emotional well-being. Many parents underestimate their influence over a child. With a good relationship, your child will come to you when they need to. With a bad relationship, your child will seek out others (such as peers) for counsel.

35. With a good parent-child relationship almost any form of discipline will work. With a poor parent-child relationship almost any form of discipline won't work.

36. Respect your child. Treat them at home as you would in front of others. This also teaches children to be respectful with others.

37. Spend some special time with your child each day, doing what they want to do. Just 20 minutes a day of special time will strengthen the bond between you and your child and make a dramatic difference in the quality of your relationship. Being available to your child will help them feel important and enhance their self-esteem.

38. Be a good listener. Find out what your child thinks *before* you tell them what you think.

39. Get down on their level when you talk with a child.

40. Speak softly to children. They're much more likely to hear you.

41. Avoid yelling at children. How do you feel when someone yells at you? It probably makes you mad, stressed, or fearful. Children are no different.

42. Keep promises to children.

43. Children learn about relationships by watching how their parents relate to each other. Are you setting a good example?

A LOVING, HELPFUL ENVIRONMENT

44. Tell your child you love them every day.

45. Touch your child every day—hug them, hold hands, rub their shoulders, or tousle their hair.

46. Establish eye contact with your child every day and inquire about their day.

47. Take the time to hug your child whenever they climb into your lap (or come into your space).

48. Listen to their music to hear what information is being fed into their mind.

49. Limit TV, video games, social media, and tablets. These are often "no-brain" activities and of little help for children.

50. Don't allow kids to watch too much of the news. It'll scare them and increase their internal sense of anxiety.

51. Use rituals (such as bedtime, mealtime, and holidays) to provide continuity, structure, and stability for children.

52. Introduce children to a multitude of experiences, even if they are hesitant.

53. Play games with your kids. Recreation is essential to a balanced, happy life.

CLEAR EXPECTATIONS

54. Be clear with what you expect from your child or teen. It is effective for families to have posted rules, spelling out the "laws" and values of the family. (See Dr. Amen's Eight Essential Rules in chapter 5.) And remember the one overarching Love and Logic rule: don't cause a problem.

NOTICE WHAT YOU LIKE A LOT MORE THAN WHAT YOU DON'T LIKE

55. When your children live up to the rules and expectations, be sure to notice them. If you never reinforce good behavior, you're unlikely to get much of it.

56. Notice the behaviors you like in your child 10 times more than the behaviors you don't like. This teaches them to notice what they like about themselves rather than growing up with a critical self-image.

57. Praise and encouragement enhance good behavior and teach children new skills. Anger and punishment suppress difficult behavior but do not teach children anything good in the long run.

58. Praise and encouragement strengthen the parent-child bond. Anger erodes the parent-child bond.

DISCIPLINE

59. Do not tell your child to do something 10 times. Expect your child to comply the first time! Be ready to back up your words with an appropriate consequence.

60. Never discipline your child when you're out of control. Take a time-out before you lose your cool.

61. Use discipline to teach your child rather than to punish or get even for bad behavior.

62. See misbehavior as a problem you're going to solve rather than "the child is just trying to make you mad."

63. It's important to have swift, clear consequences for broken rules, enforced in a matter-of-fact and unemotional way. Nagging and yelling are destructive and ineffective.

64. Remember the words *firm* and *kind*. One parent we know uses the phrase, "Tough as nails and kind as a lamb." Try to balance them at the same time.

65. When your child is stuck in negative behavior, try to distract them and come back to the issue later.

66. Deal with lying and stealing immediately.

67. Do not back away from dealing with difficult situations (sex, drugs, disrespect) with your teenager or young adult. Deal with them in a kind, firm way.

68. Avoid spanking and other forms of corporal punishment; they are detrimental.

CHOICES

69. Give your children a choice between options, rather than dictating what they must do, eat, or wear. If you make all the decisions for your children, they will be unable to make their own decisions later on.

70. Encourage your children to make independent decisions, based on the knowledge they have, rather than on what their friends might say or do.

SUPERVISION

71. Supervise your child's school experience. Get to know the teacher. Be an active part of the class. Sometimes parents are the last people to know things are going wrong. Being involved will help keep your child on track.

72. Know where your child or teen is at all times. Tell your child that you want to know who they are with, what they are doing, and what time they'll be home. Let them know that you are going to periodically check. Initially they'll complain about your intrusion, but in the long run they will appreciate your care and concern.

73. Trust is based on past experience. Let your children know that their level of freedom is based on how trustworthy they have shown themselves to be.

74. Spend time with your child's friends (even if they turn you off) to know the kind of influences they are in your child's life.

PARENTAL SUPPORT

75. Parents need to work together and support each other even if they are divorced.

76. When children are allowed to split parental authority, they have far more power than is good for them.

77. Parents need time for themselves. Parents who are drained do not have much energy left in the tank to give children their best efforts.

78. One of the best things you can do for your children is model a loving relationship with your spouse.

SELF-ESTEEM

79. Be careful of the nicknames and phrases you use to describe your children. Children live up to the labels we give them.

80. Your child's self-esteem is more important than the quality of their homework.

81. Encourage children in areas of interest to them (sports, music, etc.). Self-esteem is often based on a person's ability to feel competent.

TEACHING CHILDREN

82. Teach children values with your behavior. A significant way children learn values is by watching the behavior of their parents.

83. Teach children from your own real-life experiences.

84. Talk to your children about sex and drugs. Don't leave that responsibility up to the school, social media, TV shows, or their friends!

85. Help children learn from their mistakes. Don't berate or belittle them; otherwise, they will grow up doing that to themselves (and others).

86. Keep only healthy foods in the house, so children will learn to love foods that love them back.

87. Exercise with your child. Help them make physical activity a daily routine in their lives.

88. Teach children to notice the best about their lives.

89. Teach children that there is a beginning and an end to life to help them understand why spiritual health is important.

90. Teach children to predict the best things for themselves.

91. Don't allow children to blame others for how their life is turning out.

92. Teach children to send thank-you notes.

93. Teach your child organization skills to make their life easier. (This may mean making them keep the bedroom organized, even when they may not be naturally inclined that way.)

94. Read to children (or have them read to you) often.

95. Teach children how to use new technology responsibly, and set time limits on it.

WORK AND CHILDREN

96. Don't give children everything they ask for. Encourage them to work—doing chores, for example—for what they want.

97. Work is good for children; doing everything for them is not.

SIBLINGS

98. Encourage and reward respect among siblings. Discipline inappropriate or hostile behavior between siblings.

99. Some sibling rivalry is normal. Remember the story of the first siblings in the Bible. It didn't turn out so well.

FRIENDS AND PEERS

100. Don't fight a child's battles with their friends or peers but be available as a consultant.

101. Provide a safe and inviting home that inspires your kids to invite friends to visit.

WHEN THERE ARE PROBLEMS

102. Seek help for your child when they show signs of a brain/mental health or learning problem. Remember, it is on average 11 years from the time a person first has a mental health challenge to the time of their first appointment to get help.[1]

103. Don't sweep problems under the rug. Teach kids to talk about their struggles and what's not working in their lives.

104. Apologize to children when you make a mistake.

105. Help children see past their disabilities and weaknesses to see their strengths.

UNDERSTAND WHAT'S NORMAL

106. Act as your child's prefrontal cortex until theirs fully develops—in their mid-twenties—gradually giving them more responsibility and control as they grow.

107. Understand normal development, such as the terrible twos, independence and identity in teens, and so on.

108. When a teenager pulls away from you, pursue them with kindness, not anger.

109. Don't tell an 18-year-old what to do. They are likely to do the opposite. Suggest alternatives, listen, and help with options. Be careful with your words. They're likely to say something like "I'm 18. I can do whatever I want."

LEARN ALL YOU CAN

110. Effective parenting is a learned skill. Work to learn all you can.

111. Keep your brain sharp by continuing to learn new skills and getting out of your comfort zone.

BRAIN INTERVENTIONS

112. Make children wear helmets when riding a bike, skateboarding, rollerblading, or in high-risk situations.

113. Always make children wear seat belts in motor vehicles.

114. Feed your children a balanced diet that is low in refined sugars and simple carbohydrates. Enlist them in shopping for brain-healthy foods.

115. Teach children how to think accurate, healthy thoughts and raise healthy internal anteaters to rid themselves of ANTs (automatic negative thoughts).

116. Every day, encourage your kids to focus on the things they are grateful for in their life. Start each today with the phrase, "Today is going to be a great day."

117. At bedtime, ask kids, "What went well today?"

118. Make sleep a priority for your child. In addition, growth hormone actually works more effectively while your child is sleeping.

119. Surround children with soothing scents like lavender (for mood and anxiousness), peppermint (for energy and focus), jasmine (for mood and relaxation), and chamomile (to calm anxiousness and promote sleep).

120. Encourage children to build a mental library of wonderful life experiences. Have them make a mental list of their happiest memories so they can pull them up when they need a mood boost.

121. Eat meals with your children so they can see you enjoying healthy foods and to bolster family bonding.

122. Teach children deep-breathing techniques to help them calm and control their emotions and nervousness.

123. Help your kids, especially teens and young adults, to find their purpose in life by asking what they love to do and how it helps others.

124. Sing or hum with your children whenever you can.

125. Make beautiful music a part of your child's life.

126. Be sure your child gets regular health and dental checkups. Healthy bodies and gums are critical to brain health.

127. Keep caffeine out of your child's life.

128. Do not use much alcohol around children, and never use any illegal drugs in their presence.

129. Have children avoid contact sports where head injuries are common, and do not let them hit soccer balls with their heads.

130. Do not let children bang their head when frustrated. Teach them to love their brains.

CHAPTER 24

20 THINGS THE PARENTS OF MENTALLY STRONG KIDS *NEVER DO*

Sometimes, what you don't do is more important than what you do.

If you love your child (and we're sure you do) and want them to be successful, happy, and healthy, then it is imperative that you pay attention to your own behavior. After working with parents and their children for decades, we have come up with this list of the top 20 things the parents of mentally strong kids *never do*.

1. **Ignore your child's brain.** When you don't think about brain health, you set your child up for all sorts of potential problems at home, in school, and in relationships. Instead, you must love and care for their brain, which controls everything your child does—how they think, feel, act, and get along with other people. When their brain works right, they work right. When their brain is troubled, they are going to have trouble. As you and your child are making decisions about

any sports they may be involved in, remember to protect their brain if you want them to be happy, healthy, and mentally strong for the rest of their life.

2. **Disregard normal behavior.** When you don't understand normal childhood development, you are likely to expect more from your child, adolescent, or teen than they are ready to handle. This leads to friction, frustration, and a sense of failure. When you have a basic grasp of development, you are better able to notice when something is inside or outside of the scope of normal. For example, it is normal for teenagers to want to become more independent and to begin to make their own decisions. Knowing that is a normal part of development makes it easier for you to honor and respect it while still supervising it.

3. **Be a lousy role model.** If your motto is "Do as I say, not as I do," you are setting yourself up for trouble. If you lie, cheat, are rude or disrespectful, eat an unhealthy diet, and never address your own health, your child is going to follow your example. So model how you want your child to be.

4. **Forget what it is like to be a child or teen.** If you can't empathize with your child, you may alienate them, make them feel like they aren't being understood, or send a message that their feelings aren't valid. Remembering what it was like for you when you were your child's age and all the challenges and struggles you had will give you much more empathy for your child. You'll end up being more helpful to them than if you approach their life from an adult perspective.

5. **Be overly permissive.** Multiple studies have demonstrated that the children who grow up to have the most psychological problems had parents who never set appropriate boundaries.

6. **Diminish the other parent.** While it can be tempting, it is crucial that you not criticize, put down, or complain about your child's other parent to your child. This not only undermines the effectiveness of the other parent, but it also decreases your child's self-esteem. Your child is a product of both parents, and by saying negative things about the other parent, you are really saying negative things about your child as well.

7. **Rarely spend quality time with them.** Relationships require two things: time and a willingness to listen. If you don't spend time with them or you have a poor relationship, they are likely to develop resentment and rebel against you. If you spend quality time and have a good relationship with your child (essential for bonding), they tend to choose and emulate your morals and values. Doing things that your child enjoys and listening to them will make a huge difference in the quality of your relationship.

8. **Be a poor listener.** When you are disagreeing with your child and they are talking, do you interrupt them? Are you focusing on understanding what they are saying, or are you thinking of how you are going to respond to them? Being a bad listener sends the message that your child isn't important enough to merit your attention. And this can have devastating effects on their self-esteem. Learn how to actively listen. Don't judge or criticize what they are saying, rather repeat back what you hear. Ultimately, your child can solve a lot of their own problems.

9. **Call your children names.** There is nothing helpful about labeling your child with a negative term. They will then internalize the label and live up to the negative names that you call them. Set a good example for your children through your own conduct.

10. **Only notice what they do wrong.** Noticing all the little mistakes your child makes infuses them with a negative mindset and self-view. This can carry over into adulthood and hold them back from reaching their potential. In addition, if the only time you notice them is when they are doing something wrong, you are teaching them that doing something bad is the best way to get any attention from you. Instead, do whatever you can to catch them doing things right as often as possible. By doing that, you will reinforce their good behavior and good choices.

11. **Give in to tantrums or other bad behaviors.** By doing so, even once, you will teach them what you will tolerate. They will then learn the lesson that misbehaving works to get them what they want. They need to know that they are not able to manipulate you with their behavior.

12. **Be reactive.** When your parenting style is largely reactive, you can send mixed messages to your child. To avoid this, outline your goals for your child. What kind of child do you want to raise? What kind of parent do you want to be? For example, if you want to raise a child who is kind, competent, and makes a great contribution to society, then you must model that as well as reinforce behaviors that support those goals as opposed to simply reacting from moment to moment.

13. **Fail to supervise them.** Lack of supervision means children are left on their own to make important decisions even though their brains are not yet fully developed. This can result in poor decisions regarding alcohol, drugs, sex, and more that impact mental fortitude. In the meantime, you need to know where your children are and who they are with—and then check on them. When it comes to your children, think back to what President Ronald Reagan said: "Trust, but verify." If they know you are going to check, their decisions are going to be better than if they know you never check.

14. **Never get to know your child's friends.** During adolescence, the most influential people in your teen's life are the friends they spend the most time with—not you. That is why you want to know the values of the people they are hanging out with. Understand that trying to control your child's friendships can backfire. If you are unhappy with what you discover, then get your child involved in activities with kids who have values that you appreciate. Try inviting their friends to your home so they can benefit from your family's values and loving relationships.

15. **Feed your child the standard American diet (SAD).** The human brain uses 20 to 30 percent of the calories a person consumes. If you feed your child a fast-food diet, they're going to have a fast-food mind, which is associated with ADHD, depression, and dementia later in life. Focus on feeding your child brain-healthy foods so they are able to have optimal brain development and function.

16. **Keep kids up too late.** Children need much more sleep than most parents realize for optimal brain development and function. A lack of sleep saps focus and energy; decreases academic and sports performance; increases bad moods, stress, and anxiousness; and leads to poor decision-making.

17. **Tell kids how to think.** If a child is unable to have freedom to explore different ways of thinking and seeing the world and instead feels micromanaged, they are much more likely to rebel and have a conflicted relationship with you. To avoid this, when it comes to your kids, adopt this philosophy: "Be curious, not furious." In essence, this means letting your kids think for themselves while you act as a good coach rather than a dictator.

18. **Tell your child they are smart.** If you do this and they end up failing to learn something (which they likely will at some point in their lives), then they will tell themselves that they really aren't smart and will become more likely to give up. Instead, point out how hard they work. That way, when something in their life is hard, they will persevere and work harder because their self-esteem comes from hard work, not smarts.

19. **Ignore their mental health issues.** Mental health issues, such as ADHD, anxiety, depression, bipolar disorder, obsessive-compulsive disorder (OCD), and more can have a devastating impact on your child's life. These types of problems can rob them of their mental strength, happiness, self-esteem, motivation, and focus. As their parent, pay attention and take them for an evaluation if you have any concerns.

20. **Ignore your own mental health issues.** It can devastate a child if you are struggling with untreated symptoms of a brain-based issue, such as depression, anxiety, or addiction. In order to be the best parent you can be, you must take care of your own health—including mental health. It can change the trajectory of your child's life if your own mental health is addressed.

Dr. Amen's Gratitude and Appreciation

So many people have been involved in creating *Raising Mentally Strong Kids*. I want to first thank my best friend, partner, and wife, Tana Amen, who embraced all of Jim Fay's and Dr. Foster Cline's Love and Logic programs to help us raise a healthy, ambitious, responsible, driven, cool child together. Tana was amazing at learning and teaching Love and Logic to others. Of course, I have to thank my friend and mentor, Jim Fay, and I have been able to develop deep affection, gratitude, and respect for Dr. Charles Fay, my wonderful partner and cowriter and developer of this endeavor.

In addition, Frances Sharpe, our amazing chief storyteller at Amen Clinics, helped to masterfully blend Charles's and my voices. Andrea Vinley Converse is a very special editor who helps make us better and the work more accessible.

I am also grateful to the tens of thousands of patients and families who have come to Amen Clinics and allowed us to help them on their healing journey, with special thanks to the patients who allowed me to tell part of their stories in this book.

I am grateful to the amazing staff at Amen Clinics who work hard every day serving our patients and help us get the word of our work out to the world, especially Kim Schneider, Christine Perkins, Rob Patterson, Jim Springer, Natalie Buchoz, Stephanie Villafuerte, Jeff Feuerhaken, and James Gilbert for their input, love, and support. I am also grateful to my literary agent Greg Johnson and to the whole team at Tyndale, especially Jan Long Harris, in helping getting this work out into the world.

Dr. Fay's Gratitude and Appreciation

In writing this book, God has blessed me by giving me the support, guidance, and encouragement of countless people. Without them, this book would never have been written. Thanks to Daniel Amen, MD, who graciously provided me with the opportunity to coauthor this book with him. Your kindness and wisdom made this project possible.

Great thanks to my father, Jim Fay, and Foster Cline, MD, who pioneered the Love and Logic approach when I was just a child. Dad, your great affection, guidance, and professional contributions have been an amazing blessing to millions. Foster, your friendship and knowledge have been life changing. You also have changed millions of lives.

Thanks to Frances Sharpe for your great assistance throughout the process of writing and editing the manuscript. Your great skill and positive attitude made a challenging process fun. Andrea Vinley Converse (To the Point Editorial Services) and Janis Long Harris (Tyndale executive publisher-at-large) also deserve great praise. Your very helpful assistance made a world of difference.

To my wife, Monica. You are the love of my life! Your great patience, grace, and endless hard work have made it possible for me to grow and to help others. Thanks for being an amazing wife, mother, friend, and helper. You are a gift from God.

About Daniel G. Amen, MD

Dr. Amen is a physician, board-certified child and adult psychiatrist, award-winning researcher, and 19-time national bestselling author. His online videos about brain and mental health have been viewed over half a billion times. Sharecare named him the web's No. 1 most influential expert and advocate on mental health, and the *Washington Post* called him the most popular psychiatrist in America.

He is the founder and CEO of Amen Clinics with locations nationwide. Dr. Amen is the lead researcher on the world's largest brain imaging and rehabilitation study on professional football players. His research has not only demonstrated high levels of brain damage in players, but also the possibility of significant recovery for many with the principles that underlie his work.

Together with Pastor Rick Warren and Dr. Mark Hyman, Dr. Amen is also one of the chief architects of The Daniel Plan, a program to get the world healthy through religious organizations that has been done in thousands of churches, mosques, and synagogues.

Dr. Amen is the author or coauthor of over 80 professional articles, 9 book chapters, and over 40 books, including 19 national bestsellers and 12 *New York Times* bestsellers, including the No. 1 *New York Times* bestseller *The Daniel Plan* and the over one million copy bestseller *Change Your Brain, Change Your Life*, which The VOU listed as one of the best self-help books of all time, along with *The End of Mental Illness*; *Healing ADD*; *Change Your Brain, Change Your Body*; *Memory Rescue*; *Your Brain Is Always Listening*; *You, Happier*; and *Change Your Brain Every Day*. His books have been translated into 46 languages.

Dr. Amen's published scientific articles have appeared in many prestigious scientific journals. In January 2016, his team's research on distinguishing PTSD from TBI on over 21,000 SPECT scans was featured as one of the top 100 stories in science by *Discover* magazine. In 2017, his team published a study on over 46,000 scans, showing the difference between male and female brains; and in 2018, his team published a study on how the brain ages on 62,454 SPECT scans.

Dr. Amen has written, produced, and hosted 18 national public television programs about brain health, which have aired more than 150,000 times across North America.

Dr. Amen has appeared in movies, including *Quiet Explosions, After the Last Round,* and *The Crash Reel* and was a consultant for *Concussion.* He appeared in the docuseries "Justin Bieber: Seasons" and has appeared regularly on Dr. Phil and The Dr. Oz Show. He has been featured on the *Today* show, *Good Morning America, The Early Show,* CNN, Fox, and *The Doctors,* and appeared in the Emmy-winning show *The Truth About Drinking.*

In addition, Dr. Amen is one of the most visible and influential experts on brain health and mental health with millions of followers on social media. In 2020 Dr. Amen launched his digital series "Scan My Brain" featuring high-profile actors, musical artists, athletes, entrepreneurs, and influencers that airs on YouTube and Instagram. Over 100 episodes have aired, turning it into viral social media content with collectively millions of views.

He has also spoken around the world, with prestigious lectures in Canada, Brazil, Israel, and Hong Kong. He has spoken for the National Security Agency (NSA); the National Science Foundation (NSF); Harvard's Learning and the Brain Conference; the Department of the Interior; the National Council of Juvenile and Family Court Judges; the Supreme Courts of Ohio, Delaware, and Wyoming; and large corporations such as Merrill Lynch, Hitachi, Bayer Pharmaceuticals, GNC, NBA Referees, Miami Heat coaching staff; and many others. In 2016 Dr. Amen gave one of the prestigious Talks at Google.

Dr. Amen's work has been featured in the *New York Times,* the *New York Times Magazine, Washington Post Magazine, MIT Technology, Newsweek, Time, Huffington Post,* ABC World News, *20/20,* BBC, *London Telegraph, Parade* magazine, *World Economic Forum, LA Times, Men's Health, Bottom Line, Vogue, Cosmopolitan, LA Style,* NPR, and many others.

In November 2017, an anonymous post of Dr. Amen's passion story (6 minutes) went viral and had over 40 million views. His two TEDx talks have more than 25 million views.

Dr. Amen is married to Tana, the father of six children, and grandfather to five. He is an avid table tennis player.

About Charles Fay, PhD

Charles Fay, PhD, is a parent; a specialist in child, adolescent, and family psychotherapy; internationally recognized author; consultant; highly skilled public speaker; and president of the Love and Logic Institute, Inc., which became part of Amen Clinics Inc. in 2020.

Millions of educators, mental health professionals, and parents worldwide have benefited from Dr. Fay's practical and down-to-earth solutions to the most common and frustrating behaviors displayed by youth of all ages. These methods come directly from years of research and clinical experience serving severely disturbed youth and their families in psychiatric hospitals, public and private schools, and homes.

Dr. Fay's interest in education and psychology were piqued as a child from years of exposure to some of our nation's most dynamic experts in these fields. This early exposure came as a result of participation in training events with his father, Jim Fay. Jim is one of the nation's leading experts on child discipline and has over 50 years of experience in public education. The internationally recognized Love and Logic approach was literally developed around Charles Fay as he grew. Now, he jokes, "I think that's why I became a psychologist . . . just to figure out what they were doing to me as a kid. But . . . let me be clear . . . I absolutely adore my mom and dad as a result."

Dr. Fay earned his PhD with highest honors from the University of South Carolina. Prior to and during his university training in school and clinical psychology, he enjoyed extensive experience working with children in psychiatric, public school, and mental health settings.

Dr. Fay currently works full-time as an author, consultant, public speaker, and president of the Love and Logic Institute. Because of his high-powered sense of humor and storytelling skills, audiences experience the most memorable and life-changing form of learning—learning that's mentally connected to joy and real-life examples. Many conference attendees have written, "The time went so fast . . . a very entertaining speaker," and "I'm so relieved that he gave us things we can actually use rather than lots of theory and impractical stuff," and "I first heard Dr. Fay 15 years ago. I'm still using the skills I learned all those years ago!"

Resources

AMEN CLINICS, INC.

AMENCLINICS.COM

Amen Clinics, Inc. (ACI), was established in 1989 by Daniel G. Amen, MD. ACI has locations nationwide and specializes in innovative diagnosis and treatment planning for a wide variety of behavioral, learning, emotional, cognitive, and weight issues for children, teenagers, and adults. Brain SPECT imaging is one of the primary diagnostic tools used in our clinics. ACI has the world's largest database of brain scans for emotional, cognitive, and behavioral problems. It has an international reputation for evaluating brain-behavior problems, such as ADHD, depression, anxiety, school failure, traumatic brain injury and concussions, obsessive-compulsive disorders, aggressiveness, marital conflict, cognitive decline, brain toxicity from drugs or alcohol, and obesity, among others. In addition, we work with people to optimize brain function and decrease the risk for Alzheimer's disease and other age-related issues. ACI welcomes referrals from physicians, psychologists, social workers, marriage and family therapists, drug and alcohol counselors, and individual patients and families. For more information, visit our website or call our toll-free number (888) 288-9834.

LOVE AND LOGIC

LOVEANDLOGIC.COM

Love and Logic, founded in 1977, is the global leader in practical resources for parents, educators, and other professionals worldwide. With its research-driven, whole-child philosophy, the Love and Logic Institute is dedicated to making parenting and teaching fun and rewarding, instead of stressful and chaotic. We provide practical tools and techniques that help adults achieve respectful, healthy relationships with their children. All of this work is based on a psychologically sound parenting and teaching philosophy called Love and Logic.

BRAINMD

BRAINMD.COM
Since 2010, BrainMD has been offering the highest-quality, science-backed, brain-directed supplements and functional foods, as well as a wide variety of brain health education products such as books, videos, music, and more.

AMEN UNIVERSITY

AMENUNIVERSITY.COM
In 2014, Dr. Amen formed Amen University with courses on practical neuroscience, with topics including overall brain health, ADHD, anxiety, depression, memory, emotional trauma, head injuries, developing healthy brains in children and adolescents, autism, insomnia, and happiness. Amen University also offers brain health certification courses for medical and mental health professionals as well as for coaches and trainers. To date, we have certified brain health coaches in 56 countries.

Notes

INTRODUCTION

1. Diana Baumrind, "Effects of Authoritative Parental Control on Child Behavior," *Child Development* 37, no. 4 (December 1966): 887–907, https://www.jstor.org/stable/1126611.

CHAPTER 1: HEALTHY BRAINS: THE FOUNDATION OF MENTAL STRENGTH, RESPONSIBILITY, EMOTIONAL CONTROL, AND SUCCESS

1. Daniel G. Amen, *Change Your Brain, Change Your Life* (New York: Harmony Books, 2015), 26.

2. Amen, *Change Your Brain, Change Your Life*, 3, 27.

3. Jonathan Day et al., "Influence of Paternal Preconception Exposures on Their Offspring: Through Epigenetics to Phenotype," *American Journal of Stem Cells* 5, no. 1 (May 15, 2016): 11–18, https://www.ncbi.nlm.nih.gov/pmc/articles/PMC4913293/.

4. These principles and more are introduced in Daniel G. Amen, *Making a Good Brain Great* (New York: Harmony, 2005) and Amen, *Change Your Brain, Change Your Life*, chap. 1.

5. These concepts are introduced in Daniel G. Amen, *Memory Rescue* (Carol Stream, IL: Tyndale, 2017).

6. Wanze Xie et al., "Chronic Inflammation Is Associated with Neural Responses to Faces in Bangladeshi Children," *NeuroImage* 202 (November 15, 2019): 116110, https://www.sciencedirect.com/science/article/pii/S1053811919307013.

7. Virginia A. Rauh and Amy E. Margolis, "Research Review: Environmental Exposures, Neurodevelopment, and Child Mental Health—New Paradigms for the Study of Brain and Behavioral Effects," *Journal of Child Psychology and Psychiatry* 57, no. 7 (March 14, 2016): 775–793, https://acamh.onlinelibrary.wiley.com/doi/full/10.1111/jcpp.12537.

8. "Mental Health by the Numbers," National Alliance on Mental Illness (NAMI), last updated June 2022, https://nami.org/mhstats.

9. Marco Colizzi, Antonio Lasalvia, and Mirella Ruggeri, "Prevention and Early Intervention in Youth Mental Health: Is It Time for a Multidisciplinary and Trans-diagnostic Model for Care?" *International Journal of Mental Health Systems* 14 (March 24, 2020): 23, https://ijmhs.biomedcentral.com/articles/10.1186/s13033-020-00356-9.

10. Sarah L. O'Dor et al., "A Survey of Demographics, Symptom Course, Family History, and Barriers to Treatment in Children with Pediatric Acute-Onset Neuropsychiatric Disorders and Pediatric Autoimmune Neuropsychiatric Disorder Associated with Streptococcal Infections," *Journal of Child and Adolescent Psychopharmacology* 32, no. 9 (November 2022): 476–487, https://pubmed.ncbi.nlm.nih.gov/36383096/.

11. Institute of Medicine, "Extent and Health Consequences of Chronic Sleep Loss and Sleep Disorders," in *Sleep Disorders and Sleep Deprivation: An Unmet Public Health Problem*, ed. Harvey R. Colten and Bruce M. Altevogt (Washington, DC: National Academies Press, 2006), chap. 3, https://www.ncbi.nlm.nih.gov/books/NBK19961/.

    Jamie Cassoff, Sabrina T. Wiebe, and Reut Gruber, "Sleep Patterns and the Risk for ADHD: A Review," *Nature and Science of Sleep*, no. 4 (May 29, 2012), 73–80, https://www.ncbi.nlm.nih.gov/pmc/articles/PMC3630973/.

12. Adam Winsler et al., "Sleepless in Fairfax: The Difference One More Hour of Sleep Can Make for Teen Hopelessness, Suicidal Ideation, and Substance Use," *Journal of Youth and*

Adolescence 44, no. 2 (February 2015): 362–378, https://pubmed.ncbi.nlm.nih.gov /25178930/.

13. Jesus Pujol et al., "Breakdown in the Brain Network Subserving Moral Judgment in Criminal Psychopathy," *Social Cognitive and Affective Neuroscience* 7, no. 8 (November 2012): 917–923, https://pubmed.ncbi.nlm.nih.gov/22037688/.

Lena Hofhansel et al., "Morphology of the Criminal Brain: Gray Matter Reductions Are Linked to Antisocial Behavior in Offenders," *Brain Structure and Function* 225, no. 7 (September 2020): 2017–2028, https://pubmed.ncbi.nlm.nih.gov/32591929/.

CHAPTER 2: MENTALLY STRONG KIDS LIVE BY CLEARLY DEFINED GOALS

1. United States Census Bureau, "Census Bureau Releases New Estimates on America's Families and Living Arrangements," press release no. CB22-TPS.99, November 17, 2022, https://www.census.gov/newsroom/press-releases/2022/americas-families-and-living -arrangements.html.

2. Keita Umejima et al., "Paper Notebooks vs. Mobile Devices: Brain Activation Differences during Memory Retrieval," *Frontiers in Behavioral Neuroscience* 15 (March 19, 2021), https://www.frontiersin.org/articles/10.3389/fnbeh.2021.634158/full.

3. Gail Matthews, "Goals Research Summary" (presentation, Ninth Annual International Conference on Psychology, Athens Institute for Education and Research, Athens, Greece, May 25–28, 2015), Dominican University of California, https://www.dominican.edu/sites /default/files/2020-02/gailmatthews-harvard-goals-researchsummary.pdf.

4. For example, Daniel G. Amen, *Change Your Brain, Change Your Life*, rev. ed. (New York: Harmony Books, 2015), 194–197.

CHAPTER 3: IS YOUR PARENTING STYLE BREEDING MENTAL STRENGTH OR WEAKNESS?

1. Diana Baumrind, "Effects of Authoritative Parental Control on Child Behavior," *Child Development* 37, no. 4 (December 1966): 887–907, https://www.jstor.org/stable/1126611.

Diana Baumrind, "Authoritarian vs. Authoritative Parental Control," *Adolescence* 3, no. 11 (1968): 255–272.

Diana Baumrind, "Current Patterns of Parental Authority," *Developmental Psychology* 4, no. 1, pt. 2 (1971): 1–103, https://psycnet.apa.org/record/1971-07956-001.

Diana Baumrind, "Rearing Competent Children," in *Child Development Today and Tomorrow*, ed. William Damon (San Francisco: Jossey-Bass, 1989), 349–378.

Diana Baumrind, "The Influence of Parenting Style on Adolescent Competence and Substance Abuse," *Journal of Early Adolescence* 11, no. 1 (1991): 56–95, https://psycnet .apa.org/record/1991-18089-001.

Christopher Spera, "A Review of the Relationship among Parenting Practices, Parenting Styles, and Adolescent School Achievement," *Educational Psychology Review* 17, no. 2 (2005), 125–146, https://psycnet.apa.org/record/2005-07205-002.

Sofie Kuppens and Eva Ceulemans, "Parenting Styles: A Closer Look at a Well-Known Concept," *Journal of Child and Family Studies* 28, no. 1 (2019): 168–181, https://pubmed .ncbi.nlm.nih.gov/30679898/.

2. Jim Fay, *Helicopters, Drill Sergeants, and Consultants: Parenting Styles and the Messages They Send* (Golden, CO: Cline/Fay Institute, 1986), audiocassette.

Foster Cline and Jim Fay, *Parenting with Love and Logic: Teaching Children Responsibility* (Colorado Springs, CO: Piñon Press, 1990), 23–25.

Jim Fay and David Funk, *Teaching with Love and Logic: Taking Control of the Classroom* (Golden, CO: Love and Logic Press, 1995), 22–25.

3. Robert I. Sutton, *The No Asshole Rule: Building a Civilized Workplace and Surviving One That Isn't* (New York: Warner Business Books, 2007).

4. Jim Fay and Charles Fay, *Teaching with Love and Logic: Taking Control of the Classroom*, rev. ed. (Golden, CO: Love and Logic Institute, 2016), 19–28.

5. Jim Fay, *Helicopters, Drill Sergeants, and Consultants: Parenting Styles and the Messages They Send* (Golden, CO: Cline/Fay Institute, 1986), audiocassette.

Foster Cline and Jim Fay, *Parenting with Love and Logic: Teaching Children Responsibility* (Colorado Springs, CO: Piñon Press, 1990), 23–25.

Jim Fay and David Funk, *Teaching with Love and Logic: Taking Control of the Classroom* (Golden, CO: Love and Logic Press, 1995), 22–25.

6. Donald Meichenbaum, *Stress Inoculation Training* (New York: Pergamon Press, 1985).

7. Qutaiba Agbaria, Fayez Mahamid, and Guido Veronese, "The Association between Attachment Patterns and Parenting Styles with Emotion Regulation among Palestinian Preschoolers," *SAGE Open* 11, no. 1 (February 10, 2021), https://journals.sagepub.com/doi/10.1177/2158244021989624.

8. Analisa Arroyo and Chris Segrin, "Family Interactions and Disordered Eating Attitudes: The Mediating Roles of Social Competence and Psychological Distress," *Communication Monographs* 80, no. 4 (September 17, 2013): 399–424, https://www.tandfonline.com/doi/abs/10.1080/03637751.2013.828158.

9. Agbaria, Mahamid, and Veronese, "Association between Attachment Patterns and Parenting Styles."

CHAPTER 4: NOTHING WORKS WITHOUT RELATIONSHIP

1. National Research Council and Institute of Medicine, *Preventing Mental, Emotional, and Behavioral Disorders among Young People: Progress and Possibilities* (Washington, DC: National Academies Press, 2009), https://www.ncbi.nlm.nih.gov/books/NBK32775/.

2. J. Silk and D. Romero, "The Role of Parents and Families in Teen Pregnancy Prevention: An Analysis of Programs and Policies," *Journal of Family Issues*, 35 (10: 2014): 1339–1362, https://doi.org/10.1177/0192513X13481330.

3. Mary D. Salter Ainsworth et al., *Patterns of Attachment: A Psychological Study of the Strange Situation* (New York: Psychology Press, 2015).

John Bowlby, *Attachment* (New York: Basic Books, 1969).

Foster W. Cline, *Conscienceless Acts Societal Mayhem: Uncontrollable, Unreachable Youth and Today's Desensitized World* (Golden, CO: Love and Logic Press, 1995), 51–55.

4. Tyler Schmall, "Most Parents Think Their Kids Avoid Talking to Them," *New York Post*, September 7, 2018, https://nypost.com/2018/09/07/most-parents-think-their-kids-avoid-talking-to-them/.

5. This concept is introduced in Daniel G. Amen, *Change Your Brain, Change Your Life*, rev. ed. (New York: Harmony Books, 2015), 125–126.

6. Jim Fay, *Helicopters, Drill Sergeants, and Consultants: Parenting Styles and the Messages They Send* (Golden, CO: Cline/Fay Institute, 1986), audiocassette.

Jim Fay, *Four Steps to Responsibility* (Golden, CO: Cline/Fay Institute, 1986), audiocassette.

Foster Cline and Jim Fay, *Parenting with Love and Logic: Teaching Children Responsibility* (Colorado Springs, CO: Piñon Press, 1990), 96–111.

Foster Cline and Jim Fay, *Parenting Teens with Love and Logic: Preparing Adolescents for Responsible Adulthood* (Colorado Springs, CO: Piñon Press, 1992), 39.

7. Sabrina Suffren et al., "Prefrontal Cortex and Amygdala Anatomy in Youth with Persistent Levels of Harsh Parenting Practices and Subclinical Anxiety Symptoms over Time during Childhood," *Development and Psychopathology* 34, no. 3 (August 2022): 957–968, https://pubmed.ncbi.nlm.nih.gov/33745487/.

University of Montreal, "Does 'Harsh Parenting' Lead to Smaller Brains?" *ScienceDaily*, March 22, 2021, https://www.sciencedaily.com/releases/2021/03/210322085502.htm.

8. Kun Meng et al., "Effects of Parental Empathy and Emotion Regulation on Social Competence and Emotional/Behavioral Problems of School-Age Children," *Pediatric Investigation* 4, no. 2 (June 2020): 91–98, https://mednexus.org/doi/full/10.1002/ped4.12197.

9. Jean Decety and Meghan Meyer, "From Emotion Resonance to Empathic Understanding: A Social Developmental Neuroscience Account," *Development and Psychopathology* 20, no. 4 (Fall 2008): 1053–1080, https://pubmed.ncbi.nlm.nih.gov/18838031/.

10. Kamila Jankowiak-Siuda, Krystyna Rymarczyk, and Anna Grabowska, "How We Empathize with Others: A Neurobiological Perspective," *Medical Science Monitor* 17, no. 1 (2011): RA18–RA24, https://www.ncbi.nlm.nih.gov/pmc/articles/PMC3524680/.

11. Daniel G. Amen, *Feel Better Fast and Make It Last* (Carol Stream, IL: Tyndale, 2018), 135–136.

12. These principles are introduced in Amen, *Feel Better Fast*, 132–133.

13. Amen, *Change Your Brain, Change Your Life*, 198–199.

14. Fay, *Four Steps to Responsibility*.
Cline and Fay, *Parenting Teens with Love and Logic*, 139–140.

CHAPTER 5: LIMITS AND RULES BUILD MENTAL FORTITUDE

1. Rafaela Costa Martins et al., "Effects of Parenting Interventions on Child and Caregiver Cortisol Levels: Systematic Review and Meta-analysis," *BMC Psychiatry* 20 (2020): 370, https://bmcpsychiatry.biomedcentral.com/articles/10.1186/s12888-020-02777-9.

2. Diana Baumrind, "Effects of Authoritative Parental Control on Child Behavior," *Child Development* 37, no. 4 (December 1966): 887–907, https://www.jstor.org/stable/1126611.

3. Matthew T. Birnie and Tallie Z. Baram, "Principles of Emotional Brain Circuit Maturation," *Science* 376, no. 6597 (June 2, 2022): 1055–1056, https://www.science.org/doi/10.1126/science.abn4016.

4. Daniel G. Amen, *Healing ADD*, rev. ed. (New York: Berkley Books, 2013), 297–298.

5. B. F. Skinner, "Two Types of Conditioned Reflex: A Reply to Konorski and Miller," *Journal of General Psychology* 16, no. 1 (1937): 272–279, https://www.tandfonline.com/doi/abs/10.1080/00221309.1937.9917951.

6. Amen, *Change Your Brain, Change Your Life*, 110–112.

7. Cline and Fay, *Parenting with Love and Logic*, 60–63.

8. K. A. Cunnien, N. Martinrogers, and J.T. Mortimer, "Adolescent Work Experience and Self-efficacy," International Sociological Social Policy, no. 29 (March/April 2009):164–175, doi: 10.1108/01443330910947534. PMID: 19750144; PMCID: PMC2742471.

9. Jim Fay and Charles Fay, *Love and Logic Magic for Early Childhood: Practical Parenting from Birth to Six Years*, rev. ed. (Golden, CO: Love and Logic Institute, 2015), 88–92.
Jim Fay and Charles Fay, *Early Childhood Parenting Made Fun! Creating Happy Families and Responsible Kids from Birth to Six*, kit (Golden, CO: Love and Logic Institute, 2005).

CHAPTER 6: LOVING DISCIPLINE LEADS TO MENTAL STRENGTH

1. Carl Lindberg, "The Kurt Lewin Leadership Experiments," Leadershipahoy, August 20, 2022, https://www.leadershipahoy.com/the-kurt-lewin-leadership-experiments/.

2. Joan Durrant and Ron Ensom, "Physical Punishment of Children: Lessons from 20 Years of Research," *Canadian Medical Association Journal* 184, no. 12 (September 4, 2012): 1373–1377, https://www.cmaj.ca/content/184/12/1373.

3. Jorge Cuartas et al., "Corporal Punishment and Elevated Neural Response to Threat in Children," *Child Development* 92, no. 3 (2021): 821–832, https://psycnet.apa.org/record/2021-43033-001.

4. Cline and Fay, *Parenting with Love and Logic*, 197.

CHAPTER 7: MENTAL HYGIENE IS CRITICAL FOR PARENTS AND KIDS

1. Daniel G. Amen, *Change Your Brain, Change Your Life*, rev. ed. (New York: Harmony Books, 2015), 109.

2. Amen, *Change Your Brain, Change Your Life*, 112.

3. Amen, *Change Your Brain, Change Your Life*, 116.

4. Bernard Weiner, "Attribution Theory, Achievement Motivation, and the Educational Process," *Review of Educational Research* 42, no. 2 (Spring 1972): 203–215, https://journals.sagepub.com/doi/10.3102/00346543042002203.

   Carol S. Dweck, *Mindset: The New Psychology of Success* (New York: Random House, 2006).

5. John Sabini, Michael Siepmann, and Julia Stein, "The Really Fundamental Attribution Error in Social Psychological Research," *Psychological Inquiry* 12, no. 1 (2001): 1–15, http://www.jstor.org/stable/1449294.

6. Howard J. Markman, Scott M. Stanley, and Susan L. Blumberg, *Fighting for Your Marriage: A Deluxe Revised Edition of the Classic Best Seller for Enhancing Marriage and Preventing Divorce* (San Francisco, CA: Jossey-Bass, 2010), 50–54.

7. Tristen K. Inagaki et al., "The Neurobiology of Giving versus Receiving Support: The Role of Stress-Related and Social Reward–Related Neural Activity," *Psychosomatic Medicine* 78, no. 4 (May 2016): 443–453, https://www.ncbi.nlm.nih.gov/pmc/articles/PMC4851591/.

8. Byron Katie, with Stephen Mitchell, *Loving What Is: Four Questions That Can Change Your Life* (New York: Harmony Books, 2002), 18–19.

9. Amen, *Change Your Brain, Change Your Life*, 114.

CHAPTER 8: RAISING STRONG AND CAPABLE KIDS

1. Kenneth D. Stewart and Paul C. Bernhardt, "Comparing Millennials to Pre-1987 Students and with One Another," *North American Journal of Psychology* 12, no. 3 (2010): 579–602, https://psycnet.apa.org/record/2011-04684-012.

2. Simine Vazire and David C. Funder, "Impulsivity and the Self-Defeating Behavior of Narcissists," *Personality and Social Psychology Review* 10, no. 2 (2006): 154–165, https://journals.sagepub.com/doi/10.1207/s15327957pspr1002_4.

3. Donald Meichenbaum, *Stress Inoculation Training* (New York: Pergamon Press, 1985).

   Teri Saunders et. al., "The Effect of Stress Inoculation Training on Anxiety and Performance," *Journal of Occupational Health Psychology* 1, no. 2 (April 1996): 170–186, https://psycnet.apa.org/record/1996-04478-005.

   Fahimeh Kashani et al., "Effect of Stress Inoculation Training on the Levels of Stress, Anxiety, and Depression in Cancer Patients," *Iranian Journal of Nursing and Midwifery Research* 20, no. 3 (May-June 2015): 359–364, https://www.ncbi.nlm.nih.gov/pmc/articles/PMC4462062/.

4. Peter L. Benson, Judy Galbraith, and Pamela Espeland, *What Kids Need to Succeed: Proven, Practical Ways to Raise Good Kids*, rev. ed. (Minneapolis, MN: Free Spirit Publishing, 1998).

5. Eric S. Kim et. al., "Sense of Purpose in Life and Likelihood of Future Illicit Drug Use or Prescription Medication Misuse," *Psychosomatic Medicine* 82, no. 7 (September 1, 2020): 715–721, https://europepmc.org/article/med/32697442.

   Viktor E. Frankl, *Man's Search for Meaning* (Boston: Beacon Press, 2006), 141–143.

   George Kleftaras and Irene Katsogianni, "Spirituality, Meaning in Life, and Depressive Symptomatology in Individuals with Alcohol Dependence," *Journal of Spirituality in Mental Health* 14, no. 4 (November 2012): 268–288, https://www.researchgate.net/publication/268511923_Spirituality_Meaning_in_Life_and_Depressive_Symptomatology_in_Individuals_with_Alcohol_Dependence.

6. Patricia A. Boyle et al., "Effect of a Purpose in Life on Risk of Incident Alzheimer Disease and Mild Cognitive Impairment in Community-Dwelling Older Persons," *Archives of General Psychiatry* 67, no. 3 (March 2010): 304–310, https://www.ncbi.nlm.nih.gov/pmc/articles/PMC2897172/.

7. Anthony L. Burrow and Nicolette Rainone, "How Many *Likes* Did I Get? Purpose Moderates Links between Positive Social Media Feedback and Self-Esteem," *Journal of*

Experimental Social Psychology 69 (March 2017): 232–236, https://www.sciencedirect
.com/science/article/abs/pii/S0022103116303377.

8. Viktor E. Frankl, *Man's Search for Meaning* (1946; Boston: Beacon Press, 2006).

9. Laila Kearney, "Later Retirement Linked to Lower Risk of Alzheimer's, Study
Shows," Reuters, July 15, 2013, https://www.reuters.com/article/us-usa-alzheimers
-retirement/later-retirement-linked-to-lower-risk-of-alzheimers-study-shows
-idUSBRE96F02M20130716.

10. Deanna L. Tepper, Tiffani J. Howell, and Pauleen C. Bennett, "Executive Functions
and Household Chores: Does Engagement in Chores Predict Children's Cognition?"
Australian Occupational Therapy Journal 69, no. 5 (October 2022): 585–598, https:
//pubmed.ncbi.nlm.nih.gov/35640882/.

    Elizabeth M. White, Mark D. DeBoer, and Rebecca J. Scharf, "Associations between
Household Chores and Childhood Self-Competency," *Journal of Developmental and
Behavioral Pediatrics* 40, no. 3 (April 2019): 176–182, https://pubmed.ncbi.nlm.nih
.gov/30507727/.

11. Walter Mischel, *The Marshmallow Test: Mastering Self-Control* (New York: Little, Brown,
2014).

CHAPTER 9: HELPING KIDS DEVELOP AND MAINTAIN HEALTHY BODIES FOR STRONGER MINDS

1. University of Warwick, "Fruit and Veggies Give You the Feel-Good Factor," ScienceDaily,
July 10, 2016, https://www.sciencedaily.com/releases/2016/07/160710094239.htm.

    Redzo Mujcic and Andrew J. Oswald, "Evolution of Well-Being and Happiness after
Increases in Consumption of Fruit and Vegetables," *American Journal of Public Health* 106,
no. 8 (August 1, 2016): 1504–1510, https://ajph.aphapublications.org/doi/full/10.2105
/AJPH.2016.303260.

2. Dr. Amen covers these food rules in his books and talks because they are the foundation
of brain health at any age.

3. Matthew T. Gailliot et al., "Self-Control Relies on Glucose as a Limited Energy Source:
Willpower Is More Than a Metaphor," *Journal of Personality and Social Psychology* 92, no. 2
(2007): 325–336, https://psycnet.apa.org/record/2007-00654-010.

4. Centers for Disease Control and Prevention (CDC), "New Research Uncovers Concerning
Increases in Youth Living with Diabetes in the U.S.," press release, August 24, 2021,
https://www.cdc.gov/media/releases/2021/p0824-youth-diabetes.html.

5. Lawrence E. Armstrong et al., "Mild Dehydration Affects Mood in Healthy Young Women,"
Journal of Nutrition 142, no. 2 (February 2012): 382–388, https://www.sciencedirect
.com/science/article/pii/S0022316622028899.

    Matthew S. Ganio et al., "Mild Dehydration Impairs Cognitive Performance and Mood of
Men," *British Journal of Nutrition* 106, no. 10 (November 2011): 1535–1543, https:
//pubmed.ncbi.nlm.nih.gov/21736786/.

6. Klaus W. Lange, "Omega-3 Fatty Acids and Mental Health," *Global Health Journal* 4,
no. 1 (March 2020): 18–30, https://www.sciencedirect.com/science/article/pii
/S241464472030004X.

7. Daniel G. Amen, with Brendan Kearney (illustrator), *Captain Snout and the Super Power
Questions* (Grand Rapids, MI: Zonderkidz, 2017).

8. László Harmat, Johanna Takács, and Róbert Bódizs, "Music Improves Sleep Quality in
Students," *Journal of Advanced Nursing* 62, no. 3 (May 2008): 327–335, https://pubmed
.ncbi.nlm.nih.gov/18426457/.

    Tabitha Trahan et al., "The Music That Helps People Sleep and the Reasons They
Believe It Works: A Mixed Methods Analysis of Online Survey Reports," *PLOS One* 13,
no. 11 (November 14, 2018): e0206531, https://www.ncbi.nlm.nih.gov/pmc/articles
/PMC6235300/.

9. Institute of Medicine, *Educating the Student Body: Taking Physical Activity and Physical Education to School* (Washington, DC: National Academies Press, 2013).

10. Jaana T. Kari et al., "Childhood Physical Activity and Adulthood Earnings," *Medicine and Science in Sports and Exercise* 48, no. 7 (July 2016): 1340–1346, https://pubmed.ncbi.nlm .nih.gov/26871991/.

11. Francesco Recchia et al., "Comparative Effectiveness of Exercise, Antidepressants and Their Combination in Treating Non-severe Depression: A Systematic Review and Network Meta-analysis of Randomised Controlled Trials," *British Journal of Sports Medicine* 56, no. 23 (December 2022): 1375–1380, https://pubmed.ncbi.nlm.nih.gov /36113975/.

12. Ian M. McDonough et al., "The Synapse Project: Engagement in Mentally Challenging Activities Enhances Neural Efficiency," *Restorative Neurology and Neuroscience* 33, no. 6 (2015): 865–882, https://content.iospress.com/articles/restorative-neurology-and -neuroscience/rnn150533.

13. Daniel G. Amen, *You, Happier* (Carol Stream, IL: Tyndale, 2022), 15, 218.

CHAPTER 10: WHEN PARENTS HAVE DIFFERENT STYLES: CREATING A UNITED TEAM

1. Lucas S. LaFreniere and Michelle G. Newman, "Probabilistic Learning by Positive and Negative Reinforcement in Generalized Anxiety Disorder," *Clinical Psychological Science* 7, no. 3 (2019): 502–515, https://journals.sagepub.com/doi/10.1177/2167702618809366.

Evgenia Stefanopoulou et al., "Are Attentional Control Resources Reduced by Worry in Generalized Anxiety Disorder?," *Journal of Abnormal Psychology* 123, no. 2 (May 2014): 330–335, https://psycnet.apa.org/fulltext/2014-22133-005.html.

Kelly Trezise and Robert A. Reeve, "Worry and Working Memory Influence Each Other Iteratively over Time," *Cognition and Emotion* 30, no. 2 (2016): 353–368, https://www .tandfonline.com/doi/abs/10.1080/02699931.2014.1002755.

2. Sandra J. Llera and Michelle G. Newman, "Worry Impairs the Problem-Solving Process: Results from an Experimental Study," *Behaviour Research and Therapy* 135 (December 2020): 103759, https://www.sciencedirect.com/science/article/abs/pii /S0005796720302138.

CHAPTER 11: REACHING THE UNDERACHIEVING CHILD

1. David A. Sousa, *How the Brain Learns*, 4th ed. (Thousand Oaks, CA: Corwin, 2011).

2. Abraham H. Maslow, *Motivation and Personality*, 2nd ed. (1954; New York: Harper and Row, 1970).

3. Gökhan Baş, Cihad Şentürk, and Fatih Mehmet Ciğerci, "Homework and Academic Achievement: A Meta-analytic Review of Research," *Issues in Educational Research* 27, no. 1 (2017): 31–50, https://www.iier.org.au/iier27/bas.pdf.

4. Martin Pinquart, "Associations of Parenting Styles and Dimensions with Academic Achievement in Children and Adolescents: A Meta-analysis," *Educational Psychology Review* 28, no. 3 (2016): 475–493, https://psycnet.apa.org/record/2015-41312-001.

5. Bernard Weiner, "Attribution Theory, Achievement Motivation, and the Educational Process," *Review of Educational Research* 42, no. 2 (1972): 203–215, https://psycnet.apa .org/record/1973-10105-001.

6. Carol S. Dweck, *Mindset: The New Psychology of Success* (New York: Random House, 2006).

David Scott Yeager and Carol S. Dweck, "Mindsets That Promote Resilience: When Students Believe That Personal Characteristics Can Be Developed," *Educational Psychologist* 47, no. 4 (2012): 302–314, https://psycnet.apa.org/record/2012-28709-004.

7. Brian A. Fallon et al., "Lyme Borreliosis and Associations with Mental Disorders and Suicidal Behavior: A Nationwide Danish Cohort Study," *American Journal of Psychiatry*

178, no. 10 (2021): 921–931, https://ajp.psychiatryonline.org/doi/10.1176/appi.ajp
.2021.20091347.

CHAPTER 12: TECHNOLOGY MISUSE AND ADDICTION

1. Dimitri A. Christakis, "The Challenges of Defining and Studying 'Digital Addiction' in Children," *JAMA* 321, no. 23 (June 18, 2019): 2277–2278, https://jamanetwork .com/journals/jama/article-abstract/2734210.

   Tim Schulz van Endert, "Addictive Use of Digital Devices in Young Children: Associations with Delay Discounting, Self-Control and Academic Performance," *PLOS One* 16, no. 6 (2021): e0253058, https://www.ncbi.nlm.nih.gov/pmc/articles/PMC8219150/.

   Fazida Karim et al., "Social Media Use and Its Connection to Mental Health: A Systematic Review," *Cureus* 12, no. 6 (2020): e8627, https://www.ncbi.nlm.nih.gov/pmc/articles /PMC7364393/.

2. Associated Press in Washington, "Asiana Airlines Crash Caused by Pilot Error and Confusion, Investigators Say," *Guardian*, June 24, 2014, https://www.theguardian .com/world/2014/jun/24/asiana-crash-san-francsico-controls-investigation-pilot.

3. Daniel G. Amen, *Your Brain Is Always Listening* (Carol Stream, IL: Tyndale, 2021), 185–186.

4. Ken C. Winters and Amelia Arria, "Adolescent Brain Development and Drugs," *Prevention Researcher* 18, no. 2 (2011): 21–24, https://www.ncbi.nlm.nih.gov/pmc/articles /PMC3399589/.

5. C. B. Ferster and B. F. Skinner, *Schedules of Reinforcement* (New York: Appleton-Century -Crofts, 1957).

6. Irem Metin-Orta, "Fear of Missing Out, Internet Addiction and Their Relationship to Psychological Symptoms," *Addicta: The Turkish Journal on Addictions* 7, no. 1 (2020): 67–73, https://www.addicta.com.tr/en/fear-of-missing-out-internet-addiction-and-their -relationship-to-psychological-symptoms-13150.

7. Associated Press and Matthew Wright, "Boy, 11, Rampages through His Home Shooting His Cop Father [. . .]," *Daily Mail*, March 7, 2019, https://www.dailymail.co.uk/news /article-6782651/Investigators-Indiana-boy-shot-trooper-dad-video-games.html.

8. Marvin Fong, "Daniel Petric Killed Mother, Shot Father Because They Took Halo 3 Video Game, Prosecutors Say," *Plain Dealer*, Cleveland.com, December 15, 2008, https://www .cleveland.com/metro/2008/12/boy_killed_mom_and_shot_dad_ov.html.

CHAPTER 13: WHEN NOTHING SEEMS TO BE WORKING: HELP FOR BRAIN HEALTH ISSUES

1. Lydie A. Lebrun-Harris et al., "Five-Year Trends in US Children's Health and Well-Being, 2016–2020," *JAMA Pediatrics* 176, no. 7 (2022): e220056, https://jamanetwork.com/ journals/jamapediatrics/fullarticle/2789946.

2. "Mental Health Conditions," National Alliance on Mental Illness (NAMI), accessed March 31, 2023, https://www.nami.org/about-mental-illness/mental-health-conditions.

3. Daniel G. Whitney and Mark D. Peterson, "US National and State-Level Prevalence of Mental Health Disorders and Disparities of Mental Health Care Use in Children," *JAMA Pediatrics* 173, no. 4 (2019): 389–391, https://jamanetwork.com/journals/jamapediatrics /fullarticle/2724377.

4. Michelle V. Porche et al., "Childhood Trauma and Psychiatric Disorders as Correlates of School Dropout in a National Sample of Young Adults," *Child Development* 82, no. 3 (2011): 982–998, https://www.ncbi.nlm.nih.gov/pmc/articles/PMC3089672/.

5. Linda A. Teplin et al., "Psychiatric Disorders in Youth in Juvenile Detention," *Archives of General Psychiatry* 59, no. 12 (December 2002): 1133–1143, https://www.ncbi.nlm.nih .gov/pmc/articles/PMC2861992/.

6. Centers for Disease Control and Prevention, "U.S. Teen Girls Experiencing Increased Sadness and Violence," press release (February 13, 2023), https://cdc.gov/media/relases /2023/p0213-yrbs.html.

7. "Distribution of the 10 Leading Causes of Death among Teenagers Aged 15 to 19 Years in the United States in 2019," Statista, October 25, 2021, https://www.statista.com /statistics/1017959/distribution-of-the-10-leading-causes-of-death-among-teenagers/.

8. Centers for Disease Control and Prevention, *Youth Risk Behavior Survey 2011–2021*, 66, https://www.cdc.gov/healthyyouth/data/yrbs/pdf/YRBS_Data-Summary-Trends _Report2023_508.pdf.

9. *Youth Risk Behavior Survey 2011–2021*, 68.

10. *Youth Risk Behavior Survey 2011–2021*, 70.

11. *Youth Risk Behavior Survey 2011–2021*, 66, 68, 70.

12. "Teen Trend Report," High School, Stage of Life, March 2014, https://www.stageoflife .com/StageHighSchool/TeensandMentalIllness.aspx.

13. "Teen Trend Report."

14. "Teen Trend Report."

15. Ronald C. Kessler et al., "Age of Onset of Mental Disorders: A Review of Recent Literature," *Current Opinion in Psychiatry* 20, no. 4 (July 2007): 359–364, https://www.ncbi .nlm.nih.gov/pmc/articles/PMC1925038/.

16. Anika Knüppel et al., "Sugar Intake from Sweet Food and Beverages, Common Mental Disorder and Depression: Prospective Findings from the Whitehall II Study," *Scientific Reports* 7 (2017): 6287, https://www.nature.com/articles/s41598-017-05649-7.

17. Brad J. Bushman et al., "Low Glucose Relates to Greater Aggression in Married Couples," *Proceedings of the National Academy of Sciences of the United States of America* 111, no. 17 (April 29, 2014): 6254–6257, https://pubmed.ncbi.nlm.nih.gov/24733932/.

   Sue Penckofer et al., "Does Glycemic Variability Impact Mood and Quality of Life?" *Diabetes Technology and Therapeutics* 14, no. 4 (April 2012): 303–310, https://pubmed .ncbi.nlm.nih.gov/22324383/.

18. Ashley Abramson, "Children's Mental Health Is in Crisis," *Monitor on Psychology* 53, no. 1 (January 1, 2022): 69, https://www.apa.org/monitor/2022/01/special-childrens-mental -health.

19. Robert F. Anda et al., "The Enduring Effects of Abuse and Related Adverse Experiences in Childhood. A Convergence of Evidence from Neurobiology and Epidemiology," *European Archives of Psychiatry and Clinical Neuroscience* 256, no. 3 (April 2006): 174–186, https: //www.ncbi.nlm.nih.gov/pmc/articles/PMC3232061/.

20. Martin Sack et al., "Intranasal Oxytocin Reduces Provoked Symptoms in Female Patients with Posttraumatic Stress Disorder Despite Exerting Sympathomimetic and Positive Chronotropic Effects in a Randomized Controlled Trial," *BMC Medicine* 15, no. 1 (February 2017): 40, https://www.ncbi.nlm.nih.gov/pmc/articles/PMC5314583/.

   Jessie L. Frijling, "Preventing PTSD with Oxytocin: Effects of Oxytocin Administration on Fear Neurocircuitry and PTSD Symptom Development in Recently Trauma-Exposed Individuals," *European Journal of Psychotraumatology* 8, no. 1 (April 11, 2017): 1302652, https://www.ncbi.nlm.nih.gov/pmc/articles/PMC5400019/.

   David Cochran et al., "The Role of Oxytocin in Psychiatric Disorders: A Review of Biological and Therapeutic Research Findings," *Harvard Review of Psychiatry* 21, no. 5 (September/October 2013): 219–247, https://journals.lww.com/hrpjournal/fulltext /2013/09000/the_role_of_oxytocin_in_psychiatric_disorders_a.1.aspx.

21. Lebrun-Harris et al., "Five-Year Trends in US Children's Health."

22. Lebrun-Harris et al., "Five-Year Trends in US Children's Health."

23. Ahsan Nazeer et al., "Obsessive-Compulsive Disorder in Children and Adolescents: Epidemiology, Diagnosis and Management," *Translational Pediatrics* 9, supplement 1 (February 22, 2020): S76–S93, https://tp.amegroups.com/article/view/31620/28326.

CHAPTER 14: COMMON CHALLENGES: MAKING POTTY TRAINING A POSITIVE EXPERIENCE

1. "American Academy of Pediatrics, "The Right Age to Potty Train," HealthyChildren.org, last updated May 24, 2022, https://www.healthychildren.org/English/ages-stages /toddler/toilet-training/Pages/The-Right-Age-to-Toilet-Train.aspx.

2. Timothy R. Schum et al., "Sequential Acquisition of Toilet-Training Skills: A Descriptive Study of Gender and Age Differences in Normal Children," *Pediatrics* 109, no. 3 (March 2002): E48, https://pubmed.ncbi.nlm.nih.gov/11875176/.

3. Richard J. Butler and Jon Heron, "The Prevalence of Infrequent Bedwetting and Nocturnal Enuresis in Childhood. A Large British Cohort," *Scandinavian Journal of Urology and Nephrology* 42, no. 3 (2008): 257–264, https://pubmed.ncbi.nlm.nih.gov/18432533/.

4. Srirangram Shreeram et al., "Prevalence of Enuresis and Its Association with Attention -Deficit/Hyperactivity Disorder among U.S. Children: Results from a Nationally Representative Study," *Journal of the American Academy of Child and Adolescent Psychiatry* 48, no. 1 (January 2009): 35–41, https://www.sciencedirect.com/science/article/abs/pii /S0890856708601689.

5. People v. Peoples, no. S090602 (Supreme Court of California, 2016), https://caselaw. findlaw.com/ca-supreme-court/1725241.html.

CHAPTER 15: COMMON CHALLENGES: SIBLING RIVALRY

1. Lucy Bowes et al., "Sibling Bullying and Risk of Depression, Anxiety, and Self-Harm: A Prospective Cohort Study," *Pediatrics* 134, no. 4 (October 2014): e1032–e1039, https: //pubmed.ncbi.nlm.nih.gov/25201801/.

CHAPTER 16: COMMON CHALLENGES: WHEN YOUR CHILD IS TEASED OR BULLIED

1. Stephen B. Karpman, *A Game Free Life: The Definitive Book on the Drama Triangle and the Compassion Triangle by the Originator and Author* (San Francisco: Drama Triangle Publications, 2014).

2. Sally Northway Ogden, *"Words Will Never Hurt Me": Helping Kid Handle Teasing, Bullying and Putdowns* (Seattle, WA: Elton-Wolf Publishing, 2004).

3. Dan Olweus, *Bullying at School: What We Know and What We Can Do* (Malden, MA: Blackwell, 1993), 57–58.

4. Rebecca R. Winters, Jamilia J. Blake, and Siqi Chen, "Bully Victimization among Children with Attention-Deficit/Hyperactivity Disorder: A Longitudinal Examination of Behavioral Phenotypes," *Journal of Emotional and Behavioral Disorders* 28, no. 2 (2020): 80–91, https://journals.sagepub.com/doi/10.1177/1063426618814724.

CHAPTER 17: COMMON CHALLENGES: KEEPING SPORTS HEALTHY AND FUN

1. Katherine B. Owen et al., "Sport Participation and Academic Performance in Children and Adolescents: A Systematic Review and Meta-analysis," *Medicine and Science in Sports and Exercise* 54, no. 2 (February 1, 2022): 299–306, https://pubmed.ncbi.nlm.nih.gov /34559728/.

   Geneviève Piché et. al., "Associations between Extracurricular Activity and Self -Regulation: A Longitudinal Study from 5 to 10 Years of Age," *American Journal of Health Promotion* 30, no. 1 (2015): e32–e40, https://journals.sagepub.com/doi/10.4278/ajhp .131021-QUAN-537.

2. Christopher S. Sahler and Brian D. Greenwald, "Traumatic Brain Injury in Sports: A Review," *Rehabilitation Research and Practice* 2012 (July 9, 2012): 659652, https://www .hindawi.com/journals/rerp/2012/659652/.

3. "High School Athletes Playing College Sports," RecruitLook, August 3, 2019, https: //recruitlook.com/what-percentage-of-high-school-athletes-play-college-sports/.

4. Eric Ortiz, "Little League Legends Who Became Big League Stars," Stadium Talk,

October 28, 2022, https://www.stadiumtalk.com/s/best-mlb-players-who-played-in-little
-league-baseball-world-series-8582eb74a7bb483e.

CHAPTER 18: COMMON CHALLENGES: FRIENDS AND PEER PRESSURE

1. Joseph P. Allen et al., "When Friendships Surpass Parental Relationships as Predictors of Long-Term Outcomes: Adolescent Relationship Qualities and Adult Psychosocial Functioning," *Child Development* 93, no. 3 (May 2022): 760–777, https://www.ncbi.nlm.nih.gov/pmc/articles/PMC9167890/.

    Koji Ueno, "The Effects of Friendship Networks on Adolescent Depressive Symptoms," *Social Science Research* 34, no. 3 (September 2005): 484–510, https://www.sciencedirect.com/science/article/abs/pii/S0049089X04000419.

    G. David Batty et al., "The Aberdeen Children of the 1950s Cohort Study: Background, Methods and Follow-up Information on a New Resource for the Study of Life Course and Intergenerational Influences on Health," *Paediatric and Perinatal Epidemiology* 18, no. 3 (May 2004): 221–239, https://pubmed.ncbi.nlm.nih.gov/15130162/.

    Sara Brolin Låftman and Viveca Ostberg, "The Pros and Cons of Social Relations: An Analysis of Adolescents' Health Complaints," *Social Science and Medicine* 63, no. 3 (August 2006): 611–623, https://pubmed.ncbi.nlm.nih.gov/16603298/.

2. Robert Rosenthal and Lenore Jacobson, Pygmalion in the Classroom: Teacher Expectation and Pupils' Intellectual *Development* (New York: Holt, Rinehart and Winston, 1968).

CHAPTER 19: COMMON CHALLENGES: WHEN YOUR KID WANTS TO BEGIN DATING

1. Andreas Bartels and Semir Zeki, "The Neural Basis of Romantic Love," *NeuroReport* 11, no. 17 (November 27, 2000): 3829–3834, https://journals.lww.com/neuroreport/Fulltext/2000/11270/The_neural_basis_of_romantic_love.46.aspx.

CHAPTER 20: COMMON CHALLENGES: KEEPING YOUR PARENTING HEALTHY WHEN YOU DIVORCE

1. Richard A. Warshak, *Divorce Poison: How to Protect Your Family from Bad-mouthing and Brainwashing*, rev. ed. (New York: Harper, 2010).

CHAPTER 21: COMMON CHALLENGES: YOUR ROLE AS A STEPPARENT

1. Henry Cloud and John Townsend, *Boundaries: When to Say Yes, How to Say No to Take Control of Your Life*, rev. ed. (Grand Rapids, MI: Zondervan, 2017).

CHAPTER 22: ADULT CHILDREN AND ADULTS WHO ACT LIKE CHILDREN

1. J. Benjamin Hinnant et al., "Permissive Parenting, Deviant Peer Affiliations, and Delinquent Behavior in Adolescence: The Moderating Role of Sympathetic Nervous System Reactivity," *Journal of Abnormal Child Psychology* 44, no. 6 (August 2016): 1071–1081, https://www.ncbi.nlm.nih.gov/pmc/articles/PMC4909613/.

    Karin S. Nijhof and Rutger Engels, "Parenting Styles, Coping Strategies, and the Expression of Homesickness," *Journal of Adolescence* 30, no. 5 (October 2007): 709–720, https://onlinelibrary.wiley.com/doi/10.1016/j.adolescence.2006.11.009.

    Deborah A. Cohen and Janet Rice, "Parenting Styles, Adolescent Substance Use, and Academic Achievement," *Journal of Drug Education* 27, no. 2 (1997): 199–211, https://journals.sagepub.com/doi/10.2190/QPQQ-6Q1G-UF7D-5UTJ.

2. C. Knight Aldrich, *An Introduction to Dynamic Psychiatry* (New York: Blakiston Division, McGraw-Hill, 1966).

3. K. Kameguchi, "Chaotic States of Generational Boundaries in Contemporary Japanese Families," in *Research on Family Resources and Needs across the World*, ed. Mario Cusinato (Milan: Edizioni Universitarie di Lettere Economia Diritto, 1996).

4. Salvador Minuchin, *Families and Family Therapy* (Cambridge, MA: Harvard University Press, 1974).

5. Henry Cloud and John Townsend, *Boundaries: When to Say Yes, How to Say No to Take Control of Your Life*, rev. ed. (Grand Rapids, MI: Zondervan, 2017).

CHAPTER 23: 130 BEST THINGS YOU CAN DO TO HELP YOUR CHILD GROW UP TO BE MENTALLY STRONG

1. Philip S. Wang et al., "Delays in Initial Treatment Contact after First Onset of a Mental Disorder," *Health Services Research* 39, no. 2 (April 2004): 393–415, https://www.ncbi.nlm.nih.gov/pmc/articles/PMC1361014/.